COOPERATION IN CRIME

THE CATHOLIC UNIVERSITY OF AMERICA
CANON LAW STUDIES
No. 156

Cooperation in Crime

AN HISTORICAL CONSPECTUS AND COMMENTARY

A DISSERTATION

Submitted to the Faculty of Canon Law of the Catholic University of America in Partial Fulfillment of the Requirements for the Degree of

DOCTOR OF CANON LAW

BY

LOUIS ANTHONY ELTZ, A.B., J.C.L.
Priest of the Archdiocese of Philadelphia

THE CATHOLIC UNIVERSITY OF AMERICA
WASHINGTON, D. C.
1942

NIHIL OBSTAT:
Joseph A. M. Quigley, J.C.D.,
Censor Librorum.
Philadelphiae, die XXXI Iulii, 1944.

IMPRIMATUR:
✠ D. Card. Dougherty,
Archiepiscopus Philadelphiensis

Philadelphiae, die I Augusti, 1944.

PRINTED IN THE UNITED STATES OF AMERICA
BY THE WATKINS PRINTING CO., BALTIMORE

TO

MY FATHER AND MOTHER

TABLE OF CONTENTS

PAGE

Foreword ix

HISTORICAL CONSPECTUS

Chapter One

Preliminary Notions 1
- Article 1. The Nature of Complicity 1
- Article 2. The Various Kinds of Complicity 6

Chapter Two

Roman Law 8
- Article 1. Preliminary Remarks 8
- Article 2. The Individual Crimes 9

Chapter Three

Germanic Law 21
- Article 1. *Leges Barbarorum* 21
- Article 2. *Capitularia Regum Francorum* 22

Chapter Four

Complicity in a Broad Sense 25
- Article 1. Complicity by Reason of Association 25
- Article 2. Necessary Complicity 34

Chapter Five

Complicity in the Strict Sense from the Apostolic Age to the *Decretum Gratiani* 39

Chapter Six

Complicity in the Strict Sense from the *Decretum Gratiani* to the Council of Trent 48
- Article 1. The Legislative Development 48
- Article 2. The Doctrinal Development 54

Chapter Seven

Complicity in the Strict Sense from the Council of Trent to the Code 58

Article 1. The Legislative Development 58
Article 2. The Doctrinal Development 61
A. The Moralists 61
B. The Canonists 63

COMMENTARY

Chapter Eight

Some Jurisprudential Aspects of Criminal Cooperation 66
Article 1. The Canonical Concept of Guilt as Applied to Cooperators in Crime 66
Article 2. The Principle of Accessoriness 69
Article 3. The Principles of Objectivity and Subjectivity 72
Article 4. Attempted Acts in Relation to Cooperation 73
Article 5. Negligence as a Source of Cooperative Guilt 76

Chapter Nine

Co-Agents 84
Article 1. The Nature of Complete Participation 84
Article 2. The Guilt of Complete Participation 94
Scholion. The Status of a Single Perpetrator Acting in Cooperation 96

Chapter Ten

Necessary Cooperators 98

Chapter Eleven

Effective Cooperators 104
Article 1. The Forms of Partial Cooperation 104
A. The *Mandans* 105
B. Moral Cooperators Other than the *Mandans* 108
C. All Other Partial Cooperators 110
Article 2. The Guilt of Effective Cooperators 114
Article 3. The Essential Characteristic of Effective Cooperators 114
Article 4. The Application of Canon 2209, § 3 120

Chapter Twelve

Facilitating Cooperators 123
Article 1. The Nature of Facilitating Cooperation 123

Article 2. The Guilt of Facilitating Cooperation 128

CHAPTER THIRTEEN

THE WITHDRAWAL OF COOPERATION 131
Article 1. The Complete Withdrawal of Cooperation 131
Article 2. The Incomplete Withdrawal of Cooperation 137
Article 3. The Application of Penalties in Cases of Withdrawn Cooperation 139

CHAPTER FOURTEEN

NEGATIVE COOPERATORS 146
Article 1. Neglect of Office in Relation to Negative Cooperation 146
Article 2. The Various Offices, the Neglect of Which Can Lead to Negative Cooperation 149
A. The General Obligation of Preventing All Crime 149
B. Particular Obligations of Preventing Certain Crimes 156
Article 3. The Guilt Attaching to Negative Cooperation 159

CHAPTER FIFTEEN

SUBSEQUENT COOPERATORS 161

CHAPTER SIXTEEN

THE CONSEQUENCES OF GUILT DERIVING FROM COOPERATION IN CRIME 168
Article 1. Damages 168
Article 2. Punishment 170
A. Legal Penalties 170
B. Discretionary Penalties 178

CONCLUSIONS 181

BIBLIOGRAPHY 185

ABBREVIATIONS 192

ALPHABETICAL INDEX 195

BIOGRAPHICAL NOTE 200

CANON LAW STUDIES 201

FOREWORD

While this work is classified as an historical conspectus and commentary, it is in effect a study in jurisprudence. General principles governing the guilt and punishment of cooperators in crime are found for the first time in ecclesiastical legislation in the Code of Canon Law. Previously, there existed particular provisions in the individual laws concerning complicity, and the reasoning of legal thinkers, but nothing with universal legal efficacy comprehending the entire subject of complicity. Accordingly, the general norms of the Code must be considered as standing without exemplars in the former law to which recourse may be had for interpretation, despite the intricate and multitudinous enactments of the previous legislation against accomplices.

But while these general norms are new as laws, canonical science, evolving from the interplay of legislation and commentary, had long elaborated the principles controlling a moral yet socially effective theory for determining and punishing cooperators in crime. From the earliest times, moreover, particular applications of these principles are found in decisions and statutes. The legal statements of the pre-Code era, and especially the doctrine of the canonists, must be studied to arrive at an understanding of the canonical concept of complicity. It is for this reason that even the historical section of this work has been termed a study in jurisprudence. The thinking of the canonists is presented for its own value in the chronological evolution of doctrine and for its worth in clarifying modern principles. The former legislation is related merely to show the presence and nature of cooperative norms. There would, therefore, be no purpose in detailing all the manifold laws regarding accomplices; for the laws as such have no value at the present time, except as indications of certain historical modes of thought.

The employment of norms of complicity in ecclesiastical legislation is seen as a matter of gradual evolution, with the doctrine being shaped by practical jurisprudence. It was developed out of the conciliar laws, the decretal letters of the popes, and the ecclesiastical trials. It would be an interesting speculation, upon which it is not possible to delay here, to estimate the source of the Church's principles in this regard. As to the laws themselves, there is the usual legislative process which can offer a sufficient, if not the ultimate answer. But the use of norms of complicity has often outstripped the pertinent legislation, especially in the very early periods of history. Accomplices were judged punishable despite the absence of legal directions in their regard. Was the criterion natural justice, the discretion of the judge, or, as time went on, the rule of former decisions? The imposing structure of Roman law, then concurrently in force, with its many ramifications regarding complicity must not be overlooked, but the early legal system of the Church was hardly prepared to adopt such intricate rules. Moreover, in a society founded on religion, the influence of ethics and moral theology cannot be passed over. No solution to this problem can be offered here but whatever the criterion, at least the practical norms may be examined, as they appear in the course of centuries.

For convenient handling, a division of the historical section is made under two general headings: complicity in the strict sense and complicity in the broad sense. It is important to observe the development of both types of complicity in order to understand historically the realization of the definite norm now in use.

The Code does not define cooperation in crime. Both this notion and the interpretation of the canonical provisions regarding cooperation may be attained only by examining the meaning and context of the pertinent canons, and by making due inference. This process is to be guided by the canonical doctrine on complicity current before the Code. Several commentators have assumed that the words of the Code are self-explanatory, or that the various cooperators could be divided into two classes by analogy with those who are liable to the punishment stated in the law and those who are subject to discretionary penalties. But these inexact generalizations are confronted by the seven provisions on cooperative guilt expressed by canon 2209, which must not be deemed invalid or nugatory. No assurance can be given that a person who has taken even a preeminent part in a crime will contract the guilt described in canon 2209, § 1-3, unless the words of these provisions are fulfilled in their strict sense. This is said to indicate that the phraseology of the canons is to be subject to the closest scrutiny. Under an inquisitive approach to the interpreting of the new law, it is to be expected that jurisprudence must still be given a wide scope in unfolding the significance of the canonized principles of complicity.

The writer herewith expresses his gratitude to Dennis Cardinal Dougherty, Archbishop of Philadelphia, Patron of the Science of Canon Law, for the opportunity of graduate study; to the Faculty of the School of Canon Law of the Catholic University of America for many valued suggestions; and to all who by encouragement and assistance have contributed to the completion of this work.

HISTORICAL CONSPECTUS

CHAPTER I

PRELIMINARY NOTIONS

ARTICLE 1. THE NATURE OF COMPLICITY

It frequently happens that the same antisocial fact — the same crime — may be attributed to several persons, either equally or in varying degrees. This concurrence of several persons in the same crime is known as complicity, or cooperation in crime.[1] Not every plurality of participants, however, comes within the scope of the criminal law. Material cooperation, for example, which consists of external action without criminal intent or negligence, or without a common purpose, is excluded from a consideration of complicity.[2]

[1] Latini, *Iuris criminalis philosophici summa lineamenta* (Taurini: Marietti, 1924), p. 151; Roberti, *De delictis et poenis* (2. ed., Romae: Custodia Libraria Pontificii Utriusque Iuris, —), I, 211; Lega, *De delictis et poenis* (2. ed., Romae, 1910), p. 72; Wernz, *Ius decretalium* (Prati, 1913), VI, 52; all these works will hereafter be cited under the authors' name; Michiels, *De delictis et poenis* (Lublin: Universitas Catholica, 1934), I, 295.

[2] Chelodi, *Ius poenale* (2. ed., Tridenti: Ardesi, 1935), p. 16; Michiels, *De delictis et poenis*, I, 307; Wernz, p. 53. The concept of material cooperation is perhaps better developed by the moralists in their treatment of cooperation in another's sin, where it is distinguished from formal cooperation; thus: Aertnys, *Theologia moralis* (7. ed., Paderbornae, 1906), I, 157-158; Gury, *Casus conscientiae* (5. ed., Lugduni, 1874), I, 105; Vermeersch, *Theologiae moralis principia, responsa, consilia* (Romae: Universitas Gregoriana, 1928), II, 105-107; Girard, "Cooperation au mal,"—*Dictionnaire Pratique des Connaissances Religieuses*, XI, 535; Genicot-Salsmans, *Institutiones theologiae moralis* (Lovaniae: Museum Lessianum, 1931), I, 182-183. Some canonists, as Coronata, Lega, do not so much as mention material cooperation, whereas Chelodi, Michiels, Roberti, and Wernz, cited above, while treating of material cooperation, do not explicitly oppose this concept with the term "formal cooperation." Augustine is of the opinion that the distinction is of no purpose in canon law—*A Commentary on Canon Law* (3. ed., 8 vols., St. Louis: Herder, 1931), VIII, 48. Beste, however, indicates the utility of the distinction in clarifying the nature of cooperation by prefacing his treatment of canon 2209 with an explanation of formal and material cooperation—*Introductio in codicem* (Collegeville, Minn.: St. John's Abbey Press, 1938), p. 883.

Evidently the criminal law is concerned only with formal cooperation in crime, which implies first, that there should be a crime participated in by all the cooperators who are united by common agreement and purpose. To establish the requirements of formal cooperation in crime it is necessary to examine the constituent elements of crime and of cooperation.

If cooperation in crime were not a form of criminal activity it would have no place in the criminal law. It must, therefore, share with other penal offenses the characteristics of crime. In church law,[3] a crime is an external and morally imputable[4] violation of the law to which is added at least an undetermined canonical sanction. In each crime three elements are verified: the objective, which is the external action; the subjective, which is the criminal intention or punishable negligence; and the juridical, which is the law forbidding an action and stating a penalty.[5]

Thus far concerning the components of delictuality; it is now necessary to consider the nexus which unites the delictuality of several persons into one common crime.

Cooperative unity requires that the several participants be joined in purpose and by agreement. The same purpose must inspire all. It is not essential that this purpose should be regarded under the same aspect by each one concerned—what is for one an immediate end, may be regarded by another as a mediate end—but what is required is that the same object be desired as an end. Besides this common end, there is need of agreement on this end through the cooperating group. Each must be bound to the other in the knowledge that all are working for the common end desired by all. This knowledge need not be explicit, resulting from special discussions; simple recognition of a

[3] Canon 2195, § 1. The jurisprudence of this study is of a positive type, following the legislation of the Church where it has conveniently settled the doctrine for canonical purposes. For a consideration of the various theories on the nature of crime, cf. Latini, pp. 65-66; Roberti, pp. 33-49.

[4] *I. e.*, imputable to the agent as responsible; one must either have the will to break the law, or else act with punishable negligence—cf. Roberti, pp. 54, 86-191.

[5] Chelodi, *Ius poenale*, p. 4.

participation in the same purpose by the cooperators, which is acquired before the completion of the crime, is sufficient. Otherwise, there would scarcely be cooperation, if several persons, intent on the same crime, all contributed to the final result without being aware of another's operation.

Formal cooperation in crime, therefore, is constituted by the realization in one act of those elements necessary to produce a crime, plus the elements required by cooperative unity.

From the viewpoint of crime, there must be:

1) a penal law prohibiting the effect which is desired by the cooperators and toward which their actions tend;[6]

2) a deliberate will on the part of the cooperators to produce this effect forbidden by the penal law, or possibly, the will to produce an act from which, because of negligence, this forbidden effect results;[7]

3) some positive, external action on the part of all the cooperators which is ordained to the forbidden effect and thus efficaciously influences its accomplishment; it is required that each cooperator actually do something—merely to will the forbidden effect, even with a manifested will, would not be enough;[8]

From the viewpoint of cooperative unity,[9] there must be:

1) a common purpose, shared by all the cooperators and motivating their actions to such an extent that these actions conspire to produce the same effect forbidden by the criminal law;[10]

[6] Canon 2195, § 1; *nullum crimen sine lege*—cf. Roberti, pp. 68-85.

[7] Michiels, *De delictis et poenis,* I, 307.

[8] Michiels, *loc. cit.;* Coronata, *Institutiones iuris canonici* (Taurini: Marietti, 1935), IV, 45; Roberti, p. 212; Wernz, p. 53.

[9] What is here required is not, as a general rule, clearly stated by the authors—best is the succinct statement of Coronata (*Institutiones,* IV, 45): "Ad concursum requiritur ut concurrentes communi consilio ex praevia conventione agant."

[10] ". . . convergentia subjectiva intentionum, vi cujus scilicet actus ab unoquoque cooperante ad eundem eventum criminosum realisandum aptus ponatur cum conscientia et intentione ita integrandi actum ab alio ad eundem scopum positum, ita ut eventus criminosus realisatus revera sit effectus activitatis materialis et moralis plurium causarum partialium conscienter associatarum et simul agentium."—Michiels, *De delictis et poenis,* I, 307.

2) a general agreement among the cooperators, by virtue of which each is aware of the other's purpose and operates, not separately, but in accord with this common knowledge.[11]

In consequence of these requirements, it is possible to exclude from the ambit of complicity material cooperation, negative cooperation, and subsequent cooperation.

1) Material cooperation occurs when a criminal effect is produced by the conjunction of several people operating together without a common criminal intent.[12] This may be due to a lack of criminal intention on the part of one of the participants, to a lack of a common agreement, or by reason of legal exception.

a) Criminal intention is lacking where the work of an innocent person is used by another in the execution of his criminal designs.[13] This occurs in cases of ignorance or unwillingness; certainly when a person is ignorant of the evil end to which his work is applied, he cannot be said to have a criminal intent; the same is true of one who is unwilling to break the law, but whose work is used, contrary to his intention, to contribute to the criminal effect. Physical violence removes all complicity.[14] With regard to moral violence or fear, it is difficult to determine the exact stage wherein one is no longer bound to observe the law. This difficulty, however, has been avoided by the law in excluding from penal competency, as a general rule, infractions of ecclesiastical law performed under grave fear, necessity, or proportionate inconvenience.[15]

b) Common agreement is lacking where several people act together without being aware that each is pursuing the same end; or where some are aware of the common purpose, but others are not. In the first case, there is not merely a plurality of agents but also a plurality of crimes. In the second case, only those are formal cooperators who are cognizant of the fact that the same purpose is motivating the

[11] Michiels, as quoted above, with special reference to *conscientia* and *conscienter*.

[12] Michiels, *De delictis et poenis*, I, 307-308; Chelodi, *Ius poenale*, p. 16.

[13] Chelodi, *loc. cit.*

[14] Canon 2205, § 1.

[15] Canon 2205, § 2.

other agents. In ignorance of the common purpose each, instead of sharing in the one common crime, is responsible for his own crime or act—which may or may not, in view of personal circumstances, be as grievous as that of the other parties concerned.[16] To satisfy the condition of a common agreement there must be an understanding, either explicit or implicit, among the participants as to the common end and mutual assistance. In other words, this understanding must be such as to promote a community of operation.[17]

c) Legal exceptions may withdraw one of the participants from the competence of the law, so that from the source of this particular legal system, there can be no question of guilt.[18] Although this makes cooperation merely material for those favored by the exemption, the full responsibility of the other participants is not affected.

2) Negative cooperation occurs when the criminal effect is produced in conjunction with the inactivity of one who is under a legal obligation to prevent the crime. This is not formal cooperation since there is no conjunction of intention and activity. The guilt arises from the dereliction of duty, which is only improperly called cooperation. If the inactivity is present in the absence of a legal obligation to prevent the crime, there is no source of responsibility. In the exceptional case of a pact intervening between the remiss official and the criminal before the crime, the true concept of complicity is verified.[19]

3) Subsequent cooperation, which consists in aid or encouragement given after the completion of the crime, does not play any effective part in the commission of the crime.[20] Such cooperation does not,

[16] Roberti, p. 213.

[17] Michiels, *De delictis et poenis*, I, 307.

[18] In Roman law members of the family could not be accused of theft when they stole from one another—D. (47, 2) 36, 1. So in canon law Cardinals (canon 2227, § 2; Chelodi, *Ius poenale*, p. 30) and children under the age of seven, even when capable of criminal intentions (canon 2201, § 1 compared with canon 88, § 3; cf. Michiels, *De delictis et poenis*, I, 145, for a detailed explanation of this complex problem), are not comprehended under the penal law.

[19] Michiels, *De delictis et poenis*, I, 308.

[20] Michiels, *loc. cit.*

therefore, come under the consideration of criminal cooperation, but by legislation, acts of subsequent cooperation may become penal offenses in themselves. In this case, such acts are held to be criminal, not because they play a part in the commission of a crime, but because they are by law constituted as crimes. The cooperative qualities of such an act belong to its physical nature, not to its juridical nature.[21]

Article 2. The Various Kinds of Complicity

There are crimes which by their nature require an accomplice. An enumeration of these would include duelling, adultery, simony, illicit marriage, sodomy, and incest. Are such offenses to be viewed as implying complicity? Certainly there is malicious cooperation in crime to such an extent that the conditions required from the standpoint of delictuality and cooperation are present. Yet some jurists [22] do not consider them as true cases of complicity. It might be said that the law has here defined the act of each participant to be a crime, whereby each is held because of an infraction of the law rather than because of participation in the crime of another. Instead of engaging in one crime, each participant, according to this view, commits his own isolated offense, while at the same time mutually supplying to the other participant the subject matter of the latter's crime.[23] True complicity, on the other hand, would require that the participants engage in the same formal criminal act—not in an act that from the standpoint of each participant is formal for him but material for his partner. But this additional requirement of the identical formality of the criminal act is not required by all jurists;[24] moreover, many legal systems, among them canon law,[25] do not distinguish between accomplices necessarily required by the nature of the crime, and those not so required, as far as cooperative guilt is concerned. Whatever the

[21] Michiels, *loc. cit.*

[22] Wernz, p. 52; Chelodi, *Ius poenale*, pp. 15-16; Ayrinhac-Lydon, *Penal Legislation* (New York: Benziger Brothers, 1936), p. 15.

[23] Michiels, *De delictis et poenis*, I, 296.

[24] Coronata, *Institutiones*, IV, 46; Michiels, *De delictis et poenis*, I, 295-296.

[25] Canon 2209, § 2; cf. Michiels, *De delictis et poenis*, I, 296.

merits of the distinction, it may be stated that in offenses marked by necessary complicity there is no jurisprudential problem in legally defining the guilt of the participants; each breaks the law in equal measure. Hence once the crime is defined, the equality of complicity is perceived.

There are other crimes which can be completed by one person, but in which several can and often do occur. Not everyone, however, concerned in the commission of these crimes offers the same type of participation. Some actually perform the physical actions which effect or facilitate the crime; these are known as physical coöperators. Others, while not involved in the actual commission of the crime, have, nevertheless, influenced the perpetrators to such an extent that they are to be considered responsible, to a varying degree, for the act committed; these are called moral cooperators. An exhaustive list of the possible types of physical and moral cooperation would be difficult to compile; variant circumstances often change the precise nature of the cooperation offered. As archtypes, however, to which nearly all kinds of cooperation may be reduced, there can be mentioned, with regard to moral participation: command, persuasion, counsel; and in reference to physical cooperation: joint participation, singular participation in conjunction with moral cooperation, and assistance.

Chapter II

ROMAN LAW

Article 1. Preliminary Remarks

It is not the purpose of this study to trace the inevitable fluctuations occurring in the application of the principles of complicity over the length of Roman history, but simply to indicate, as an antecedent to the ecclesiastical legislation, the salient norms governing complicity, especially those found in the Justinian Codification.

The Roman legislation on complicity, while both numerous and detailed, has never been systematically reduced to a body of general principles.[1] Consequently, the norms dealing with complicity are to be found attached to the various penal laws,[2] and to examine them it is necessary to have recourse to the individual laws.

This examination into the Roman notion of complicity will be confined to those laws which by their nature or phraseology indicate the joining of several people in the same crime. This is not to deny the possibility of manifold participation in other crimes not treated, but merely to present positively and without speculation the Roman legislation.

Delictual cooperation was, for the Romans, the participation of several persons in the same crime,[3] each acting with criminal intent, but not necessarily sharing in the same common intent.[4] Hence the Roman jurisprudence did not require a *commune consilium* moti-

[1] Chelodi, *Ius poenale*, p. 16; Michiels, *De delictis et poenis*, I, 298; Roberti, p. 207; Wernz, pp. 54-55.

[2] Mommsen-Duquesne, *Le Droit Penal Romain* (Paris, 1907), I, 115. This will be referred to hereafter by citing the authors followed by volume and page.

[3] Mommsen-Duquesne (I, 113): "La participation de plusieurs personnes au même délit, la complicité, comme on doit la nommer ici . . . "

[4] Mommsen-Duquesne (I, 117): "En général, on considérera comme complicité tout acte enterpris avec mauvaise intention en vue de réaliser le délit."

vating the participants.[5] All cooperators, however, whether of greater or less degree, usually incurred the same penalty,[6] with some exceptions in the legislation of the imperial period, which displayed a tendency to gradate penalties among the various classes of cooperators.[7]

Article 2. The Individual Crimes

1. *Crimes against the state.* Crimes against the state are generally so described as to include the accomplices.[8] This is indicated for the following crimes:[9] to surrender a province,[10] a city,[11] a fort,[12] or a Roman citizen [13] to the enemy; to send news to the enemy;[14] to give counsel to the enemy against the Roman people;[15] to supply arms or money to the enemy;[16] to bear arms against the state;[17] to stir up

[5] Falchi, *Diritto Penale Romano—Dottrine Generale* (Treviso: Stab. Tip. A. Vianello, 1930), p. 193; Ferrini, *Diritto Penale Romano* (Milano, 1899) pp. 302-303; Michiels, *De delictis et poenis*, I, 299.

[6] Falchi, *Dottrine Generale*, pp. 195-196; Mommsen-Duquesne, I, 117-118.

[7] Falchi, *loc. cit.*; Mommsen-Duquesne, *loc. cit.*

[8] D. (48, 4) 1, 1: "quo tenetur is, cuius opera dolo malo consilium initum erit . . . ," "cuiusve opera consilio malo consilium initum erit quo . . . " D. (48, 4) 3: "quive quid eorum, quae supra scripta sunt, facere curaverit." These phrases are indicative of complicity. Thus Mommsen points out: "Deux tournures sont principalement employées: 'Occidendum curare et dolo malo facere ut occidatur.' On peut embrasser dans ces deux formules, notamment dans la dernière toute activité qui est dans un rapport de causalité avec le delit."—Mommsen-Duquesne, I, 115, note 3. To the same effect, cf. Falchi, *Dottrine Generale*, pp. 194-195; Ferrini, *Diritto Penale Romano*, pp. 299-300.

[9] Cf. Falchi, *Diritto Penale Romano—I Singoli Reati* (Padova: R. Zannoni, 1932, pp. 97-99.

[10] D. (48, 4) 10.

[11] D. (48, 4) 10.

[12] D. (48, 4) 3.

[13] D. (48, 4) 3.

[14] D. (48, 4) 1, 1.

[15] D. (48, 4) 1, 1.

[16] D. (48, 4) 4.

[17] D. (48, 4) 1, 1.

the enemy;[18] to lead the army into ambush;[19] to prevent the enemy from coming under Roman power;[20] to incite soldiers to sedition;[21] to desert from the Roman state or army;[22] to wage unauthorized war;[23] not to surrender the army to one's successor in the province;[24] to bear arms in the City;[25] to kill *obsides* without authority;[26] to kill a magistrate.[27] Here complicity is marked for punishment by legal phraseology incidental to the statement of the crime; in the cases about to be considered, the acts forbidden are themselves a form of participation which have been legislated into independent crimes. Thus to teach barbarians the construction of ships was a crime deemed worthy of death.[28] The matter ot complicity is considered with fine detail by the imperial legislation treating of conspiracy against the life of the emperor's councillors and senators.[29] First, the parties to the conspiracy, which by its nature demands several cooperators, were executed and their goods confiscated.[30] Second, their sons were rendered incapable of receiving any inheritance and were infamous.[31] Third, those who interceded for the latter became infamous.[32] Fourth, the punishment meted out to sons of the conspirators was applied to the conspirators' satellites and servants and their sons.[33]

2. *Crimes against life.* Criminal acts against life, as described by

[18] D. (48, 4) 3.
[19] D. (48, 4) 4.
[20] D. (48, 4) 4.
[21] D. (48, 4) 1, 1.
[22] D. (48, 4) 3.
[23] D. (48, 4) 3.
[24] D. (48, 4) 3.
[25] D. (48, 4) 1, 1.
[26] D. (48, 4) 1, 1.
[27] D. (48, 4) 1, 1.
[28] C. (9, 47) 25.
[29] C. (9, 8) 5.
[30] C. (9, 8) 5 pr.
[31] C. (9, 8) 5, 1. Strictly, this was not punishment because of complicity, but by extension of the penalty to those closely associated to the criminal.
[32] C. (9, 8) 5, 2. Such intercession was treated as complicity—Mommsen-Duquesne, II, 238.
[33] C. (9, 8) 5, 6.

Justinian, come within the competence of the *lex Cornelia de sicariis et veneficis*, which treated of homicide and crime juristically related to it,[34] and of the *lex Pompeia de parricidiis*, which confined its sanctions to parricide,[35] and which will be considered later in this study. Under the *lex Cornelia* complicity was noted in the case of murder,[36] poisoning,[37] abortion,[38] castration,[39] and circumcision.[40] With regard to murder, it might be said that all positive cooperators were considered equally guilty with the author of the crime.[41] Here the texts speak of complicity in a general way.[42] In other cases specific forms of complicity are noted. Thus the manufacture, sale, or possession of poison with homicidal intent involved the guilt of poisoning.[43] While a woman who procured an abortion was exiled,[44] those who supplied the drug, even without criminal intent, were exiled with partial confiscation of goods or condemned to the mines; should the woman die, they were executed.[45] Those who castrated another, ordered it done, or permitted it to be done on their property were all equally punished by castration and exile, or, in

[34] Mommsen-Duquesne, II, 343-344.

[35] D. (48, 9) 1.

[36] C. (9, 16), 6.

[37] D. (48, 8) 3.

[38] D. (48, 19) 38, 5.

[39] D. (48, 8) 3, 2.

[40] D. (48, 8) 11 pr.

[41] Mommsen-Duquesne, II, 343. Incidentally it might be remarked that though not originally, at least under Constantine, killing a slave could be murder—Mommsen-Duquesne, II, 329-330. *Dolus*, however, was required under the *lex Cornelia*—D. (48, 8) 7; whereas a civil remedy—Buckland, *A Text-book of Roman Law from Augustus to Justinian* (Cambridge: University Press, 1921), p. 580—could be had under the *lex Aquilia*, even if only *culpa* were present—Buckland, *op. cit.* p. 581. Concerning the nature of *dolus* and *culpa*, cf. Buckland, *op. cit.* p. 551.

[42] D. (48, 8) 15: "Nihil interest, occidat quis an causam mortis praebeat;" C. (9, 16) 6: " . . . qui hominem occiderit vel cuius dolo malo factum erit commissum . . . "

[43] D. (48, 8) 1, 1; D. (48, 8) 3 pr.

[44] D. (48, 8), 8.

[45] D. (48, 19) 38, 5.

the case of women, by exile and confiscation of property.[46] With an exception in favor of the Jews, those who permitted themselves or others to be circumcised were punished probably with exile and confiscation; the physician or slave who performed the operation, with death.[47]

Legislation evolved special forms of complicity—negative co-operation in the case of the soldier who was obliged to protect his officer,[48] and presumed complicity in the case of all slaves present in the house when the master was attacked.[49]

Complicity with regard to parricide[50] was described generally,[51] but there are instances of specific cases: the son who knew of his brother's parricidal intent and failed to reveal it;[52] the physician involved;[53] those who knowingly lent, either directly or indirectly, money to be used for parricidal purpose,[54] and those who acted as an agent to obtain the money,[55] or who gave security for it.[56]

[46] N. 142, 1.

[47] D. (48, 8) 11 pr. Here it is simply stated " . . . qui hoc fecerit, castrantis poena irrogatur." The texts to which this might refer—D. (48, 8) 3, 5; D. (48, 8) 4, 2—are not in complete accord. Paul's explicit statement with regard to circumcision provides the best interpretation: "Ciues Romani, qui se Iudaico ritu uel seruos suos circumcidi patiuntur, bonis ademptis in insulam perpetuo relegantur; medici capite puniuntur."—P. Sent. (5, 22) 2, 3.

[48] D. (49, 16) 6, 8-9: "Qui praepositum suum non protexit, cum posset, in pari causa factori habendus est; si resistere non potuit, parcendum ei."

[49] D. (29, 5) 1, 18. The slaves were questioned under torture—D. (29, 5) 1 pr.; 1, 25—and failing to prove innocence, were executed—D. (29, 5) 1, 30. " . . . tout esclave de la *domus* présent au lieu du crime et qui ne peut établir l'impossibilité où il était de venir en aide à son maître, est exécuté comme complice sur le fondement de cette présomption juridique qu'il aurait pu secourir son maître."—Mommsen-Duquesne, II, 347.

[50] This crime involved a more severe penalty than simple murder, as is noted in D. (48, 9) 9.

[51] Inst. (4, 18) 6; D. (48, 9) 1; 6.

[52] D. (48, 9) 2. He, however, was only exiled.

[53] *Ibid.* He was punished with death. *Glossa* ad v. *Frater. Et medicus* suggests that his part consisted in supplying poison to the son.

[54] D. (48, 9) 7; Falchi, *I Singoli Reati*, p. 167.

[55] D. *ibid.*; Falchi, *loc cit.*

[56] D. *ibid.*; Falchi, *loc. cit.*

Accomplices to voluntary incendiarism were also comprehended under the *lex Cornelia,*[57] possibly because of the danger to human life.[58]

3. *Superstition under the Christian emperors.* With regard to pagan sacrifices, those who offered, participated in, or gave their services to them, were equally punished with death and confiscation; provincial governors who failed to punish the culprits were fined.[59] The owner who knew such sacrifices were performed on his property was stripped of military and civil dignity and forfeited his possessions; if of private condition, he was tortured and sent to the mines.[60] The complementary acts of teaching and learning witchcraft were of delictual parity;[61] to consult a practitioner of magical arts about the future made one liable to death;[62] moreover the soothsayer who entered another's house was burned to death, and the one who introduced him was punished with exile and confiscation.[63]

4. *Crimes of violence.* One who used armed men to dispossess another of lands, house, or ship,[64] or who lent men for such purposes or for other acts of violence as making attacks, robbing with arms or upon the occasion of a fire, and raping a youth or woman,[65] were all comprehended by Justinian under the *lex Julia de vi publica.* Acts of violence without the use of arms came under the *lex Julia de vi privata.*[66] If, however, only one of the group was armed, all were held under the *lex Julia de vi publica.*[67] Also guilty of *vis publica* was the magistrate who ordered the death or torture of a Roman

[57] D. (48, 8), 1 pr.

[58] Mommsen-Duquesne, II, 364-365.

[59] C. (1, 11) 7, 2-3.

[60] C. (1, 11), 8, 1.

[61] C. (9, 18) 8.

[62] C. (9, 18) 5. Cf. P. Sent. (5, 21), 34.

[63] C. (9, 18) 3 pr.

[64] D. (48, 6) 3, 6.

[65] D. (48, 6) 4.

[66] Cf. *glossa* ad D. (48, 6) 3, 6 v. *armatis.*

[67] "Per D. (43, 16) 3, 3 se di coloro che espellono violentemente taluno dal suo possesso, alcuni sono armati e altri no, la violenza si intende, per ciascuno, commessa con armi"—Falchi, *Dottrine Generali,* p. 193.

citizen who had made an appeal to a higher court.[68] Complicity was likewise noted in those who interfered with funerals,[69] who prevented a defendant from going to Rome within a certain time,[70] who precluded safe trials by proper judges.[71]

5. *The crime of fraud.* These cases of complicity were mentioned with regard to the crime of fraud: one who corrupted a judge or the judge who allowed himself to be corrupted;[72] those who participated in the suborning of witnesses;[73] those who brought about the removal, deletion, interpolation of a will or the signing or quoting of a false will; [74] those who failed to prevent counterfeiting, when able to do so; [75] who engaged in the sale or purchase of tin or lead coins; [76] who were accomplices to counterfeiting; [77] a soldier who helped the escape of a counterfeiter from jail was punished with death.[78] With regard to the house or place, where the counterfeiting was done, the law made very fine distinctions. The owner, who was nearby, even if ignorant of the crime, lost the property merely by negligence;[79] widows and wards *(pupilli)* were excepted.[80] Procurators, however, who allowed counterfeiting in the property under their care, and also slaves, inhabitants, and tenants were punished with death.[81]. Guardians *(tutores)* who were nearby, since by their office they were required to exercise vigilance, were fined as much as their wards

[68] D. (48, 6) 7.

[69] D. (48, 6) 5 pr.; D. (47, 12) 8.

[70] D. (48, 6) 8.

[71] D. (48, 6) 10 pr.

[72] D. (48, 10) 1, 2; D. (48, 8) 1, 1; Mommsen-Duquesne, II, 397. This is mentioned as a common crime participated in by the corrupter and the corrupted, but the first text cited also indicates other forms of complicity in a general way.

[73] D. (48, 13) 2; D. (48, 10) 1, 2; Mommsen-Duquesne, II, 398.

[74] D. (48, 10) 2.

[75] D. (48, 10) 9, 1.

[76] D. (48, 10) 9, 2.

[77] C. (9, 24) 1 pr.

[78] C. (9, 24) 1, 2.

[79] C. (9, 24) 1, 4.

[80] C. (9, 24) 1, 6.

[81] C. (9, 24) 1, 5.

would have lost, if subject to punishment.[82]

6. *Sexual crimes.* The man who committed bigamy was to be judged infamous.[83] A *decurio* secretly married [84] to another's slave suffered exile and confiscation; the woman was sent to the mines. If, however, the procurator of the place where the crime was committed, knew of the crime and failed to report it, he too was condemned to the mines. The owner, guilty of knowing or permitting it, lost his farm and equipment, if it happened in the country; or if in his house in town, one half of his possessions.[85] If a Christian married a Jew both were punished as guilty of *adulterium.*[86] Partners in incest committed a common crime,[87] punishable by exile.[88] Nothing could be given, either by gift or will, to the incestuous partner or children, but after death everything passed by law to the near relatives; if, however, any of the latter had given counsel regarding the crime he forfeited his share.[89]

Illicit sexual intercourse, classified as *adulterium* or *stuprum,* was comprehended under the *lex Julia de adulteriis coercendis,* in the Justinian Codification, and was punished by exile and confiscation of one-half the patrimony; in the case of married women, the confiscation became one-third the patrimony and one-half the *dos;* people of lower condition received a corporeal punishment; finally the condemned woman could not marry in the future.[90] Although a procedural matter, it might be mentioned to show the implications of the crime of *adulterium* that slaves present in the house could be examined by torture.[91] Guilty of *adulterium* was the man who knowingly married a woman convicted of *adulterium,* who did not expel an adulterous

82 C. (9, 24) 1, 7.

83 C. (5, 5) 2. Nothing was discerned against his partner.

84 *Glossa* ad v. *Cum ancillis* observes that *contubernium* not *justae nuptae* is meant.

85 C. (5, 5) 3.

86 C. (1, 9) 6.

87 D. (48, 5) 8; D. (48, 6) 40, 7.

88 Mommsen-Duquesne, II, 413-414.

89 C. (5, 5) 6.

90 Mommsen-Duquesne, II, 426.

91 C. (9, 9) 31.

wife, who accepted money for her adultery or for not revealing it, or who offered his house for the perpetration of sexual crimes.[92] This included lending the house for pederasty; [93] which in turn was punished by death for both active and passive participant.[94] A woman who had sexual relations with her own slave was condemned to death; the slave was beaten and burned to death.[95] Rape was penalized with death and loss of goods for the principal agent and for those who accompanied him; those who offered other aid or shelter were punished with death.[96]

7. *Price manipulation.* Those who formed an association to raise the price of food, or who helped to detain a ship or sailor for the same purpose were subject to a fine.[97]

8. *Theft.*[98] All participation by way of assistance and counsel induced the guilt of theft.[99] This was expressed in the famous formula *ope consilio,* which applied to the principal agent and all who lent assistance either moral or physical.[100] It was not necessary for the contribution of each cooperator to be endowed with all the characteristics of theft that each might contract the guilt; it was sufficient that the essentials be present cumulatively.[101] Moral assistance was not punishable till physical handling *(contrectatio)* had completed the crime.[102] The formula *ope consilio* included those who advised, impelled, or instructed regarding theft or who lent service and assist-

[92] D. (4, 4) 37, 1.

[93] D. (48, 5) 9.

[94] D. (47, 11) 1, 2; C. (9, 9) 30; Mommsen-Duquesne, II, 431-432.

[95] C. (9, 11) 11, 1 pr., cf. *glossa* ad v. *Verberone*: "Id est, qui post verbera comburitur . . . "

[96] C. (9, 13); C. (1, 3), 53.

[97] D. (48, 12) 2.

[98] Thus far offenses of public law, crimes, have been considered; certain offenses of private law, torts, must now be studied. Because of their relation to the subject matter, several crimes will also be included in this section, but they will be expressly noted as such.

[99] Mommsen-Duquesne, I, 116.

[100] Mommsen-Duquesne, I, 116-117; III, 48.

[101] Mommsen-Duquesne, III, 49.

[102] D. (47, 2), 52, 19; 36 pr.

ance; [103] as examples of the latter form there is mentioned one who knocks money out of another's hand or stands between him and his property that a third person might steal; one who chases or frightens animals for another to steal; one who places a ladder to a window, who breaks open windows or doors, who lends tools or ladders that another might commit theft.[104] Failure to report a thief was not punishable,[105] but to receive or hide thieves involved complicity.[106] Those who knowingly accepted stolen goods not only could be obliged to surrender them but were also guilty of theft.[107]

Those caught in the act, or while carrying off the goods *(furtum manifestum)* were condemned to a penalty of fourfold the value of the thing stolen; otherwise *(furtum nec manifestum)* when convicted of theft they were held to a penalty of double the value.[108] Judges who embezzled public money *(peculatus)*, those who aided them, and those who knowingly received such money, were punished with death.[109] In the case of the wife, son, or slave, who stole from the husband, father, or master respectively, in conjunction with others, the outsiders were held to theft, from which the former were excepted.[110] Partners in kidnapping *(plagium)* where a free person was unwillingly held or sold, or a slave held or sold without his master's consent,[111] were punished according to the gravity of the crime and generally sent to the mines.[112] If several slaves of the

[103] D. (47, 2) 50, 2-3.

[104] Inst. (4, 1) 11.

[105] D. (47, 2) 48, 1.

[106] D. (47, 16) 1; C. (9, 39) 1; reception of cattle-thieves, D. (47, 14) 3, 3.

[107] C. (5, 2) 14. These, however, like all who lent assistance, were in any case held only to *furtum nec manifestum*—Inst. (4, 1) 4; D. (47, 2) 34.

[108] Mommsen-Duquesne, III, 56-59. The thief himself upon conviction became infamous—*ibid*.

[109] C. (9, 28) 1. This—Inst. (4, 18) 9—and kidnapping—Inst. (4, 18) 10—next to be considered, are crimes, belonging to public law, but are a kind of alienation and so are treated here.

[110] D. (47, 2) 36, 1; Falchi, *Dottrine Generali*, pp. 193-194.

[111] D. (48, 15) 6, 2.

[112] D. (48, 15) 7; C. (9, 20) 16.

same master participated in theft, the master could either surrender the guilty parties or pay the pecuniary penalty a single free person would incur.[113] This choice was given only if the crime was committed without the knowledge of the master.[114] When the crime was committed at the order of the master, both slaves and master were held as principal agents.[115] The same rule applied to cases where slaves caused damage.[116]

9. *Iniuria.* Complicity in the matter of *iniuria* was indicated generally, but emphasized the case of those who gave or received a command.[117] If an injurious act was performed by several slaves, the act became proper to each; in fact, there were as many injurious acts as participants.[118] Writers and publishers of defamatory books, and their accomplices were declared incapable of making a will; the same penalty was imposed upon composers of injurious epigrams and upon those who had them bought or sold.[119] The criminal act of corrupting the praetorian book *(album)* was similar to *iniuria;* if several slaves of the same household participated, they were all held to the penalty and could not be freed, as in the case of theft and damage, by the payment of the penalty due from a single free person.[120] Those who ordered the crime received the same punishment as those who did it—a fine for those who could pay, or, for slaves whose master was willing to pay for them; otherwise, torture.[121]

10. *Damage.* The *lex Aquilia* provided for a compensation of damage to property.[122] As to complicity, moral and physical cooperation were considered, in the Justinian compilation, as of the same

[113] D. (47, 6) 1 pr.

[114] D. (47, 6) 1, 1.

[115] Mommsen-Duquesne, I, 119, n. 1.

[116] D. (47, 6) 1, 2.

[117] D. (47, 10) 11 pr.; D. (47, 10) 11, 3-6; Inst. (4, 4) 11; C. (9, 2) 5. Regarding the nature and penalties of *iniuria*, cf. Leage-Ziegler, *Roman Private Law* (2. ed., London: Macmillan, 1937), pp. 375-379.

[118] D. (47, 10) 34.

[119] D. (47, 10), 5, 9-10.

[120] D. (2, 1) 9.

[121] D. (2, 1) 7.

[122] Cf. Leage-Ziegler, *Roman Private Law*, p. 371.

class as the principal agent; when several people acted together or when it was impossible to determine the part played by each, all were held to the same penalty.[123] Slaves who committed the crime [124] of violating graves without their master's knowledge were sent to the mines; if they acted with his knowledge, they were exiled;[125] their accomplices could be fined.[126]

11. *Legal Responsibility*. Responsibility was fixed by law upon masters of ships, keepers of inns and stables for acts of guile and theft done by their slaves or employees upon their premises to the patrons,[127] and likewise upon householders for damage caused by things thrown out of the house.[128] But this is not a matter of complicity but rather of public order, providing safety against harm and security for damage.

This study of Roman complicity is brought to a close with the following observations:

1. There was no general norm governing complicity.

2. Very often complicity was indicated in a general way, by such phrases as *dolo malo facere ut . . . ; faciendum curare.*

3. On the other hand, there was much legislation, especially that derived from the later emperors, which was most specific and detailed.

4. Except for the general formulas indicated above, complicity and its forms were described by law, or at least, by the legalized opinions of the jurisconsults. This situation put a limit upon the extension of a specific law, but no limit upon the legislator.

5. As a result, the laws contain cases of complicity which according to their nature would not be considered as criminal cooperation, e.g., the negligent owner of the place where the crime was committed.

123 Mommsen-Duquesne, III, 152; D. (9, 2) 11, 2.
124 "crimen"—C. (9, 19) 1; "cessat Aquilia"—D. (47, 12), 2 and 8.
125 C. (9, 19) 2.
126 D. (47, 12) 3 pr.
127 Inst. (4, 5) 3.
128 D. (9, 3) 1 pr.

6. With regard to the influence of Roman law upon the concept of criminal cooperation in later legal systems, it may be noted, first that Roman law presented a highly developed application of cooperative principles in the penal laws, which took account not only of the external element but also of the internal element of guilt; second that the legal arguments of its legislators and the ratiocination of its juris-consults were open to selection by future jurists.

Chapter Three

GERMANIC LAW

Article 1. Leges Barbarorum

The Germanic law is divided into two classes—*Leges Barbarorum* and *Capitularia Regum Francorum.* The former represent the unwritten customs of different German peoples compiled in Latin between the fifth and eighth century—whether these various collections were official redactions or not is not clear in every case, but once they were written they were accepted.[1] Because of their common consuetudinary origin an unanimity is observed in the penal institutions of these laws, although the individual dispositions may differ in detail.

Primitively a part of private law, the penal system operated by way of self-help through private vengeance[2] called *faida.*[3] The social disorders occasioned by this system of private vengeance called for some amelioration. This was supplied by the substitution of a pecuniary composition for the corporal penalty—once this price was paid, the *faida* could no longer lawfully exist between the delinquent and the family of the injured party.[4] The penal law was largely a narration of these tariffs which went into great detail over the material qualities of the crime—especially the number and the kind of injury.[5] However, the composition was not given in full to the victim; the king kept a third, called *fredus,*[6] and thus was introduced the notion of a fine. Other penalties were introduced by the early Frankish kings. Crimes of special interest to the tribe, as treason,

[1] Chénon, *Histoire Générale du Droit Français Public et Privé dès Origine à 1815* (2 vols., Paris: Recueil Sirey, 1926-1929), I, 134-135.

[2] Chénon, *op. cit.*, I, 263.

[3] *Faida*, signifying enmity, gave the right, not only to the injured party, but also to his relatives, of personally exacting from the culprit the penalty equivalent to the injury—cf. Du Cange, "Faida,"—*Glossarium Mediae et Infimae Latinitatis.*

[4] Chénon, *op. cit.*, I, 263. This was already in force at the time of Tacitus († post 117 A. D.?)—*ibid.*

[5] Cf. Chénon, *op. cit.*, I, 266.

[6] Cf. Du Cange, "Fredus"—*Glossarium;* Chenon, *op. cit.*, I, 266.

desertion, and cowardice in battle, were punished by death.[7] Under the Merovingians, outlawry, flagellation, castration, and fines were in use, and to these were added in Carolingian times, death, mutilation (as of the nose, hand, eye), prison, exile, and confiscation.[8]

The peculiar jurisprudence of the Germanic system, noteworthy for its attention to physical details, may be observed in the matter of complicity as the following instances testify. In the *lex Burgundionum* if a slave killed a free man without his master's knowledge, the slave was killed, but the master was unharmed; [9] but if the master knew of this, he also was killed; [10] moreover if after the crime the slave was not available, his master was forced to pay a compensation, in gold coins, fixed by law, in place of the slave, to the relatives of the deceased.[11] In the *lex Alamannorum*, one who violated a girl was to pay 6 coins; those who to his advantage accompanied him were to pay 3 coins, but if they did not touch the girl, they paid only 2 coins.[12] In the *lex Visigothorum*, whoever shut up a lord or lady in a house, or whoever commanded it done, was to pay 300 gold coins and to receive 100 stripes; those who consented or aided were to pay 15 coins and receive 100 stripes; slaves who did this apart from their master's command were to receive 200 stripes.[13]

Article 2. *Capitularia Regum Francorum.*

The later class of Germanic law, the *Capitularia Regum Francorum*, were edicts of the Frankish kings of the Merovingian and Carol-

[7] This also was in use at the time of Tacitus—cf. Chénon, *loc. cit.*

[8] Chénon, *loc. cit.*

[9] Liber Constitutionum, II, c. 3—*Monumenta Germaniae Historica*, Legum Sectio, I, tom. II, pars I, *Leges Burgundionum* (ed. L. R. de Salis, Hannoverae, 1892), p. 43.

[10] C. 4—*ibid.*

[11] C. 5—*ibid.* This is an example of vicarious responsibility without personal guilt.

[12] Fragmentum III, n. 24—*MGH*, Legum Sectio, I, tom. V, pars I, *Leges Alamannorum* (ed. K. Lehmann, Hannoverae, 1888), p. 25.

[13] Lib. VIII, tit. 13, c. 4—*MGH*, Legum Sectio I, tom. I, *Leges Visigothorum* (ed. K. Zeumer, Hannoverae et Lipsiae, 1902), p. 314.

ingian periods.[14] Besides repressing necessary complicity in adultery,[15] incest,[16] and simony,[17] these laws also proceeded against complicity in specified cases.

If anyone believing a person to be a witch, who ate human beings, would for this reason, burn him, eat him, or give him to be eaten, he was to be punished with death.[18] Those who entered into counsel with the pagans against Christians or who by fraud consented to this, were killed.[19] Anyone who harbored thieves or other malefactors for seven nights broke the ban of the emperor; if a count did this, he lost his honor.[20] If one should presume to help a person unjustly litigating with another in court, he was to pay 15 coins upon conviction.[21] In a conspiracy, the authors were to be killed; those who lent aid were to be beaten and have their nose cut off.[22] If a person to whom a condemned thief had been turned over for execution, should allow him to live, he was to pay half the sum for which the thief was condemned.[23] Further, if one caught a thief, and let him go unpunished, he was, on conviction, to be held for the damage to which the thief had been liable.[24] With regard to offenses against religious chastity, the nun and her illicit consort were to be separated and put into monasteries, together with their goods, and

[14] Cf. Van Hove, *Commentarium Lovaniense in Codicem Iuris Canonici*, Vol. I, tom. I, *Prolegomena* (Mechliniae: Dessain, 1928), p. 140.

[15] Capitulare Missorum Item Speciale (a. 802?), c. 22—*MGH*, Legum Sectio II, tom. I, *Capitularia Regum Francorum* (ed. A. Boretino, Hannoverae, 1883), p. 103.

[16] Capitulare Missorum Generale (a. 802), c. 33—*ibid.*, p. 97.

[17] Capitulare Missorum Item Speciale, c. 8—*ibid.*, p. 102.

[18] Capitulatio de Partibus Saxoniae (a. 775-790), c. 6—*ibid.*, pp. 68-69. This was a particular law for the newly conquered and violently converted Saxons—cf. Stephenson, *Mediaeval History* (2 vols., New York: Harper and Brothers, 1935), I, 184-185.

[19] Capitulatio de Partibus Saxoniae, c. 10—*ibid.*, p. 69.

[20] Capitulatio de Partibus Saxoniae, c. 24—*ibid.*, p. 70.

[21] Capitulare Legibus Additum (a. 803), c. 4—*ibid.*, p. 113.

[22] Capitulare Missorum in Theodonis Villa Datum Secundum Generale, c. 10—*ibid.*, p. 124.

[23] Capitulare Italicum (a. 801), c. 4—*ibid.*, p. 205.

[24] Capitulare Italicum, c. 7—*ibid.*

with the composition which was due to the state and to her guardian *(mundoaldo)*. If the man were so poor as to be unable to support himself in a monastery, he was remitted to the custody of his relatives, who were to guard against any relapse. But if he did relapse, he was to pay 30 coins to her guardian, and she was to enter a monastery with the tax due her guardian and the composition of her adultery. If a slave took the religious habit in accordance with the will of her master, and afterwards committed adultery, the master was to pay a fine of one gold coin.[25]

When witnesses were produced against one party of a lawsuit, he had the right to oppose them with his own witnesses. If discordance ensued without either side surrendering, a champion was to be picked from each group, and these two champions were to fight with stave and shield until one yielded and was thus proclaimed guilty of perjury. For this his right hand was cut off, but the others of his side could redeem their hands with a composition, two parts of which was given to him against whom they had testified, the remaining third was collected by the state as *fredus*.[26]

In conclusion it may be remarked that relatively little account of *dolus* or criminal intention was taken in Germanic law; external relation to the crime by presence, aid, or counsel, and responsibility for the criminal were principally considered. This was due to the basis of the penal system which was indemnification, in place of guilt and punishment. With regard to its influence on the canonical jurisprudence of complicity, Germanic law, harsh as it was, is to be given some credit for the introduction of a more flexible system of penalization than that of Roman law, ranging from severe to milder penalties according to the gravity of the offense. A further influence is to be noted in the canonical development of the notion and punishment of subsequent cooperation.

[25] Capitula Italica, c. 1—*ibid.*, p. 215. Whether negligent or not, the guardian forfeited the composition to the monastery. In the last case, it seems clear that the master was held to vicarious responsibility. This and the other capitula thus far cited are ascribed to Charlemagne.

[26] Capitula Legibus Addenda Hludovici Pii (818-819), c. 10—*ibid.*, pp. 282-283.

Chapter Four

COMPLICITY IN A BROAD SENSE

The cases treated in this chapter fall into two classifications—crimes which present complicity by reason of association with the culprit and crimes which necessarily involve an accomplice. This does not imply that in the latter case practical jurisprudence may not rightly regard the reciprocal acts of the necessary accomplices as formal complicity. Since both associative and necessary complicity are not considered by legal philosophers, apart from what the law may decide in practical cases, as true cooperation in crime, it has not been felt desirable to trace the full history of these forms of complicity, but merely to show their evolution and acceptance in canon law. This is all the more reasonable in view of the fact that in these cases there is usually no jurisprudential problem involved in fixing the guilt, since in necessary complicity the accomplices are equally at fault, and in associative complicity the status of the delinquents depends on the will of the legislator.

Article 1. *Complicity by Reason of Association*

Not only participation in the crime is contemplated by the law as coming under complicity but also association with the criminal apart from the crime itself. Clearly there is no sharing in the crime here, and in order to be forbidden it should be explicitly stated by law. Since, however, it is an easy step to advance from the punishment of an offender to the penalizing of his associates, history shows frequent legal strictures against associates of criminals from the beginning of the Church.

This may be due to two reasons. First, the followers of a heretic or a schismatic, against whom most of the legal efforts of the early Church were expended, were usually as guilty as their leader; here was a case of many people committing the same crime without the possibility of determining the independent or, on the other hand, the cooperative quality of their various crimes. But it was sufficient for practical purposes that all committed the same crime, and by doing so were, in concert with the others disrupting the unity of the Church. Hence the frequent device of stating a punishment for a heresiarch or a schismatic and his companions *(socii)* or followers *(sectatores.)*

The second reason was the nature of the principal penalty developed in the early Church. Grave offenses were punished by excommunication. Now if the delinquent were cut off from the ecclesiastical society, it was only natural that the correlative of this penalty should also be stated by law—namely, that the members be forbidden to associate with excommunicates.

A consequent development of these two penalizing norms was the legislation against those who favored the criminal. These supporters may not have participated in the crime, but besides association and communion, there was the connotation of some aid, even if given after the crime, which was odious to the law and therefore to be repressed.

The first companions to be punished were those who had at least committed the same crime, if not actually shared in it cooperatively. In the third century, Felicissimus and five Carthaginlan priests, followers of his schism, were excommunicated by St. Cyprian.[1] About the year 368,[2] Pope St. Damasus I (366-384) excommunicated Ursacius, Valens, and their followers,[3] but St. Athanasius still wished him to take measures against Auxentius, the invader of the bishopric of Milan, who was not only a follower of Arianism, but also guilty of many crimes, which he had committed with Gregory, the companion of his impiety.[4]

Pope St. Celestine I (422-432) decided that the companions of Nestorius, the deposed bishop of Constantinople, should be given an opportunity to return to Catholic unity, and then, if still con-

[1] *Ep. XL. S. Cypriani*—*MPL*, IV, 332-339.

[2] Jaffé, *Regesta Pontificium Romanorum ab condita ecclesia ad annum post Christum natum MCXCVIII* (editionem secundam correctam et auctam auspiciis Gulielmi Wattenbach, curaverunt S. Loewenfeld, F. Kaltenbrunner, P. Ewald, Lepsiae, 1885), p. 37. Hereafter this work will be cited as JK, JE, or JL, depending upon the period entrusted to the editors: Kaltenbrunner, y. 1-589; Ewald, y. 590-881; Loewenfeld, y. 882-1198.

[3] " . . . aliisque qui cum illis sentirent"—*Ep. Episcoporum Aegypti et Libyae Nonaginta necnon B. Athanasii*—MPG, XXVI, 1046.

[4] *Ibid.*

tumacious, were to be condemned.[5] Dioscorus and Eutyches, the companion of his perfidy, and their associates were penalized by Pope St. Leo I (440-461).[6] Leo also requested the emperor Leo I to expel clerics of Constantinople, who were the companions of heretics.[7] He disapproved of the selection of Peter, a companion of heretics, to be bishop.[8] Misenus in a profession of faith before a Roman synod held under Pope St. Gelasius I (482-486) condemned the heresy of Eutyches together with Eutyches, Dioscorus, and all their successors, followers, and communicants.[9] Pope Hormisdas (514-523) excommunicated Nestorius, Eutyches, their companions,[10] and followers.[11] Thus was established the basis of criminal procedure against the companions of criminals, especially of heretics and schismatics.

Association was also noteworthy in a procedural matter, when the method of procedure on suspicion alone was adopted, which was especially found in the penalization for suspicion of heresey.[12] This suspicion could be based on many roots other than companionship,[13] but during the Inquisition, which was empowered to proceed on suspicion,[14] association or friendship was cause for

[5] *Ep. ad synodum Ephesinam*—Mansi, *Sacrorum Conciliorum Nova et Amplissima Collectio* (Paris), V, 269; JK n. 385, year 432. Hereafter this work will be cited as Mansi.

[6] *Ep. ad episcopos Galliorum*—Mansi, VI, 185-188; JK n. 480, year 452.

[7] *Ep. ad Leonem Augustum*—Mansi, VI, 323-327; JK n. 532, year 457.

[8] *Ep. ad Acacium episcopum Constantinopolitanum*—Mansi, VII, 992-993; JK n. 587, year 482.

[9] Synodus Romana—Mansi, VIII, 177; held in 495 according to JK p. 88.

[10] *Ep. ad Anastasium Imperatorem*—Mansi, VIII, 393-395; JK n. 775, year 515.

[11] *Ep. ad Ioannem Nicopolitanum episcopum*—Mansi, VIII, 402-403; JK n. 780, year 516.

[12] Cf. canons 2315-2316.

[13] Cf. Wernz, pp. 294-295.

[14] "Secundo, inquisitores ex commisso sibi officio possint procedere contra quoscumque hereticos, aut de pravitate heretica culpabiles, vel suspectos, seu etiam diffamatos, et contra receptores . . . "—Bernardus Guidonis, *Practica Inquisitionis Heretice Pravitatis* (c. 1324) (edited by C. Douais, Paris, 1886), p. 186.

suspicion.[15] In this connection there is an interesting case mentioned in the Decretals of Gregory IX,[16] The dean of Nevers had been denounced for heresy because of association with heretics. No convincing witness appeared against him while on trial for heresy. Accordingly, Pope Innocent III (1198-1216) ordered that if he purged himself of heresy by canonical purgation, he was to receive some benefice but in punishment for associating with heretics[17] he was to remain suspended from office until he had repaired the scandal given; if, however, he failed in the purgation, he was to be suspended from office and benefice and put in a monastery for penance.

With regard to communicating with the criminal, the First Council of Antioch (341) under pain of excommunication forbade bishops, priests, and deacons to pray with excommunicates,[18] or to celebrate any sacred rite with them.[19] Pope St. Leo I (457-474) cautioned Anatolius, bishop of Constantinople, to avoid the supporters of heretics.[20] Pope St. Felix III (483-492) warned the clergy of Constantinople to abstain from communion with the excommunicated Acacius.[21] Whoever knowingly communicated with an excommunicate was to refrain from Holy Communion until he had received a penance from the superior who had imposed the excommunication, according to Pope St. Gelasius I (429-496).[22]

The restriction of social communion was occasionally broadened

[15] Anselmus Dandinus, *De suspectis de haeresi* (Romae, 1703), praeliminare XI, *Ex amicis*, pp. 17-19; p. 436, n. 10; cf. Bernardus Guidonis, *op. cit.*, p. 122, *Forma sententiae alicujus defuncti*, where a single visit to heretics gave cause for holding a trial even after death.

[16] C. 10, X, *de purgatione canonica*, V, 34.

[17] *Glossa* ad v. *familiaritatis:* "ex qua orta fuit infamia contra eum."

[18] Canon 2—Mansi, II, 1310.

[19] Canon 4—Mansi, II, 1311.

[20] *Ep. ad Anatolium*—Mansi, VI, 341-343; JK n. 532, y. 458.

[21] *Ep. ad clerum et plebem Constantinopolitanum*—Mansi, VII, 1067; JK n. 602, y. 484.

[22] C. 37, C. XI, q. 3; JK n. 693 gives no date.

to include wicked men,[23] magicians and groups participating in the sacrifices of the dead,[24] Jews, and unbaptized pagans of the eighth century,[25] and finally the Saracens.[26] Pope Nicholas I (858-867) used this device of restricting communion to deter King Lothaire from the society of the woman he attempted to make his second wife, Waldrada—who was already excommunicated.[27] Under Innocent III (1198-1216) these measures became legally [28] repressive of true complicity when the Pope distinguished between communion with an excommunicate in the crime—by lending aid, counsel, or support—for which he was excommunicated, and communion with an excommunicate outside his crime—as by praying, talking, eating.[29] In the first case, called *communicatio in crimine criminoso,* Innocent ruled that communion brought with it all the strictures to which the excommunicate was liable; in the second case, communion merely induced an excommunication which could be absolved by a simple

[23] *Ep. Gregorii Papae I ad Serenum episcopum Massiliensem*—*MGH,* Epistolae II, pars II, *Gregorii I Registrum Epistolarum* (ed. L. M. Hartmann, Berolinii, 1895), pp. 269-272; JE n. 1800, y. 600.

[24] *Ep. Gregorii Papae III ad Optimates et populos Germaniae*—*MGH,* Epistolae III, *Epistolae Merowingici et Karolini Aevi,* tom. I (S. Bonifatii et Lulli epistolae ed. E. Dummler, Berolini, 1892), p. 291; JE n. 2236, y. 739.

[25] *Ep. Hadriani Papae I ad Egilam episcopum Illiberitanum*—Mansi, XII, 808-814; *Epistolae Merowingici et Karolini Aevi, ibid.* (Codex Carolinus ed. W. Gundlach), pp. 644-647; JE n. 2445, date: between 772 and c. 785. *Ep. Hadriani Papae I ad episcopos per Spaniam Commorantes, ibid.,* pp. 636-643; JE n. 2479, y. 785-791.

[26] *Ep. Ioannis Papae VIII ad Sergium magistrum Neapolitanum*—Mansi, XVII, 36-37; JE n. 3089, y. 877. *Ep. Ioannis Papae VIII ad (Athanasium) episcopum Neapolitanum*—Mansi, XVII, 37-38; JE n. 3090, y. 877. *Ep. Ioannis* ad Landulfum episcopum Capuanum—Mansi, XVII, 44-45; JE n. 3095, y. 877.

[27] *Ep. Nicolai Papae I ad Lotharium regem*—Mansi, XV, 321-324; also c. 10, C. XI, q. 3; JE, n. 2873, y. 867.

[28] This distinction was previously made by the decretists of the twelfth century; cf. *glossa* ad c. 19, C. XI, q. 3, v. *Excommunicetur;* under Innocent it became law, cf. Sole, *De delictis et poenis* (Romae, 1920), p. 274.

[29] *Ep. Wratislaviensi episcopo*—c. 5, X, *de poenis,* V, 37; Potthast, *Regesta Pontificum Romanorum inde ab A. post Christum natum 1198 ad A.* 1304 (Berlin, 1874-1875), n. 700, y. 1199. This work will later be cited as Potthast.

priest. This had practical significance especially in penalties *ab homine;* even if only one of those participating in the crime were liable ordinarily to a penalty, either because only he had been apprehended or because only he was subject to the penalizing prelate, nevertheless, all others concerned in the crime were subject to the same penalties as was he who had been brought to trial, immediately upon sentence being passed,[31] in the case of *communicatio in crimine criminoso.*

Repressive measures were also taken against those who gave favor or support to criminals. Such support was often given by persons in authority, who instead of proceeding against delinquents often aided them. Strictly understood, these supporters took no part in the crime; they merely favored the criminal by offering him shelter, comfort, advice, position, legal aid.

In the Second Council of Rome (251) Pope St. Cornelius (251-252) excommunicated Novatian and his supporters.[32] Leo I required the Bishop of Constantinople to avoid the supporters of heretics.[33] Pope St. Gregory I (590-604) warned civil and ecclesiastical authorities not to defend unjustly those implicated in public thefts.[34] He rebuked Serenus, Bishop of Marseilles, for protecting the practice of destroying images, which Gregory had condemned.[35] Honorius I

[31] *Glossa* ad v. *Comedendo*: Tunc in istis casibus non communicat illi in crimine, sed extra, unde propter hoc non est ligatus eadem sententia cum illo . . . " *Glossa* ad v. *Tunc erit absolutio*: "Si ego excommunico parochianum meum propter crimen et parochianus alterius ei communicat favorem impartiendo in delicto suo, in me videtur derelinquere et eadem sententia ligatur et non sententia canonis, quia tunc a suo episcopo vel proprio sacerdote absolveretur, et sic iste propter delictum ligatur sententia mea et a me debet absolvi."

[32] Mansi, I, 864-866; JK, p. 17.

[33] *Ep. ad Anatolium*—Mansi, VI, 341-343; JK n. 532, y. 457.

[34] *Ep. ad Romanum defensorem et Ioannem episcopum Syracusanum*—MGH, *Gregorii I Papae Registrum Epistolarum*, p. 95; JE, n. 1647, y. 598.

[35] *Ep. ad Serenum, episcopum Massiliensem*—Mansi, X, 255-257; JE n. 1800, y. 600.

(625-638) instructed the deacon Cyriacus to make radical corrections in a case which might also be classed under forbidden communion. Peter, Bishop of Syracuse, pleaded the cause of the city's harlots before the prefect to request the removal of their present custodian and the appointment of a new one. The fact that the bishop was accompanied by three hundred of these unsavory characters in performing this mission was especially blameworthy.[36]

The encyclical of Pope St. Martin I (649-653 or 655) anathematized all heretics with their doctrines and all who would receive or defend or write in favor of them or their doctrines.[37] Gregory II (715-731) in the Roman Synod of 721 excommunicated those who gave favor to one committing rape.[38] Thietgaud, Bishop of Treves, and Gunther, Bishop of Cologne, were excommunicated and deposed by Nicholas I (858-867) for the counsel and favor they had given the king of France, Lothaire, in his adulterous second marriage.[39] Nicholas II (1059-1061) excommunicated the supporters of the antipope, Benedict X, who had been elected and enthroned at night by several noblemen.[40] Innocent III in 1205 [41] extended the idea of favor to include legal advice and aid. Advocates, notaries, and judges were forbidden to grant the legal assistance peculiar to their office to heretics, under pain of suspension from office, infamy, and nullity of the act performed.[42] Lucius III (1181-1185) had prepared the way for this legislation by decreeing that those who favored heretics were to be repelled from all public office as laboring under infamy.[43] Innocent III also punished falsifiers of papal documents and their supporters and defenders with excommunication.[44] In the

[36] *Ep. Petro episcopo Syracusano*—Mansi, X, 585; MPL, LXXX, 481; JE n. 2029, no date.

[37] Mansi, X, 1170-1183; JE n. 2058, y. 649.

[38] Capitulum XI—Mansi, XII, 264; JE, p. 250.

[39] Concilium Romanum (863), capitulum II—Mansi, XV, 651; JE, p.351.

[40] *MGH*, Scriptores, VII, *Chronica Monasterii Casinensis* (ed. W. Wattenbach, Hannoverae, 1846), 705.

[41] Potthast n. 22532.

[42] C. 11, X, *de haereticis*, V, 7.

[43] Mansi XXII, 476-478; JL n. 15109, y. 1184.

[44] C. 7, X, *de crimine falsi*, V, 20; promulgated in 1201 according to Friedberg.

First Ecumenical Council of Lyons (1245), Innocent IV (1243-1254) threatened with excommunication and deposition those who received, defended, or concealed assassins—the same punishment as was decreed for those who commissioned the assassins.[45]

In addition to those already treated, there was penalized another criminally cooperative form—presence or attendance at the crime. Once again in this type, there was no explicit intervention in the crime, but merely attendance at its commission. It was not, therefore, complicity in the true sense but in so far as the law penalized presence because of its reference to another's delinquency, and because of the support which is lent thereby to the crime, it is here briefly considered.

In the Roman Council of 1059, Nicholas II (1059-1061) prohibited the faithful to attend mass celebrated by a priest known to have a concubine.[46] Alexaxnder III (1149-1181) ruled that Robert, a cleric, who was forced to be present at a murder, and had done penance on this account, should be absolved and promoted to orders.[47] He also decided that a youth, who, in the capacity of an acolyte, had been present at his brother's rebaptism—done superstitiously to restore his health—should receive a punishment; although this was to be slight because of his minority, nevertheless, the boy was not to be promoted to higher orders if the affair had been public, unless he entered a religious congregation.[48] In an interesting case,[49] Innocent III (1198-1216) seems to regard corporeal presence as equally culpable as mandate. A man accused of theft before the Bishop of Albenga offered to purge himself by the ordeal of hot iron, or failing, was to be hanged. When the suspect was burned in the trial, which

[45] *Constitutiones Innocentii Papae IV, de homicidio*—Mansi, XXIII, 670; c. 1, *de homicidio*, V, 4, in VI°.

[46] N. 3—Mansi, XIX, 897; JL, pp. 558-559. This was repeated by Alexander II (1061-1073), Concilium Romanum (1063), capitulum III—Mansi, XIX, 1025; JL n. 4501.

[47] *Ep. Henrico episcopo Remensi*—MPL, CC, 828; JL n. 12072, y. 1171-1172.

[48] Appendix ad Concilium Lateranense III (1179), De depositione clericorum, cap. I—Mansi XXII, 367; c. 2, X, *de apostatis et reiterantibus baptisma*, V, 9; JL n. 13940, no date.

[49] *Ep. ad Episcopum Hiponensem et Abbatem de Toleto*—c. 10, X *de excessibus praelatorum et subditorum*, V, 31; Potthast, n. 3564, y. 1208.

the bishop attended, the latter ordered the man hanged in his presence. Innocent ruled that since the bishop not only lent authority to the ordeal and execution, but also corporeal presence,[50] he was to resign or be removed as unworthy of the ministry of the altar.[51] Finally there may be mentioned the excommunication of spectators of duels.[52]

[50] The language of the text as well as of the *casus* of the *Glossa Ordinaria* places the emphasis on presence not on authority.

[51] Bernardus Parmensis de Botone († 1266) believed that the bishop was liable to punishment solely for consenting to the ordeal—*glossa* ad v. *candentis*: "Haec purgatio prohibita est supra *de cler. vel mona. sententiam,* et infra *de pur. vulg.* titulo toto—unde hoc solo quod in hoc consensit, fuit puniendus;" and further, that he broke the law by his presence—*glossa* ad v. *corporalem*: "Unde incidit in illam constitutionem, supra, *ne cler. vel mona. sententiam.*" The authorities cited, however, do not bear him out. C. 9, X, *de clericis vel monachis,* III, 50 originated in the Fourth Lateran Council in 1215, seven years after the present rule and does not precisely forbid the presence of clerics at ordeals. Bernard, of course, considered the Decretals as a whole and did not take account of the primary *fontes existentiae*. Title 35 *de purgatione vulgari* in the fifth book of Gregory IX forbids trial by combat or ordeal. As far then as general positive law, the present case may have very well set the precedent with regard to attendance.

[52] Iulius II const. "*Regis Pacifici*" 24 febr. 1509, n. 2, 3— *Codicis Iuris Canonici Fontes cures Emi. Petri Card. Gasparri* Editi (9 vols., Romae [postea Civitate Vaticana]: Typis Polyglottis Vaticanis, 1923-1939. [Vol. VII, VIII et IX ed. cura et studio Emi. Iustiniani Card. Seredi]), n. 63 (Hereafter, this work will be cited as *Fontes*); Concilium Tridentinum, Sess. XXV, *de ref.*, c. 19.

Article 2. Necessary Complicity

Among the types of complicity included under canon 2209, the crimes which necessarily require the reciprocity of several people have a decided place.[53] Strictly speaking, however, such criminal reciprocity should not be considered as complicity.[54] In practice, nonetheless, those participating in such crimes may be regarded as co-agents of the crime, provided the necessary delictual requisites exist in each case. Since the canonized jurisprudence of the Code adopts this viewpoint a brief historical exploration of the crimes entailing necessary complicity is indicated. It is not to be hoped that this study will contribute anything to the knowledge of jurisprudential evolution for once the crime is stated, the guilt and cooperation of the necessary parties are at once obvious. It may be noticed, however, that at times legislation lags behind jurisprudence, and the law may proceed against one partner without being concerned about the other. This is due to a number of factors. Previous legislation may offer the needed supplement; the special end of the law may find fulfilment through the coercion of one party especially; the special viewpoint of the law may be directed not against the ethical guilt of the several parties, but against the infraction of the peculiar social duty of one participant in particular. It is of some historical importance then to determine when a certain crime was penalized in its complete complicity. Little delay, therefore, will be made over crimes recognized as entailing complicity from the beginning, but an attempt will be ventured to assign the time for fixing the complete complicity in crimes where this concept was retarded.

Dual guilt seems to have been well recognized in sexual delinquencies. The repression of these crimes was at first done less by purely legal measures than by the penitential discipline, which during the first four centuries was public for grave sins.[55] However, the punish-

[53] Canon 2209, § 2; Michiels, *De delictis et poenis*, I, 296.

[54] Michiels, *loc. cit.*

[55] Morinus, *Commentarius Historicus de Disciplina in Administratione Sacramenti Poenitentiae Tredecim Primis Seculis in Ecclesia Occidentali, et huc usque in Orientali Observata* (Parisiis, 1651), V, cap. 8-14; Batiffol, "Les Origines de la Penitence"—*Etudes d'Histoire et de Theologie Positive*, 1re serie (4. ed., Paris, 1906), I, 200.

ment imposed, involving in this case an excommunication, was certainly the act of a juridical society, whether the penalty was solely for the spiritual welfare of the sinner,[56] or rather was vindictive in nature.[57] Fornication [58] and adultery [59] were contained under this discipline. Besides this, however, legislation made definite strictures. One of the earliest councils, Elvira ((303) denied communion for life to those who relapsed into fornication,[60] and to women who deserted their husbands and had carnal intercourse with other men.[61] Pope St. Innocent I (402-417) branded as adultery, remarriage after divorce.[62]

In sacrilegious unions, however, the dual guilt was not at first expressly stated. Following the first legislation with regard to clerical celibacy,[63] and the public vow of chastity,[64] in the Council of Elvira (303), the Council of Neocesarea (314)[65] ordered that priests who married were to be deposed, and the Fifth Council of Carthage (439) [66] required that clerics in major orders abstain from their wives. Innocent I (402-417) refused penance to sacred virgins who married, until the death of their spouse.[67] Leo I (457-474) noted that monks and nuns may not desert their resolve to practice chastity.[68] All these ordinances refer to the one directly bound by the obligation;

[56] Kober, *Der Kirchenbann* (Tuebingen, 1863), pp. 23-27.

[57] Hinschius, *System des Katholischen Kirchenrechts* (6 vols., Berlin, 1869-1897), V, 127.

[58] S. Irenaeus, *Contra haereses*, I, cap. 13, n. 5-7—*MPG*, VII, 487-591.

[59] Tertullianus, *De pudicitia*, c. 1—*MPL*, II, 981.

[60] Canon 7—Mansi, II, 7.

[61] Canon 8—Mansi, II, 7.

[62] *Ep. ad Exsuperium episcopum Tolosanum*—Mansi, III, 1038-1041; JK n. 293, y. 404.

[63] Canon 33—Mansi, II, 11. Hefele and Funk consider this the first prescription on celibacy—Hefele-Leclercq, *Histoire des Conciles* (10 vols. in 19, Paris, 1901-1938), I, 239.

[64] Canon 13—Mansi, II, 8.

[65] Canon 1—Mansi, II, 539.

[66] Canon 3—Mansi, III, 969.

[67] *Ep. ad Victricium*, n. 12—Mansi III, 1035; JK n. 286, y. 404.

[68] *Ep. ad Rusticum episcopum Narbonensem*, nn. 14 and 15 respectively—Mansi, VI, 397-407; JK n. 544, y. 458-459.

however, Pope Gelasius I (492-496) finally took cognizance of the guilty partner—he who associated sacrilegiously with a nun was to be excommunicated and to be reconciled only after public penance.[69] This rule was repeated by the Council of Tribur (895).[70] Complicity, however, was expressed in its completeness by Clement V (1305-1314) in the Council of Vienne (1311).[71] In virtue of this enactment all who contracted marriage with religious men or women or with clerics in sacred orders were excommunicated.

With regard to simony, the Council of Chalcedon (451) nullified the ordination obtained through simony and rendered the ordaining prelate liable to deposition; [72] the complete guilt was expressed by Gelasius in 494: [73] according to the Scriptures the damnation of Simon involves the one who gives and the one who accepts. Although without fault of simony himself, one, nevertheless, who knowingly received ordination from a simoniacal prelate, was deposed and subjected to penance together with his consecrator.[74]

[69] *Ep. ad episcopos Lucaniae,* c. 20—Mansi, VIII, 37-45; JK n. 636, y. 494.

[70] Canon 23—Mansi, XVIII, 144.

[71] C. un., *de consanguinitate et affinitate,* IV, in Clem.

[72] Canon II—Mansi, VII, 373, 358-359.

[73] *Ep. ad Episcopos Lucaniae,* c. 24—Mansi, VIII, 43-44; JK n. 636.

[74] Nicolaus II (1059-1061), Synodus Romana—Mansi, XIX, 899; held in 1059, cf. JL, under this date. It does not seem necessary that the ordination be simoniacal, since the law was directed against those known to be guilty of simony. The germane subject of ordination by an excommunicated prelate was much discussed. Ioannes Faventinus and Rufinus held that orders conferred by an excommunicate were valid but were not to be exercised, provided the ordainer was consecrated a bishop while in the Catholic Church; if he were not consecrated in the Catholic Church, neither licit exercise nor validity of orders were conferred—cf. Kuttner, "Eine Dekretsumme des Johannes Teutonicus"—*Zeitschrift Der Savigny-Stiftung fuer Rechtsgeschichte,* kan. abt., XXI (1932), 141-189; *Die Summa Decretorum des Magister Rufinus* herausgegeben von Heinrich Singer (Paderborn, 1902), pp. 298-299. Ioannes Teutonicus (Kuttner, *loc. cit.*) shows that this view does not accord with C. I, q. 7, and points out that if the excommunicate has been validly ordained a bishop, he can confer valid orders, but not the licit exercise of orders. Now simoniacal ordination became involved in this question by Gratian's inclusion of Urban II's response (c. 4, C. IX, q. 1) which tolerated those ordained by excommunicates if there was no simony regarding the ordination or the ordainer, cf. *casus* ad c. 4, C. IX, q. 1.

While the name of Gregory VII (1073-1085) is prominently associated with the struggle over lay investiture, he directed his legislative strictures against the cleric receiving the investiture.[75] It was under Paschal II (1099-1118) that both members of this crime were explicitly comprehended by the law.[76]

With regard to the alienation of church property, Paschal II decreed that in the case of those who obtained church offerings through the civil power, both the giver and the receiver were judged to be sacrilegious thieves.[77] There was a previous statute passed in the synod under Hadrian II (867-872) requiring those who bought or received any of the Church's revenue to restore it under pain of anathema.[78] The complete complicity of giver and receiver was however first developed in this regard by Psuedo-Isidore.[79] It was in his apocryphal letter ascribed to Lucius I (252-253) [80] that this concept [81] was first set forth, and strangely enough, whereas the genuine law of Paschal II was neglected by the canonical collections, the forgery of Pseudo-Isidore was incorporated into the *Decretum* of Gratian [82] after many previous reproductions.[83]

While those who fought duels suffered excommunication, infamy, and confiscation of property after the Council of Trent (1545-1563) [84] this legislation was preceded by strictures against tourna-

[75] Synodus Romana, c. 2—Mansi, XX, 509; held in 1078—JL under this date.

[76] Concilium Trecense (1107), *Ep. Paschalis Papae II ad Reinhardum episcopum Halberstadensem*—Mansi, XX, 1221-1222; Synodus Beneventi (1108) —Mansi, XX, 1231-1232; cf. JL under these dates.

[77] "raptor et sacrilegus"—*Ep. Canonicis S. Martini*—Mansi, XX, 1074; JL n. 6598, y. 1099-1118.

[78] C. 15—Friedberg, note to c. 13, C. XII, q. 2.

[79] The identity of this forger is much discussed; the date of his collection is set between 847 and 857; cf. Van Hove, *Prolegomena*, pp. 143-147.

[80] JK n. 123.

[81] Hinschius, *Decretales pseudo-Isidorianae et capitula Angilrami* (Lipsiae, 1863), p. 179.

[82] C. 5, C. XVII, q. 4.

[83] Cf. Friedberg's note to c. 5, C. XVII, q. 4.

[84] Sess. XXV, *de reform.*, c. 19.

ments,[85] duels on papal territory,[86] and trial by combat.[87].

[85] Innocent II (1130-1143), Synodus apud Clarummontem (1130) c. IX —Mansi XXI, 439; cf., JL under this date.

[86] Celestine III (1191-1198), c. 1, X *de purgatione vulgari*, V, 35; JL n. 17626, no date.

[87] Honorius III (1216-1227), c. 3, X *de purgatione vulgari*, V, 35; Potthast n. 6910, y. 1222.

CHAPTER FIVE

COMPLICITY IN THE STRICT SENSE, FROM THE APOSTOLIC AGE TO THE *DECRETUM GRATIANI*

Under this heading, complicity in the strict sense, will be considered all actions which fall under the name complicity, whether it be formal, negative, or subsequent. What is here recorded may be regarded as the prototype of the entire canon 2209, except insofar as necessary complicity is concerned. An endeavor will be made to offer a description sufficiently clear so that the cooperation may in each instance be recognized as formal, negative, or subsequent.

Pope St. Victor (190?-c. 202) proceeded against guilty joint agents by excommunicating members of an Asiatic council who had decided to celebrate Easter on the fourteenth day of the Jewish month Nisan, whether a Sunday or not, contrary to the practice prescribed by Rome.[1]

In the middle of the third century the excesses of schismatics presented an interesting episode replete with complicity. Novatian with the help of two associates brought three provincial bishops to a banquet, where surrounded by Novatian's prepared followers and overcome with wine, they were forced to consecrate the schismatic rigorist as anti-pope.[2] All who took part in the affair were excommunicated and the bishops were also deposed. One of these bishops returned to the Church and was received by the pope to lay communion. In this story are indicated the principal, Novatian, his two associates who procured the bishops, the men who had been prepared to extort the consecration, and the three bishops who acted under compulsion and in a confused state of mind.

Joint agents were again punished by Pope St. Stephan I (253-257), who excommunicated those who agreed to the rebaptism of heretics

[1] Concilium Asiaticum—Mansi, I, 719; Cicognani, *Canon Law* (authorized English version by O'Hara and Brennan, 2. ed., Philadelphia: The Dolphin Press, 1935), p. 137.

[2] *Ep. Cornelii papae ad Fabium episcopum Antiochenum*—Mansi, I, 817-830; JK n. 106, y. 251?

in an African synod.[3]

While, strictly speaking, one cannot claim evidence of complicity in the warning given by Pope St. Damasus (366-384) to the bishop of Thessalonica against allowing the *statuta maiorum* to be contravened,[4] nevertheless, there is indicated here the possibility of negative cooperation.

Out of all concerned in a crime, the most reprehensible are those who institute it. These authors of the crime were noticed by Pope St. Siricius (384-398) who excommunicated various heresiarchs—Iovianus, Auxentius, Genialis, and several others, as *novae haeresis incentores*.[5]

The conciliar legislation of the fourth century is not overabundant with rules governing complicity. The Council of Elvira (303) refused communion for life to pimps.[6] According to the same council, when a wife committed adultery with the knowledge of her husband, he was to receive the same punishment as the adulterers—excommunication for life—unless he should leave his wife, and in this case he was to be received to communion after ten years of penance.[7] The Council of Ancyra (314) prescribed ten years of penance to those who supplied drugs for abortion or who consented to abortion, as well as the woman committing it.[8] By the same council, five years of penance were decreed for those who brought magicians into their houses for magical or superstitious purposes.[9] More in the nature of an irregularity than a penalty was the ordinance of the Council of Neocaesarea (314) regarding the husband of an adulterous wife: if he were still a layman, he could not enter the clerical state; if the adultery occurred after ordination, he was obliged either to dismiss her or to refrain from his ministry.[10]

[3] Synodus Romana—Mansi, I, 934; JK p. 20, y. 256?

[4] *Ep. ad Acholium episcopum Thessalonicensem*—Mansi, VIII, 749-750; JK n. 237, y. 380.

[5] *Ep. Siricii papae ecclesiae Mediolanensi*—Mansi, II, 663-664; JK n. 260, y. 390.

[6] Canon 12—Mansi, II, 7-8.

[7] Canon 70—Mansi, II, 17.

[8] Canon 21—Mansi, II, 519, 526.

[9] Canon 23—Mansi, II, 527, 528.

[10] Canon 8—Mansi, II, 541.

With the fifth century ushering in a new period of external liberty for the Church, increased legislative and judicial activity may be observed.

Considering the case of a man illicitly made bishop, the First Council of Orange (441) condemned his consecrators as the authors of the crime and, if he had been willing, the one so consecrated; the former were also to be deposed. If, however, the recipient had been unwilling, he was to be installed in the place of one of his consecrators, provided he were worthy.[11]

Pope St. Leo I (440-461) ruled that clerics who assented to any detriment to the possessions of the Church should be deprived both of their order and of communion.[12] He based his efforts for the suppression of disturbing crowds of Palestine monks, who were followers of Eutyches and Dioscorus, on the fact that they were authors of seditionary riots.[13]

The Synod of St. Patrick (450 or 456) [14] in Ireland decreed that the father, who, having once given his daughter in marriage, would consent to her illicit love for another man and take a gift in consideration of it, should together with his daughter be excluded from the Church.[15]

The Council of Chalcedon (451) proceeded against agents or intermediaries in the matter of simony: clerics were to be degraded; monks and laymen excommunicated.[16] The same council noted coauthors by degrading monks or clerics who conspired against their

[11] Canon 21—Mansi, VI, 439.

[12] *Ep. Leonis papae I ad episcopos per Siciliam constitutos*—*MPL*, LIV, 703; JK n. 415, y. 447.

[13] "incentores seditionum"—*Ep. ad Iulianum Episcopum Coensem*—Mansi, VI, 212-214; JK n. 486; y. 452. "auctores seditionum"—*Ep. ad Iulianum Episcopum Coensem*—Mansi, VI, 234-236; JK n. 493, y. 453. "incentores cruentarum seditionum"—*Ep. ad eundem Iulianum Coensem Episcopum*—Mansi, VI, 237- 238; JK n. 494, y. 453.

[14] Cf. Hefele-Leclercq, *Histoire des Conciles*, II, 888.

[15] Canon 22—Mansi, VI, 517.

[16] Canon 2—Mansi, VII, 373, 359.

bishop or fellow-clerics.[17] Those who consented to the crime of rape were punished equally with the perpetrators by excommunication.[18]

The Second Council of Arles (452) declared sacrilegious the bishop who neglected to eradicate idolatry in his diocese; the owner of land on which were situate idolatrous remains, if unwilling to remove them, was to be excommunicated.[19]

Asellus, an archdeacon, was suspected of cooperating in the murder of his bishop and in the theft of ecclesiastical goods. He was ordered removed from office by Pope St. Gelasius I (492-496) on the definite charge of failing to report the murder of the bishop, whom he intended to succeed.[20]

Pope St. Hormisdas (514-523) required Dorotheus, Bishop of Thessalonica, as author of a murder, to be deprived of the episcopacy and to be exiled or sent to Rome.[21]

For a conspiracy two deacons, Rusticus and Sebastianus, together with their associates, were deprived of their office by Pope Vigilius (537-555).[22]

Menna, Bishop of Constantinople, together with all the bishops of the patriarchate who assented to the excesses of Theodorus, Bishop of Caesarea in Cappadocia, now excommunicated and deposed, were also excommunicated by Vigilius.[23]

Pelagius I (555-560) indicated forty days of strict penance and seven years of lighter penance for one who perjured himself or

[17] Canon 18—Mansi, VII, 366, 378; c. 21, C. XI, q. 1. Conspiracy is difficult to classify; insofar as several persons are required, it can be considered as necessary complicity; but it is also possible to regard the conspirators as co-agents, since no definite number is required, and since they all join in the same act rather than complete each other's act.

[18] Canon 27—Mansi, VII, 369; c. 1, C. XXXVI, q. 2.

[19] Canon 23—Mansi, VII, 881. This may be regarded as negative cooperation.

[20] *Ep. Iohanni episcopo*—Mansi, VIII, 126-127; Ivo, *Decretum*, X, C. 13; JK n. 724, y. 496.

[21] *Ep. ad Germanum episcopum Capuanum*—Mansi, VIII, 477-478; JK n. 840, y. 519.

[22] *Ep. ad Rusticum et Sebastianum*—Mansi, IX, 351-359; JK n. 927, y. 550.

[23] *Fragmentum Damnationis Theodori*—Mansi, IX, 58-61; JK n. 930, y. 551.

knowingly led others into perjury, and for all other accomplices.[24] He also delayed the consecration of the Bishop of Syracuse until the latter promised not to usurp the goods of the Church either through himself, his children, his wife, his servants, his relatives, or any other person.[25]

The Council of Macon I (581) refused communion till death to those who induced another to give false testimony; those who consented to perjury were made incapable of testifying and were considered infamous.[26]

Gregory I (590-604) imposed a penance on Opilio, deacon, and Servus-dei and Crescentius, clerics, who together had sold two silver chalices and other furnishings of the Church of Vanafra, and he further desired the Jew who had bought them to be compelled by the civil judge to restore them.[27]

Honorius I (625-628) announced that unless Hypatius, Bishop of Nicopolis in Epirus, would swear that he was not involved in the murder of his predecessor, Sotericus, he would not be given the pallium.[28]

The Seventeenth Council of Toledo (694) punished with perpetual exile the priest who said mass for another's death, and also the person who induced him to do so.[29] The one committing rape and those consenting to the crime were excommunicated by Gregory

[24] C. 4, C. XXII, q. 5; Thiel, *Epistolae Romanorum Pontificum Genuinae* (Brunsbergae, 1868), I, 613: ascribes this to Pelagius I; cf. JK n. 967, no date.

[25] *Ep. ad Cethagum patricium*—Mansi, IX, 733-734; JK n. 992, no date. This was a precautionary measure by the pope. The only man capable of being bishop was married; so the pope wanted to have some security that his consent to the consecration would not bring detriment to the possessions of the Church. It is not intended to show cooperation in crime here, but merely consciousness on the part of ecclesiastical authority, of the possibility of cooperation.

[26] Canon 17—Mansi, IX, 935.

[27] *Ep. ad Anchimium, subdeaconum*—Mansi, IX, 1075-1076; JE n. 1135, y. 591; *MGH, Gregorii I Papae Registrum Epistolarum*, p. 87.

[28] *Ep. ad Ioannem, Andream, Stephanum, Donatum, episcopos Epiri*—Mansi, X, 581-582; JE n. 2010, y. 625.

[29] Capitulum 5—Mansi, XII, 99.

II (715-731).[30] Gregory III (731-741) applied the penance given for homicide to those who sold slaves to the pagans to be sacrificed.[31]

Although his ambassador was involved, Carloman was cleared by Pope Stephan IV (768-772) of complicity in an attempt against the pope's life.[32]

Leo IV (847-855) rejected presumed complicity. A priest had been deprived of his benefice by another priest who had obtained it through simony. The jealous relatives of the injured priest, apart from his will and counsel however, put out the eyes of the simoniacal invader, and on this account, the innocent priest had been excommunicated. The pope decided that, if found innocent, he was to be absolved.[33]

Nicholas I (858-867) prescribed three years of penance for Burgandus and his accomplices who stole sacred vessels and put holy chrism to common use.[34]

John VIII (872-882) pointed out to Duke Domagol, under whose name pirates were operating, that unless he repressed their depradations, he would share in their guilt.[35] He also tried to put down several conspiracies by the bishops and nobles against the emperor, Charles the Bald.[36] In the Synod of Ravenna (877) he threatened

[30] Synodus Romana, c. 10-11—Mansi, XII, 264; held in 721 according to JE, under this date.

[31] *I. Ep. ad Bonifacium archiepiscopum*, c. 8—Mansi, XII, 278-279; MGH, *Epistolae Merowingici et Karolini Aevi*, pp. 279-280; JE n. 2239, y. 732.

[32] *Ep. ad Bertradam, deo consecratam et Carolum regem Francorum*—Mansi, XII, 691-693; JE n. 2388, y. 771.

[33] *Ep. ad Ebrunium et Adelfredum episcopos*—c. 5, C. I, q. 4; JE n. 2624, no date.

[34] *Ep. ad Frontarium archiepiscopum Burdegalensem*—Mansi, XV, 400-401; c. 17, C, XII, q. 2; JE n. 2840, no date.

[35] *Ep. ad Demagum Ducem gloriosum*—Mansi, XVII, 243; c. 12, C. XXIII, q. 8; JE n. 2998, y, 873-882. This is an example of negative complicity.

[36] *Ep. ad episcopos et comites in regno Caroli constitutos*—Mansi, XVII, 233-234; JE n. 3037, y. 876. *Ep. ad episcopos qui a Carolo deciscentes Ludovico regi adhaeserant*—Mansi, XVII, 234-235; JE n. 3038. *Ep. ad episcopos in regno Ludovico regis Bajoariae constitutos*—Mansi, XVII, 227, 230; JE n. 3039, y. 876. *Ep. ad Comites in regno Ludovici regis Bajoariae constitutos*—Mansi, XVII, 230-233; JE n. 3040, y. 876. Synodus Romana—Mansi, XVII, 236.

with excommunication those who commit homicide, mutilation, incendiarism, or who command or consent to them,[37] likewise those who perform, command, or consent to pillaging.[38] Those who kidnapped the son of Count Wipert and ravaged his land were to be excommunicated.[39] The pope exhorted Count Hugo to restore what had been stolen by his men.[40] The Bishop of Pavia was ordered to excommunicate Godfrey, son of a nobleman, Iselbert, a subdeacon, and Heribald, a notary, for the rape of Gausilda.[41] John ruled that certain monks, at whose instigation a boy was murdered, were gradually to be restored to the exercise of orders after due penance.[42] Helpers of Bertilda, who had deserted her husband, were excommunicated; but she was ordered to appear before the pope.[43] Count Liudtefried and his wife were excommunicated for persuading a nun to leave the monastery.[44] Romanus, Archbishop of Ravenna was called to a synod for giving the wife of Count Deusdedit to another man.[45]

The synod held at Rome by John IX (898-900) excommunicated those who had agreed together to violate the corpse of Formosus, unless they should have repented.[46] Those who confessed they were forced to be present at Pope Stephan's synod, at which this violation occurred, were pardoned.[47] Notice the different *modus agendi* of John here and of Pope Cornelius toward the consecrators of Novatian.

[37] c. 7—Mansi, XVII, 338.

[38] c. 8—Mansi, XVII, 338.

[39] *Ep. Ioannis papae ad Theodoricum archiepiscopum et Isaac episcopum*—Mansi, XVII, 101; JE n. 3214, y. 878-879.

[40] *Ep. ad Hugonem Comitem*—Mansi, XVII, 101; JE n. 3215, no date.

[41] *Ep. ad Ioannem episcopum Papiensem*—Mansi, XVII, 102; JE n. 3193, y. 878-879.

[42] *Ep. ad episcopum Bellovacensem*—Mansi, XVII, 105; JE n. 3197, y. 878-879.

[43] *Ep. ad Aimarum et Widonem episcopos*—Mansi, XVII, 105; JE n. 3198, y. 878-879.

[44] *Ep. ad Liudtefridum*—Mansi, XVII, 113; JE n. 3235, y. 879.

[45] *Ep. ad Romanum, Archiepiscopum Ravennatem*—Mansi, XVIII, 202; JE n. 3348, y. 881.

[46] C. IX—Mansi, XVIII, 225; held in 898 according to JL.

[47] C. II—Mansi, XVIII, 223.

It was probably a question of policy to a large extent with John, because of the number of important bishops present at the shameful occurrence.

In the Roman Council of Gregory V (996-999) a sentence of excommunication was passed against the Archbishop of Turin, who performed the ceremony, and the other bishops who consented to the illicit marriage of Robert, king of France, and Bertha, a relative.[48]

Leo IX (1048-1054) announced that the clergy and people of Osino were under anathema for following the custom of plundering the house of the bishop upon his death.[49]

Gregory VII (1073-1085) had to deal with several schisms and conspiracies.[50] In the Roman Synod of 1078, it was ruled that bishops were to be suspended from office who, for money or because of persuasion, would consent to fornication committed by priests, or to the crime of incest, or who did not proceed against such offenses with the authority of their office.[51]

Gregory warned Count Robert of Flanders not to give aid to Lambert, the simoniacal invader of the church of Therouanne.[52] He anathematized the antipope Clement III and his creator, Henry IV of Germany.[53]

Paschal II (1099-1118) excommunicated those who counseled Henry, king of England, to persist in the practice of lay investiture.[54] He pointed out that those who out of ignorance or necessity communicated with excommunicates were not guilty before the Eternal

[48] C. II—Mansi, XIX, 225.

[49] Mansi, XIX, 672-673; JL n. 4210, y. 1047-1054.

[50] Synodus Romana (1076)—Mansi, XX, 467; *Ep. ad Udonem archiepiscopum Trevirensem et Theodericum Virdunensem et Herimannum Metensem*—Mansi, XX, 319; JL n. 4986, y. 1076. *Ep. ad Hugonem abbatem Cluniacensem*—Mansi, XX, 315-316; JL n. 5173, n. 1080.

[51] C. 11—Mansi, XX, 510.

[52] *Ep. ad Robertum, comitem Flandrensium*—Mansi, XX, 370-371; JL n. 5242, y. 1082.

[53] Concilium Romanum—Mansi, XX, 589-590; JL assigns this council to the year 1083.

[54] Concilium Lateranense—Mansi, XX, 1183-1184; y. 1105 according to JL under this date.

Judge.[55] The clerics who conspired against the bishop of Florence were deprived of their dignities.[56]

Gelasius II (1118-1119) excommunicated the emperor, Henry V, and Burdinus, Archbishop of Braga, whom Henry made antipope under the name of Gregory VIII.[57]

Similarly, the Synod of Liege under Innocent II (1130-1143) excommunicated the antipope Anacletus II, King Conrad and his brother Frederick.[58]

The Second General Council of the Lateran, held in 1139, excommunicated those who set fire to buildings, or had such incendiarism committed, or knowingly gave counsel or help to those committing it. Further, they were not to be absolved until they had made reparation according to their ability, and then a penance was to be imposed, consisting of a year's service in Jerusalem or Spain.[59] This is a splendid piece of legislation dealing competently with complicity, and marks the beginning of detailed laws on complicity similar to those of the later Roman emperors.

With this climax is brought to a close the formative period of Canon Law. It was a time of scattered legislation and judicial rulings which laid the foundation of an ecclesiastical jurisprudence of complicity. During this period nearly every type of cooperation has been explored, and many laws were fortified with provisions concerning complicity. From earliest times ecclesiastical jurisprudence recognized varying degrees of responsibility even among the same type of cooperators. A new period began with the publication of Gratian's Decretum. Law now tended, because of the popularity of this work, to confine itself within certain fixed forms. Gratian brought to a close the inchoative, unsystematized and formative period of ecclesiastical legal history and ushered in a new period of codified and relatively centralized law.[60]

[55] *Ep. ad (Gebeardum) episcopum Constantiensem*—Mansi, XX, 1083-1084; JL n. 6252, y. 1101-1110.

[56] *Ep. ad Florentinum*—Mansi, XX, 1053-1054; JL n. 6508, y. 1116.

[57] *Ep. ad C(ononem) episcopum Praenestinum*—Mansi, XXI, 173; JL n. 6642, y. 1118.

[58] Mansi, XXI, 473; y. 1131, JL under this date.

[59] Canons 18-19—Mansi, XXI, 531.

[60] Cf. Van Hove, *Prolegomena*, p. 165; Cicognani, *Canon Law*, p. 282.

Chapter Six

COMPLICITY IN THE STRICT SENSE FROM THE DECRETUM GRATIANI TO THE COUNCIL OF TRENT

Article I. The Legislative Development

A general statement or concordance of norms of complicity, such as was offered with regard to the direct crimes themselves, is not to be found in the Decretum Gratiani, completed about the year 1140. The ample but not novel treatment of criminal cooperation, which Gratian presented, was predominantly incidental to his treatment of other legal problems.

Gratian's method was by way of compiling various legal texts, arranging them by subject, and integrating them by his own notes or *dicta.* The texts which he used had only their own inherent authority,[1] but legal science profited by his arrangement and explanations.

While treating of irregularity, Gratian pointed out that with regard to murder, precept or counsel were equivalent to the act.[2] In solving the possibility of marriage between a woman and the man who had raped her, he noted the parity of consent or favor with actual commission as a basis of responsibility.[3] In Distinction 83, however, consent is treated explicitly, but here regard is not always had to consent sufficient to effect participation in crime but often to consent to another's transgressions unworthy of priests and especially bishops. This, however, and the many other texts dealing with consent[4] laid the foundation for a jurisprudence of complicity.

[1] Van Hove, *Prolegomena*, pp. 165-166; Cicognani, *Canon Law*, pp. 302-303.

[2] Rubric, c. 8, D. L.

[3] Rubric, c. 1, 4, 5, C. XXXVI, q. 2.

[4] The majority of Gratian's texts dealing with complicity are concerned with complicity by means of consent. Included is consent to rape (c. 1, 4, C. XXXVI, q. 2, to sinning (c. 100, C. XI, q. 3), to stealing church property (c. 10, C. XII, q. 2; c. 5, C. XVII, q. 4), to mayhem or incendiarism (c. 31, 33, C. XXIII, q. 2).

More directly in line with criminal cooperation was the culpable negligence of officials.[5] Concerning heresy, it was noted that to defend was even worse than to err.[6] A norm of true complicity was delineated in discussing the responsibility of the bishop who forced his archdeacon to perjure himself.[7] Clerics who removed or handed over to adversaries of the Church ecclesiastical documents were mentioned under alienation of property.[8] While the morality of consent to another's sin was declared in connection with obedience,[9] consent was proclaimed as requisite for guilt in relation to the toleration of the wicked.[10]

Although this grouping of opinions and legal statements under his own headings may be considered, in the fullest sense, Gratian's contribution to the jurisprudence of complicity, yet it does not mark the full value of the Decretum in this regard. Apart from Gratian's notes there are many texts [11] which treated of complicity, and which by their inclusion in Gratian's work, received new currency and influenced the legal thinking and practice of the Church.

Various other collections followed, as the need arose to compile the ever increasing legislation of this period. But this legislation will be presented here according to its original promulgation, with citations to the various collections in which it is to be found. In due course, proper attention will be given to the influence which the principal collections exercised in regard to the development of the canonical theory of complicity.

Pope Alexander III (1159-1181) wrote to the Bishop of Exeter in regard to those involved in the murder of St. Thomas of Canterbury.[12]

[5] Rubric, c. 12, C. XXIII, q. 8.

[6] Rubric, c. 32, C. XXIV, q. 3.

[7] Dicta ante c. 1, C. XXII, q. 5.

[8] Rubric, c. 33, C. XII, q. 2.

[9] Dicta ante c. 100, C. XI, q. 3; Rubric, *ibid.*

[10] Rubric, c. 8, C. XXIII, q. 4.

[11] All references to the Decretum cited above for Gratian's notes also indicate texts dealing with complicity.

[12] Comp. I, c. 7, *de homicidio voluntario vel casuali,* V, 10; c. 6, X, *h. t.*, V, 12; Mansi, XXII, 391-392; JL n. 12180, y. 1171-1173.

In summary,[13] the instructions in this letter may be recognized as presenting an unusually complete treatment of the modes of complicity and their penalization. One who accompanies a murderer with the intention of killing, even though he may not strike a blow, is held almost to the same penalty as the murderer; one who accompanies a murderer only with the intention of preventing him from being impeded, is held to a slightly less penalty; as to one inciting murder, he is punished more mildly than the murderer; but if he incites to a definite murder and this is effected, he is considered a murderer. Those guarding the belongings of the murderers and aware of their purpose, are not immune from the penalty of murder. Those who take possesion of the property of the victim are not thereby guilty of homicide but they must make due restitution. Those who communicate with the excommunicated killers are punished according to the mode of communication. Clerical accomplices and companions are to be deposed. The pope also pointed out that in punishing accomplices the subjective dispositions of each are to be weighed; not only the gravity of the crime, but also the age, intelligence, sex, and condition of the delinquent is to be considered, so that the same excess is to be more severely punished in one than in another.

The same pontiff replied to the query of the bishop of London, that judges with papal delegation may proceed against all those who abet persons on trial in manifest hindrance of justice.[14] The reason for this extension of authority was, according to the pope, the usual basis for penalizing all complicity, namely, that those who do and those who consent are to be punished by the same penalty.[15]

According to the Third Council of the Lateran (1179) heretics, and those defending or receiving them were excommunicated, and it was forbidden under pain of excommunication to keep heretics in one's house or on one's lands, or to have business dealings with

[13] Cf. Panormitanus (†1435), *Commentaria in quinque libros decretalium* (5 vols. in 7, Venetiis, 1588), V, c. 6, *h. t.*, n. 1.

[14] Comp. I, c. 2, *de officio et potestate iudicii delegati*, I, 21; c. 1, X, *h. t.*, I, 29; JL n. 13770, y. 1159-1181.

[15] *Glossa ordinaria* ad c. 1, X, h. t., I, 29, v. *Impedire*.

them.[16] The same council punished with excommunication and confiscation those who engaged in commerce with the Saracens.[17]

Lucius III (1181-1185) in the Council of Verona (1184) ordered strict penalties against secular princes who refused to swear to defend the Church against heretics.[18] Innocent III (1198-1216) proceeded against lawyers, notaries, and judges who performed acts of their office in favor of heretics, and also against those who elected heretics to public offices.[19]

Moreover, in solving the question of irregularity for a priest who had hit with a spade the robber of a church, who was to expire later under the attack of the people, Innocent gave a rule [20] which was occasionally invoked in matters of complicity, though not originally concerned with it. In summary,[21] this reply stated that one who has struck another lethally, incurs irregularity when the wounded person expires under the attack of others; irregularity is also contracted by all concerned, when it is not clear who gave the mortal wound, or again, when a person acting with homicidal intent gave a slight wound to one who died from the wounds of others.[22]

The Fourth Council of the Lateran (1215) used the formula believers,[23] defenders, and supporters in punishing the accomplices of

[16] Concilium Lateranense III, c. 27—Comp. I, c. 6, *de haereticis*, V, 6; c. 8, X, *h. t.*, V, 7.

[17] Concilium Lateranense III, c. 24, 16—Comp. I, c. 6, *de Iudaesis et Sarracenis et eorum servis*, V, 5; c. 6, X, *h. t.*, V, 6.

[18] Comp. I, c. 11, *de haereticis*, V. 6; c. 9, 13, X, *h. t.*, V, 7.

[19] Comp. III, c. 2, *de haereticis*, V, 4; c. 11, X, *h. t.*, V, 7; Potthast n. 2532, y. 1205.

[20] Comp. IV, c. 2, *de homicidio voluntario vel casuali*, V, 6; c. 18, X, *h. t.*, V, 12; Potthast n. 3757, y. 1209.

[21] Cf. Panormitanus, *Commentaria*, V, c. 18, *h. t.*

[22] Cf. *lex Aquilia*: "Sed si plures servum percusserint, utrum omnes quasi occiderint teneantur, videamus. et si quidem apparet, cuius ictu perierit, ille quasi occiderit tenetur; quod si non apparet, omnes quasi occiderint teneri . . . "—D. (9, 2) 11, 2.

[23] "Illi [credentes] enim dicuntur, et sunt omnes, qui haeresim credant, aut defendant (quo casu haeretici sunt) implicite tamen, verbis, vel factis credunt erroribus illis, quos sciunt esse contra fidem: ut si quis generaliter credat veram esse doctrinam Lutheri, quam scit fidei esse contrariam; licet

heretics.[24] This council also specified forbidden aid to Saracens in noting as punishable the supplying of ships or implements of war, and the giving of aid in nautical or military operations.[25]

Several modes of effecting the same criminal result were detailed by Honorius III (1216-1227) when he extended the penalty of excommunication imposed on those who introduced or enforced legislation against the liberty of the Church, or handed down judgment according to this legislation, and he applied this penalty to those who wrote such laws and judgment.[26]

In 1234 a new and authentic collection, now called the Decretales of Gregory IX, was promulgated.[27] Its purpose was the unification of ecclesiastical legislation which since the time of Gratian had been scattered through five collections or *Compilationes*.[28] The legislation just reviewed in chronological order was included first in one of the Five Compilations, and finally brought together in the collection of Gregory, as may be seen from the citations.

The collection of Gregory IX was followed by the authentic Liber Sextus of Boniface VIII (1294-1303). The notable texts on complicity in this collection emanated from the same pontiff, and are related here under the date of the promulgation of the Liber Sextus in 1298.

First may be mentioned the decree against the persecutors of cardinals.[29] Making them guilty of *lèse majesté*, as did the Justinian

in particulari nullum errorem sequatur, dicetur haereticus ex eo, quod implicite sic credit haeresibus."—Gonzalez-Tellez, *Commentaria perpetua*, (5 vols., Venetiis, 1699), IV, c. 13, X, *h. t.*, V, 7, n. 6.

[24] Concilium Lateranense IV, c. 3—Comp. IV, c. 2, *de haereticis*, V, 5; c. 13, X, *h. t.*, V, 7.

[25] C. 17, X, *de Iudaeis et Sarracenis et eorum servis*, V, 6; not in Compilatio IV.

[26] Comp. V, c. 2, *de const.*, I, 1; c. 49, X, de *sententia excommunicationis*, V, 39; Potthast n. 6469, y. 1220.

[27] Concerning the nature and authority of the *Decretales*, cf. Van Hove, *Prolegomena*, p. 174-176.

[28] Cicognani, *Canon Law*, p. 298.

[29] C. 5, *de poenis*, V, 9, in VI°.

Code with the murderers of the emperor's councillors and senators,[30] the pope decreed infamy, banishment, incapacity to succeed to or to will property, and the censure of excommunication against those performing the hostile act, their companions, those who commanded it done, or who ratified it, those who gave counsel, or favor or who afterwards knowingly sheltered or defended the delinquent. Moreover the male descendents within the second degree of those just mentioned were deprived of all benefices and declared incapable of obtaining others, and were also subjected to all the effects of infamy. Those who gave non-effective counsel or favor were subject to arbitrary penalties to be determined according to their guilt. Finally the penalties of this constitution could, at the discretion of the pope, be extended to the brothers, nephews, and grand nephews of those mentioned.

The same pontiff's rule on the ratification of another's crime legally settled a previous discussion among canonists. According to Boniface,[31] those who ratify violence to clerics done in their name but not at their request, incur the same excommunication as those performing the crime.

The last official canonical collection to be issued before the Council of Trent was the Constitutions of Clement V, promulgated in 1317. This contained complete dispositions regarding complicity in attacks on bishops and in the extortion of benefices from clerics.[32]

Following the Clementine Decretales, came two private collections, the *Extravagantes* of John XXII and the *Extravagantes Communes*.[33] Contributing little to the development of complicity, these collections contained texts repressing conspiracy and its various cooperators.[34]

[30] C. (9, 8) 5.

[31] C. 23, *de sententia excommunicationis, suspensionis, et interdicti,* V, 11, in VI°.

[32] Const. "*Si quis suadente diabolo,*" promulgated in the Council of Vienne (1317)—c. 1, *de poenis,* V, 8, in Clem. This is an extension of the famous constitution of the Second Lateran Council, c. 15—c. 29, C. XVII, q. 4.

[33] Cf. Van Hove, *Prolegomena,* pp. 180-181.

[34] C. un., *de poenis,* XII, in Extravag. Ioan. XXII; c. 3, 5, *de poenitentiis et remissionibus,* V, 9, Extravag. com.

Article 2. The Doctrinal Development

With the systematization given by Gratian to ecclesiastical law, the science of canon law arose, and was cultivated and augmented by the glossators and commentators who based their teachings on Gratian's *Decretum.*[35] The decretists laid the foundation of the ecclesiastical jurisprudence of complicity by their teaching on consent to another's act, whereby the one consenting was considered to make the act of another his own.[36] The act of the will, the consent, and not the form of participation, which was indeed discussed [37] was the principal point of the teaching of the decretists.[38] Consent involved guilt; this and not an examination of the causality of participation was the fundamental assumption even in detailed discussions of modes of cooperation.[39] When, however, the voluntary element as indicated by consent, was established in the law, the canonists would proceed to detail the forms in which the motion of the will was manifest, whether by cooperation, defense, counsel, the lending of authority or approbation.[40] The act of the will was furthermore the

[35] Cf. Kuttner, "The Father of the Science of Canon Law"—*The Jurist* I (1941), 2-19, especially, 15-18.

[36] Kuttner, *Kanonistische Schuldlehre von Gratian bis auf die Dekretalen Gregors IX* (Città Del Vaticano: Biblioteca Apostolica Vaticana, 1935), pp. 41-42. From the many authors cited by Kuttner, there may be selected as representative Simon de Bisiniano, writing about 1177-1179: "Immo tua per consensum; et nota quod rem alienam et peccatum alterius possumus nostrum facere per consensum"— *Summa* ad c. 3, C. XXXII, q. 5.

[37] Cf. Panormitanus, *Commentaria*, V, c. 6, X, *de homicidio voluntario vel casuali*, V, 12.

[38] Kuttner, *loc. cit.*

[39] Kuttner, *op. cit.* p. 42.

[40] Ioannes Teutonicus (†1245 or 1246), *glossa ordinaria* et *casus* ad c. 10, C. XII, q. 2, v. *Qui consentit;* Guido de Baysio (Archidiaconus, †1313), Additio ad ibid.; Bernardus Parmensis de Botone (†1263): "Ad hoc nota quod quadruplex est consensus, s. negligentiae, consilii, cooperationis, et auctoritatis seu defensionis. In primo casu, s. negligentiae, minus peccat consentiens quam faciens, nisi forte negligentia nimis crassa fuerit, ut in praelato. In secundo casu, s. consilii minus punitur: plus tamen quam negligens. . . . In tertio casu cooperationis aequaliter peccant facientes et consentientes, et in hoc intelliguntur omnes auctoritates, quae dicunt quod aequaliter puni-

distinguishing criterion for the imputation of the guilt of omission; whoever omits an act that is commanded, is similar to one who commits a forbidden act, but only insofar as he is conscious of it and is bound, and insofar as his omission implies an act of the will.[41] The determination of the legal obligation to perform an act as the condition for contracting the guilt of omission was a matter of dispute; thus it was debated by the decretists whether the duty of impeding crimes was incumbent only on the holders of official power and prelates or on all.[42]

Besides the fundamental nature of cooperation and the elaboration of cooperative forms, the canonists also developed particular doctrines regarding complicity.

Bernardus Parmensis de Botone (†1263) noted that fear reduces punishment, or in cases of violence, removes it; [43] also that one who participates gladly *(affective)* is to receive a greater punishment;[44] and that ignorance, unless it be crass, excuses.[45]

This decretalist also declared that the will to commit a crime, even when this had not been put into effect, was punishable provided the one so willing accompanied those who committed the deed, for in that case he contributed to the crime by cooperating.[46]

untur. In quarto casu auctoritatis seu defensionis, magis peccat consentiens defendendo et auctoritatem praestando quam faciens, et magis puniendus . . . "—*glossa ordinaria* ad c. 1, X, *de officio et potestate iudicis delegati*, I, 29, v. *pari poenia;* cf. *glossa ordinaria* ad c. 10, X, *de excessibus praelatorum et subditorum*, V, 31, v. *Auctoritate vel mandato; glossa ordinaria* ad c. 47, X, *de sententia excommunicationis*, V, 39, v. *consentientes* (*auxilium* is here considered as one mode of consent); *glossa ordinaria* ad c. 6, X, *de homicidio voluntario vel casuali*, V, 12, v. *Consilium*: " . . . aut committitur homicidium voluntate, aut casu, aut necessitate: si voluntate quod fit tribus modis, facto, praecepto, et consilio."

41 Kuttner, *op. cit.*, p. 43.

42 Kuttner, *op cit.*, p. 45.

43 *Glossa ordinaria* ad c. 6, X, *de homicidio voluntario vel casuali*, V, 12, v. *timore.*

44 *Glossa ordinaria, ibid.*, v. *affective.*

45 *Glossa ordinaria, ibid.*, v. *ignoranter.*

46 *Glossa ordinaria, ibid.*, v. *Mors.* Cf. also Ioannes Andreae (†1348) *glossa ordinaria ad* c. 5, *de poenis*, V. 9, in VI°, v. *socius.*

Counsel was interpreted strictly to mean necessary counsel so that without it the crime would not be committed.[47]

Mandate was extinguished by death;[48] otherwise the mandate perdured until revocation. Despite repentance, the *mandans* comes under the law, unless he should have revoked the mandate and the notice of this revocation should have reached the mandatary.[49] Ioannes Andreae (†1348) specifically required that the revocation take place *re integra*.[50] This decretalist also showed that mandate may be punished as a separate crime, and in this case, revocation does not remove penalty.[51] He further pointed out that the question of incurring excommunication for the ineffective revocation of a mandate was still unsettled: Bernardus Parmensis de Botone claimed that the excommunication was incurred by the *mandans* when notice of the withdrawal of mandate failed to reach the mandatary in time; Hostiensis († 1271) denied this but made the *mandans* liable to arbitrary penalties; Ioannes Andreae himself inclined the compromise of Bartholomaeus Brixiensis († 1258) to the effect that the *mandans* was not held in the sight of God, but was excommunicated in the sight of the Church.[52]

Reference has previously been made to the legal solution of an early thirteenth century controversy regarding the penalization of ratification *(ratihabitio)*. Alanus and Tancredus writing in this period, held that ratification of the crime of striking clerics did not come under the canon since nothing was expressed in the law con-

[47] *Glossa ordinaria ad* c. 29, X, *de sententia excommunicationis*, V, 39, v. *Consilium impendendo;* cf. *glossa ordinaria ad* c. 6, X, *de homicidio voluntario vel casuali*, V, 12, v. *Provocassent*.

[48] *Glossa ordinaria ad* c. 6, X, *de sententia excommunicationis*, V, 39. v. *Auctoritate vel mandato*: "Sed pone quod mandator ante iniectionem manuum moriatur; tunc non erit excommunicatus, quia mandatum morte extinguitur . . . " This was an adaptation of Roman Private Law — Leage-Ziegler, *Roman Private Law*, p. 340.

[49] *Glossa ordinaria, ibid.*

[50] *Glossa ordinaria* ad c. 1, *de homicidio*, V, 4, in VI°, v. *Mandaverit*.

[51] *Glossa ordinaria* ad c. 1, *de poenis*, V, 8 in Clem., v. *Mandaverit;* ad c. 1, *de homicidio*, V, 4, in VI°, v. *Mandaverit*.

[52] *Glossa ordinaria* ad c. 23, *de sententia excommunicationis, suspensionis, et interdicti*, V, 11, in VI°, v. *Mandato*.

cerning it.[53] Ioannes Galensis agreed provided that the crime had not been done in the name of the person ratifying.[54] Damasus, however, argued that ratification was equivalent to communication *crimini et criminoso* and so rendered one liable to the penalty of the law.[55] Bernardus Parmensis de Botone excluded guilt by way of ratification.[56] Afterwards Boniface VIII decreed that those who ratify violence to clerics done in their name but not at their request, incur the same excommunication as those performing the crime.[57] Ioannes Andreae noted thereupon that this penalty was incurred at the time of the ratification *(ex nunc)*, not at the time of the commission of the crime *(ex tunc)*; for although the law makes ratification retroactive, the sentence of excommunication is not retroactive.[58]

In this period, beginning with the Decretum of Gratian and terminating with the Council of Trent, the greatest evolution in the matter of complicity occurred. The legal texts incorporated multiple and intricate provisions for accomplices in crime. Canonists established consent as the basis for penalizing complicity and explored the modes of cooperation. Subjective factors in the imputability of cooperators and the withdrawal of cooperation were also considered.

[53] Kuttner, "Damasus als Glossator"—*Zeitschrift der Savigny-Stiftung fuer Rechtsgeschichte*, kan. abt. XXIII (1934), 387, 384 note 1.

[54] Kuttner, *op. cit.*, p. 387.

[55] *Questiones et glossa* ad Compl. I, c. 7, *de sententia excommunicationis*, V, 34—Kuttner, *op. cit.*, p. 386-387.

[56] *Glossa ordinaria* ad c. 6, X, *de sententia excommunicationis*, V, 39, v. *Auctoritate vel mandato*: " . . . cum hoc fecerit causa sui et eius nomine, secus si potuit prohibere et non prohibuit."

[57] C. 23, *de sententia excommunicationis, suspensionis, et interdicti*, V, 11 in VI°.

[58] *Glossa ordinaria* ad c. 23, *h. t.*, V, 11, in VI°, v. *incurris*.

Chapter Seven

COMPLICITY IN THE STRICT SENSE FROM THE COUNCIL OF TRENT TO THE CODE

Article 1. The Legislative Development

Benefiting by the exquisite treatment of complicity in previous legislation, the reforming Council of Trent (1545-1563) made some very competent provisions in this regard.

Those who personally or through others whom they coerced by force or fear, or through an intermediary, should convert to their own use or usurp ecclesiastical property, funds, or revenue, were to be subject to anathema and the loss of the *jus patronatus*; any cleric who was the author *(fabricator)* of this fraud or usurpation, or who consented to it was subject to the same penalty together with the loss of all benefice and suspension from orders.[1]

A notary who practised any fraud in presenting the judicial acts to an appellant was to be deprived of office at the discretion of his ordinary and pay double the damages of the suit, and the judge who knew of this or took part in it was likewise held to double damages.[2]

Anathema was decreed against those who forced a woman, except in cases specified by law, to enter the religious life, or who knowing of her unwillingness, lent presence, consent, or authority to the affair.[3]

The penalty for the principals who engaged in a duel has already been stated; the others sharing in the delict will now be considered. Previous to the Council of Trent, the penalization of duelling was confined to papal territory,[4] though Paul IV (1555-1559), antecedently to the Tridentine enactment,[5] subjected to major excommunication

[1] Sess. XXII, *de ref.*, c. 11.

[2] Sess. XXIV, *de ref.*, c. 20.

[3] Sess. XXV, *de regularibus*, c. 18.

[4] Iulius II, const. "Regis Pacifici" 24 febr. 1509, §§ 2, 3—*Fontes*, n. 63.

[5] Const. "Ea quae a praedecessoribus" 13 nov. 1560, §4—*Fontes*, n. 101. Session 25 of the Council of Trent was held December 3, 4, 1563 — cf. Cicognani, *Canon Law*, p. 360.

not only the duellers but also those provoking the duel, or assigning a place for it, the spectators, the followers and supporters of the contestants, those giving counsel, writing announcements of the duel, affixing them to public buildings or publishing them. The conciliar decree, however, embraced only temporal rulers who assigned a place for duelling, the contestants, their seconds, and those who counseled, persuaded or attended.[6]

Among the papal decrees relating to complicity given after the Tridentine Synod there may be recounted, first, the constitution of Gregory XIII (1572-1585) which repeated the penalties of Trent in regard to duels, and further specified that temporal rulers who permitted duels or did not as fully as possible prohibit them, and all those who commanded, instigated, lent aid, counsel, or favor to duels or knowingly provided horses, arms, money, transportation, or other supplies, were to be subjected to the same censures and penalties as the principals.[7] Next, Sixtus V (1585-1590) applied all divine, ecclesiastical, and civil penalties for homicide to those who personally or through another committed abortion, including the guilty mother, the principles, those who as companions in crime knowingly wrote letters, receipts, or otherwise helped by words or signs, or gave advice.[8]

Two details may be noted about a later enactment by Clement VIII (1592-1605) against duelling. He extended the penalties of all the forms of physical and moral cooperation to the writing of duelling notices, and declared subject to papal interdict all cities, lands, territories in which duels were tacitly or expressly allowed.[9]

However, the outstanding legal influence in penal matters during this period was the famous Bullae "*In Coena Domini,*" originating about the beginning of the fourteenth century [10] and continued by successive popes down to Clement XIV, who on his election in 1769 found it inopportune to issue this list of papally reserved excommuni-

[6] Sess. XXV, *de ref.*, c. 19.

[7] Const. "*Ad tollendum*" 5 dec. 1582—*Fontes*, n. 149.

[8] Const. "*Effraenatam*" 29 oct. 1588, §§ 1, 2, 3, 7—*Fontes*, n. 165.

[9] Const. "*Illius vices*" 17 aug. 1592, §§ 6, 7—*Fontes*, n. 176.

[10] Cappello, *De censuris* (2. ed., Taurinorum Augustae: Marietti, 1925), p. 10.

cations.[11] As representative of the present period there may be selected from this series the constitution "*Pastoralis Romani Pontificis*" of Urban VIII (1623-1644)[12] in which excommunication and anathema were decreed against: 1) those appealing to a general council over the Roman Pontiff, and those giving aid, counsel, and favor to them; 2) those supplying the Saracens with war materials, or giving them information, aid, counsel, or favor; 3) those harming pilgrims to Rome, or giving aid, counsel, or favor to those doing so; 4) those harming ecclesiastical authorities, or ordering or ratifying such harm, and also those giving aid, counsel, or favor to the former; 5) those who impeded ecclesiastical jurisdiction, who ordered or executed such interference, or gave counsel, patronage, or favor to this effect; 6) those taxing ecclesiastical property or revenue without papal permission, or receiving such tax, and those giving aid, counsel, or favor in this matter; 7) those invading papal territory, their followers, supporters, defenders, and those giving aid, counsel, or favor.

After the lapse of a century, a definitive collection of existing censures was made by Pius IX (1846-1878), who in his well known Constitution "*Apostolicae Sedis,*"[13] while retaining many provisions of the Bullae "*In Coena Domini,*" with little modification as far as as complicity was concerned,[14] extended the simplification of cooperative forms. The new provisions of "*Apostolicae Sedis*" penalized those giving aid, counsel, or favor to those interfering with the officers and processes of the Holy Office; those commanding the violation of asylum or the burial either of notorious heretics or of

[11] Pennacchi, *Commentaria in Constitutionem Apostolicae Sedis,* (Romae, 1883), I, 67.

[12] Promulgated April 1, 1627 — *Bullarum Diplomatum et Privilegiorum Sanctorum Romanorum Pontificum Taurinensis Editio* (Augustae Taurinorum, 1867-1872), XIII, 530-537 (hereafter cited as *Bullarium Romanum*). This was the final revision of the *Bullae Coenae* — Cappello, *De censuris,* p. 10, note 32 — yet the stability of these papal censures may be noted by comparing it with Paul V's (1605-1621) const. "*Pastoralis* 8 apr. 1610—*Bullarium Romanum,* XI, 617-623—which agrees with Urban's in all points here treated.

[13] Const. "*Apostolicae Sedis*" 12 oct. 1869—*Fontes,* n. 173.

[14] The penalties against aid to the Saracens and against the disturbers of pilgrims, and those taxing ecclesiastical property were discontinued.

those excommunicated or interdicted by name; all accomplices to a duel, including the spectators and those failing to prohibit it. With regard to abortion,[15] Pius limited the punishment to those actually committing the crime to the omission of the accomplices.[16]

Pius IX climaxed the post-tridentine movement towards the abbreviation of the more exaggerated extensions of the notion of complicity. This is the best quality to be seen in the legislation before the Code. Except for censures, penal legislation was in a disorganized state, and even with regard to censures, complicity had in each case, through the lack of general norms, to be found by consulting the legal texts themselves.

Article 2. The Doctrinal Development

A. *The Moralists*

Account must now be taken of a collateral development in the theory of complicity. Following St. Thomas Aquinas († 1274)[17] moral theologians explored the concept of complicity in relation to responsibility for restitution.[18] Later, the tract on scandal was enlarged by a treatment of cooperation in another's sin.[19] Here was evolved the notion of formal and material cooperation, as may be

[15] Gregory XIV (const. "*Sedis Apostolicae*" 31 maii 1591—*Fontes*, n. 173) —had already tempered the provisions of Sixtus V.

[16] Pennacchi, *Commentaria*, II, 3. The Code retains the words of the Constitution, "*Apostolicae Sedis*": "procurantes abortum," but by virtue of canon 2209, this provision now embraces the effective accomplices—a striking example of the force of principles of complicity incorporated into law.

[17] 2a 2ae, q. LXII, art. VII—cooperation in damage and responsibility for indemnification.

[18] Cf. Martinus Bonacina (†1631), *Operum de morali theologia et omnibus conscientiae nodis in tres tomos distributorum tomus secundus* (Ventiis, 1687), *de cooperatione*, pp. 363-375.

[19] St. Thomas did not treat of this, despite his tracts on Scandal (2a 2ae, q. XLIII, art. 1), Adulation (2a 2ae, q. CXV, art. II), Defense of an Unjust Cause by a Lawyer (2a 2ae, q. LXXI, art. III), The External Causes of Sin (1a 2ae, q. LXXV, art. III), Failure to Resist Detraction (2a 2ae, q. LXXIII, art. IV).

seen in the writings of Busembaum (†1668).[20]

While all this helped to clarify the nature of complicity, a distinct contribution to legal science was made when the moralists, in accord with their desire to establish the state of conscience, engaged a strictly legal subject—the requisites for incurring a penalty through cooperative forms. Relying on the principle, *poenae sunt restringendae,* Busembaum [21] stated that mandate, counsel, and help, do not contract the penalty for homicide, unless this crime was actually effected; but he noted that a distinction must be made regarding mandate and counsel when punished principally and these same forms when punished accessorially; for in the former case, the penalty is incurred even without the effect being attained. St. Alphonsus († 1787) [22] related that this was accepted by the Salmanticenses, (1664-1724), who further stated that one was excused from censures who gave a simple mandate or counsel to a person already determined to perform the delict. While St. Alphonsus held even ineffective recall of mandate or counsel excepted one from censure, his importance rests on the honor, attributed to him by Aertnys (†1915),[23] of being the first to give an accurate notion of formal and material cooperation.

D'Annibale († 1892)[24] examining the question of the incurrence of penalties, took the position that since penalties are not to exceed their proper case, no cooperator was held by any law unless expressly named therein; thus the perpetrator would not be liable to the penalty stated for the mandator, but all accomplices, though unnamed, may be punished by a discretionary penalty, generally of a milder nature, not mentioned in the law.[25] This became the prevailing position in pre-Code jurisprudence, as adopted by Wernz without qualification, and by Lega in practice.[26]

Moral theology, therefore, did much to refine the concept of

[20] *Medulla theologiae moralis* (ed. novissima, Venetiis, 1698), p. 57.
[21] *Op. cit.*, p. 464.
[22] *Theologia moralis* (nova ed., Vesuntione, 1828), VII, 20.
[23] *Theologia moralis* (7. ed., 2 vols., Paderbornae, 1906), I, 157.
[24] *Summula theologiae moralis* (3 vols., Reate, 1874), I, 180-181.
[25] Wernz, p. 58, note 17.
[26] Wernz, *loc. cit.*

complicity; it introduced the distinction between formal and material cooperation; a moralist is credited with the best solution in the application of the pre-Code legal penalties, insofar as only those accomplices were considered subject to the legal penalty, who were mentioned in the law.

B. *The Canonists*

Thesaurus († 1655)[27] solved the question of the incurrence of a penalty when the penalty as stated by law was directed against another form of criminal participation, by considering separately *latae sententiae* penalties and *ferendae sententiae* penalties; in the case of the former, accomplices do not, unless mentioned, incur the penalties stated against the agents of the delict; in the case of the latter, effective cooperators are to be punished by the ordinary penalty of the law, non-effective cooperators are to be punished by extraordinary penalties. The reason for this division was the rule that *latae sententiae* penalties were subject to the strictest interpretation, and were not to be extended even for identical cause; on the other hand, *ferendae sententiae* penalties, according to Thesaurus, embrace not only the perpetrator of the delict, but also the less principal causes of the crime—these cooperators who efficaciously influenced the entire result.

A systematic treatment of complicity, to be desired in the work of this canonist, was offered in a book by Franciscus De Angelis[28] which contained whole chapters on physical[29] and moral[30] participation. Although this work was not purely canonical since it also treated of Roman and Neapolitan law, yet it offered an excellent

[27] *De poenis ecclesiasticis praxis absoluta et universalis, cum notis et accessionibus earundem poenarum ab anno MDCLIII ad currentem usque MDCCLX inflictorum locupletata ab Ubaldo Giraldi a S. Cajetano* (Romae, 1760), p. 11.

[28] *Tractatus Criminalis de Delictis* (Neapoli, 1741).

[29] *De auxilio et ope praestita ad delictum*—*op. cit.*, pp. 29-30.

[30] *De consilio, persuasione, instigatione, inflamatione, et instructione ad delinquendum*—*op. cit.*, pp. 44-46; *De mandato, seu ordine ad delinquendum*—*op. cit.*, pp. 138-140.

treatment of complicity, despite the fact that it seems exclusively concerned with the external forum.

Schmalzgrueber († 1735)[31] discussed the incidence of censure in cooperative forms other than those specifically named by law. He considered as more probable the opinion that a censure directed against one committing a crime did not affect those participating by mandate or counsel, unless this was expressed in the law. This was Kober's opinion, also, with regard to excommunication.[32]

Lega († 1935)[33] distinguished between canonical theory and practice. Considering the intention of the law, he rejected D'Annibale's opinion as an inept generalization with respect to *ferendae sententiae* penalties. The opinion of Thesaurus, on the other hand, responded accurately to the mind and intention of the canons, because in *ferendae sententiae* penalties the prudence of the judge is to be somewhat indulged that he might punish those who have violated the intent rather than the letter of the law. To this Lega noted as an exception an express clause limiting the penalty to the agent of the crime—here the penalty was not to be extended beyond its own case. With regard to practice, however, these distinctions were not of great weight, he admitted, since the judge could always proceed against the accomplices with extraordinary penalties.

Wernz († 1914)[34] rejected with D'Annibale the distinction between *latae sententiae* penalties and *ferendae sententiae* penalties as illogical and without foundation in the sources. There is no juridical reason why cooperators in a delict punished with a *ferendae sententiae* penalty should be in a worse condition than those cooperating in an offense punished with a *latae sententiae* penalty; moreover, according to the mind of the Church, *latae sententiae* penalties are expected to be the more efficacious. Without any distinction, therefore, cooperators other than the actual agents, when not mentioned by the law,

[31] *Jus ecclesiasticum* (5 vols. in 12, Romae, 1845), lib. XI, pars IV, tit. 39, n. 69.

[32] *Der Kirchenbann*, pp. 135-136.

[33] *De delictis et poenis*, pp. 75-77.

[34] *Ius decretalium*, VI, 58-60.

are immune from its penalties, but are subject to extraordinary penalties.

Both Lega [35] and Wernz [36] present a comprehensive treatment of complicity. But besides systematizing the principles of criminal co-operation then in use, Wernz [37] explicitly called for a legislated norm to remove the uncertainty of the law at that time:

> "Quodsi incertitudo iuris in hac parte esset tollenda *de lege ferenda* facile posset statui principium: delinquentes accessorios eadem poena legis (sive latae sive ferendae sententiae) teneri, qua principales, nisi lex aliud expresse dicat, quando sine ipsorum opera delictum commissum non fuisset, minori poena esse puniendos si sine ipsorum concursu delictum etiam commissum fuisset et idcirco suo concursu solum reddiderunt facilius delictum, salva etiam contraria legis dispositione."

This statement remarkable in its own right as an admirable expression of jurisprudence, is even more noteworthy insofar as it lays down the principle adopted by the Code in canons 2209 and 2231.

The influences of the pre-Code period may be summarized as a simplification of the law, a systematization of theory, and an articulated need for an official solution of the problems of penalization of complicity.

[35] *De delictis et poenis*, pp. 72-80.
[36] *Ius decretalium*, VI, 52-64.
[37] *Op. cit.*, p. 60.

Chapter Eight

SOME JURISPRUDENTIAL ASPECTS OF CRIMINAL COOPERATION

A commentary on canon 2209 may be best orientated by a preliminary consideration of several fundamental concepts related to the nature of cooperation in crime. Treated in order are canonical guilt as applied to cooperation in crime, the question of adopting the principle of accessoriness, the application of the principles of objectivity and subjectivity, the problem of attempted acts considered in respect to cooperation in crime, and finally, negligence as a source of cooperative guilt. From a consideration of these topics, a complete concept of cooperative guilt may reasonably be expected insofar as the various problems which have arisen in regard to the imputability of cooperators are conveniently reviewed under these titles.

Article 1. The Canonical Concept of Guilt as Applied to Cooperators in Crime

In the first chapter a definition of cooperation in crime was arrived at by listing the constituent elements required by the nature of the ecclesiastical crime and by the nature of cooperative unity. Here it was stated that one of the essential elements of crime is moral imputability [1] by which the violation of the law is ascribed to each accomplice as to a moral cause.[2] This imputability is derived either from a deliberate will to violate the law or from negligence to

[1] Moral imputability, as distinguished from physical imputability, which is the attribution of an effect to its physical cause, may be defined as the attribution of an effect to its moral cause, or the responsibility of a rational creature for a freely willed act. It is a constitutive element of the canonical delict—canon 2195, § 1: " . . . moraliter imputabilis legis violatio." When described for legal purposes, which are less extensive than those of moral theology, it is known as juridical imputability. The conditions for juridical imputability in the Code are set down in Book Five in the title: *De imputabilitate delicti, de causis illam aggravantibus vel minuentibus et de iuridicis delicti effectibus.* Cf. Michiels, *De delictis et poenis,* I, 98-100.

[2] Cf. canon 2195, § 1.

which the violation of the law is due.[3] Because of this deliberate will of violating the law or because of this criminal negligence in the persons involved, the crime is imputed to all accomplices who have, as free agents, acted in cooperation, to bring about, either directly or indirectly, the criminal effect.

In canon law guilt is constituted by the external violation of a penal law which is morally imputable.[4] Two points are to be emphasized here in connection with cooperation in crime. First, the external violation of the law is found in each cooperator, who has, at least, placed some external act, either by word or deed, which is directed toward the violation of the law. It must be noted that this external act must have some effect, however slight, upon the commission of the crime; otherwise, this activity is futile as far as cooperation is concerned and shows merely the desire to cooperate, rather than the fact of cooperation. Second, moral imputability of the crime is verified in each accomplice who in cooperation with the others has voluntarily performed an external act directed towards the violation of the law. This is equivalent to saying that a cooperator is guilty of a crime to which he has contributed some external act while willing the violation of the law or while acting with criminal negligence. This statement is valid, however, only when the crime is, as a matter of fact, effected by the cooperation of several persons. Where there is no cooperation, the external violation of the law must be completed by one person, except in cases where provision has been made for attempted crime according to canon 2212, § 4. When, on the other hand, several persons commit a crime in cooperation, the external violation may be physically divisible among the cooperators, even though morally, the whole crime is ascribed to each cooperator. By moral imputability, therefore, one and the same crime is ascribed to several cooperators.[5] This was be-

[3] Canon 2199.

[4] Cf. canon 2195, § 1.

[5] "Paricipatio seu concursus in crimen habetur cum *unum delictum* habet *plures auctores.* Schola classica in participatione constanter unum delictum vidit. Schola positiva, ut propius prospiceret delinquentibus, conata est scindere crimina, ita ut tot aestimarentur esse delicta quot auctores Verum communiter in concursu delinquentium doctores unum tantum crimen esse cen-

cause each person involved has, by cooperating, made himself responsible for the activity of the others, and thus for the whole crime. Hence several cooperators may be guilty of a crime, despite the fact that none of them singly has performed the complete external violation of the law. Accordingly, the basic norm in the imputation of guilt is moral, insofar as the cooperators are guilty not because of their external actions considered separately, but because of the cooperative action of all involved, to which every cooperator assents and to which he contributes by his own external act. The moral imputation of guilt considers the cooperators as free agents who by means of cooperation effect the crime.[6]

This statement of guilt by way of cooperation has as yet been confined to the existence of guilt itself, without inquiring into the various grades of guilt. It is clear that certain cooperators may be more responsible for the crime than others, not because the former willed the crime more intensely, but because their contribution had greater efficacy in effecting the crime. Thus account must also be taken of the individual activity of each cooperator, which cumulatively produces the violation of the law. This activity may be such that by it, in conjunction with the cooperation of others, the crime is either effected or merely facilitated. According to the relative importance of his activity, each cooperator incurs a corresponding degree of guilt. This relation between activity and degree of guilt

sent."—Roberti, pp. 211-212; also, Wernz-Vidal, *Ius canonicum* (Romae: Apud Aedes Universitatis Gregorianae, 1937), VII, 132. This problem of the multiple authorship of one crime had been discussed by the Roman jurists: "Si duo pluresue unum tignum furati sunt, quod singuli tollere non potuerint, dicendum est omnes eos furti in solidum teneri, quamuis id contrectare nec tollere solus potest et ita utimur: neque enim potest dicere pro parte furtum fecisse singulos, sed totius rei uniuersos: sic fiet singulos furti teneri."—D. (47, 2) 21, 9.

[6] Not every legal system has found it convenient to adopt this moral norm completely. Because of the comparative facility of proving external facts, a legal system may employ some physical standard of guilt. Thus the Anglo-American system distinguishes between principals and accessories before the fact chiefly by presence or non-presence at the commission of the crime—cf. *May's Law of Crimes* (4. ed. by Sears-Weihofen, Boston: Littic, Brown and Company, 1938), n. 66, n. 68.

is detailed in canon 2209. It is sufficient now to indicate the existence of this relation insofar as the various provisions of canon 2209 will be explained at length in the course of this commentary.

Here then in brief is the nature of guilt due to cooperation in crime. It is a moral imputation of the crime to the accomplice because of his cooperation. The cooperator must act as a free agent; he must work in conjunction with others; he must intend the crime, or at least intend the act from which the crime results because of negligence; he must perform some external act which has positive effect upon the commission of the crime. As a result of his acting in this manner, the whole crime will be attributed to the accomplice, and not merely his own external act. His guilt, however, will vary according to the relative importance of the external act in the commission of the crime.

Article 2. The Principle of Accessoriness

The canonical theory of complicity is an adaptation of moral imputability as ordinarily applied to a single perpetrator with modifications requisite to the case of several persons acting together. But whether in singular action or in cooperation, the free agent is held responsible for his voluntarily unlawful act; in singular action, however, the agent must complete the violation of the law, whereas in cooperative action, the accomplice need only contribute externally to the general effort by which the crime is effected. Since, however, the free agent has, in both cases, to a greater or less degree, brought about the infraction of the law, he incurs moral imputability for the crime.

This concept of complicity, however, should, according to some jurists,[7] be subject to modification by the principle of accessoriness,[8] according to which the cooperation of all except the actual perpetra-

[7] Baumer, "De iure poenali pro delinquentibus minoris aetatis in Codice iuris canonici et novissimo schemate Codicis poenalis helvetici,"—*Apollinaris* VI (1933), 478-481.

[8] The principle of accessoriness originating in continental legislation in the French Penal Code was introduced into the Prussian Penal Code in 1851—Baumer, *art. cit.*, p. 478, note 116.

tors of the deed is considered a specific crime, dependent for existence upon the action of the perpetrators, but punishable because of the criminal character of cooperation itself.[9] Accordingly, the guilt of the various accomplices depends upon the establishment of the guilt of the actual perpetrators of the crime.[10] The crime actually committed is ascribed to the perpetrators, while the crime of cooperation is assigned to their accomplices. In applying this principle of accessoriness to the canonical prescriptions on cooperation in crime, Baumer admits the principle with regard to co-agents as contemplated by canon 2209, §·1, but denies it in cases of partial cooperation as considered by canon 2209, § § 3, 4.[11] Michiels, on the other hand, from the viewpoint of jurisprudence, admits the possibility of accessoriness in cases of partial participation, although, as a matter of fact, he points out, no provision is made in canon law for the application of this principle.[12] According to Michiels, it is difficult to understand why the perpetrators and the cooperators should be held equally guilty and liable to the same penalty, as is the case in canon law,[13] if they are considered guilty not of the same crime but of the separate crimes—the perpetrators, of the principal crime;

[9] Michiels, *De delictis et poenis,* I, 315-316. Less explicitly Baumer states the requirements: ". . . concursus dependet a capacitate poenali alius, qui sit plene responsabilis actor et a facto principali, quod sit poenale."—*art. cit.* p. 478.

[10] As in Anglo-American criminal law, cf. *May's Law of Crimes,* n. 68.

[11] Baumer, *art. cit.*, pp. 479-480. This author has especially in mind the cooperation of minors, but his arguments in this matter have general value as regards cooperation in crime. In conjunction with the non-operation of the accessorial principle in cases of partial cooperation, he cites in favor of his opinion Luenenborg, "Der Versuch im Strafrecht des Codex iuris canonici" —*Archiv fuer Katholisches Kirchenrecht* CXI (1931), 395—*art. cit.*, p. 480, note 124. It may be noted here that by the term complete participation is meant activity which includes both moral and physical contribution toward the crime, as is the case with the co-agents of canon 2209, § 1. By partial participation is indicated either moral or physical aid towards the crime, as is found described in canon 2209, § § 3, 4.

[12] Michiels, *De delictis et poenis,* I, 315-316; Dreyer, *Die akzessorische Teilnahme* (Borna-Leipzig, 1911), pp. 7 ff., 20 ff., 36-40.

[13] Canons 2209, § 3; 2230; 2231.

the cooperators, of the crime of cooperation.[14] The fundamental reason, however, for denying accessoriness is found in the interpretation of the pertinent canons.[15] According to the obvious sense of these canons, the guilt and punishment of cooperators is not considered secondarily and dependently to the status of the perpetrators of the crime; in fact, according to canon 2230, when the perpetrator is excused from the penalty because of impuberty, those who induced him to commit the crime or who cooperated in it with him according to canon 2209, § § 1, 2, 3 are subject to the penalty due the principal crime. This rule hardly indicates the operation of the principle of accessoriness. Moreover, the very wording of canon 2209 would tend to exclude the principle of accessoriness from the nature of cooperative guilt. In paragraph 3, it is stated that the cooperators under certain conditions incur no less imputability than the perpetrator of the crime; according to paragraph 4, the cooperators contract less imputability than the perpetrator. These norms remain unmodified by accessoriness, as is indicated by the use of the word *imputability*. This term cannot rightly be used without referring to an object as well as to a subject. Something must be imputed to the subject. In this case, the object must reasonably be, not the separate crime of cooperation which would have to be expressly stated, but the same crime as was commmitted by the perpetrator. The identical crime is imputed to the various cooperators, but in variant degrees according to paragraphs 3 and 4. This interpretation is confirmed by paragraph 7 wherein the phrase *delicti patrati imputabilitatem* is found.

The principle of accessoriness is somewhat alien to canonical jurisprudence, insofar as it is not mentioned by the pre-Code authors, nor has it been applied to the legislation of the Code except by Baumer.[16] Its application, therefore, in the interpretation of the

[14] Michiels, *ibid.*, p. 316. This argument is not altogether cogent; in point of fact, according to the Anglo-American system, "the accessory before the fact was considered guilty of as reprehensible conduct as the principal in the first or second degrees—at least, he was subject to the same punishment"—*May's Law of Crimes*, n. 68.

[15] Canons 2209; 2212, § § 3, 4; 2230; 2231.

[16] A careful distinction must be made between the application of accessoriness to the rules governing cooperative guilt and between accessorial crimes.

canonical principles of cooperation in crime could be justified only by clear directions from the words of the law itself.[17] These are lacking, and the principle of accessoriness must be rejected for the present.

ARTICLE 3. THE PRINCIPLES OF OBJECTIVITY AND SUBJECTIVITY

For canonical purposes, therefore, guilt of juridical imputability will be the moral imputability of each cooperator as defined by the law. In determining this notion, a useful jurisprudential device is found in the application of the principles of objectivity and subjectivity. These principles do not qualify the canonical concept of guilt as the principle of accessoriness would have done, but rather subject this unmodified concept of guilt to separate scrutiny in its external and internal phases respectively. The objective guilt is derived from the effect in point of fact one has had in the commission of the crime, either by direct participation and aid, or by influence on others; thus it is guilt in its objective phase. The subjective guilt is based on the dispositions of mind and will of the delinquent; and so is guilt considered subjectively. Neither objective guilt or subjective guilt are self-sufficient, but they must be conjoined so as to present the concrete guilt, which is guilt as it actually exists in a person. The purpose of considering guilt in its separate phases, however, is to determine conveniently the various attributes of the concrete guilt as derived from the principles of objectivity and subjectivity.

For cooperators in crime the objective guilt is one and indivisible: one in the sense that the same criminal fact with all its circumstances is communicable to all; and indivisible insofar that this guilt cannot be divided proportionally or quantitatively among the co-

The latter are the subject of special legislation but depend for their existence upon the preexistence of the principal crime—cf. Lega, pp. 78-79. Thus, commanding an unlawful act could by legislation be made a special crime, but unless the law stated otherwise, the issuance of the command would not be considered a crime until the unlawful act so commanded had itself been effected. It is claimed in this article that accessoriness does not influence the norms of cooperative guilt; the presence in the Code of accessorial crimes does not prejudice this view..

[17] Cf. canons 6, nn. 2, 3, 4; 18.

operators, but is attributed wholly to each.[18] On the other hand, the subjective guilt is personal and not communicable to others. A cooperator is not held for acts committed by others apart from the common will, but even in the case of acts willed in common, the responsibility of each is to be determined according to the personal circumstances which increase or diminish guilt.[19]

Article 4. Attempted Acts in Relation to Cooperation

Two matters are to be considered here: attempted cooperation in crime, and cooperation in attempted crime. When a person intending to cooperate in a crime performs an act which, because it is in itself insufficient or because it is in fact superfluous, contributes nothing to the crime either physically or morally, then there is only attempted cooperation in crime. A necessary element required by the concept of cooperation in crime is missing—efficacy whereby the act of cooperation actually makes some positive contribution towards the accomplishment of the crime. Only efficacious acts induce the guilt of cooperation. Hence separate provision must be made for ineffectual acts or attempted cooperation in crime. There is, moreover, the case of cooperation in attempted crime. Here the cooperation offered is efficacious. It makes a positive contribution towards the accomplishment of the crime, but because of the failure of the other accomplices or because of other external factors, the crime itself is not effected. Hence there is an attempted crime, and the ordinary rules for cooperation in crime are not to be applied absolutely since they contemplate a perfected crime.[20] Attempted cooperation is exemplified in the person who persuades another to commit a crime, when as a matter of fact, the latter is already determined to commit the crime; it may also be illustrated in a person who leaves a door open for a robber who breaks open a window for his own entrance. Cooperation in attempted crime is found in the person who actually

[18] Michiels, *De delictis et poenis*, I, 316.

[19] Michiels, *ibid.*, p. 317. This diverges from Anglo-American law; cf. *May's Law of Crimes*, n. 67.

[20] In all the paragraphs of canon 2209, the word *delictum* is used and must be interpreted strictly, as defined in canon 2195, § 1, which speaks of a violation of the law, not an attempted violation of the law.

persuades another to commit a crime which through some failure of circumstances is never effected; it is to be noted also in the person who provides the necessary equipment for committing the crime which likewise is never accomplished.

The provisions of canons 2212 and 2213, which deal with attempted crime, are to be applied to the problems of attempted cooperation and cooperation in attempted crime. Thus according to canon 2212, § 4, attempted crime becomes a true crime if it is punished by law with its own penalty.

With regard to attempted cooperation, it must be stated that by the very nature of the matter such attempted cooperation is not true cooperation. Hence acts of attempted cooperation are to be considered separately, apart from the acts of other cooperators. Attempted moral cooperation approaches the nature of attempted crime according to canon 2212, § 3.[21] The majority of authors do not identify this attempted suasion with attempted crime because of the wording of the canon, *accedit,* but point out that this kind of attempted cooperation merely approaches attempted crime.[22] For this reason, Vermeersch-Crusen [23] state that attempted suasion is to be penalized only because of great scandal. Accordingly, it would form an exception from any generic punishment of attempted crime which did not expressly describe attempted suasion.[24] Attempted physical co-

[21] "Conatui delicti accedit actio illius qui alium ad delictum committendum inducere studuerit, sed inefficaciter."

[22] Ayrinhac-Lydon, *Penal Legislation,* p. 21; Augustine, *A Commentary on the New Code of Canon Law,* p. 56; Blat, *Commentarium textus codicis iuris canonici, Liber V, De delictis et poenis* (Romae: Collegio Angelico, 1924), p. 41: "*Conatui delicti* proprio accedit illius naturam participans, quin iure obtineat . . .;" Coronata, *Institutiones,* IV, 62; Wernz-Vidal, *Ius canonicum,* VII, 163. To the contrary, Michiels (*De delictis et poenis,* I, 279-280) disregards the force of *accedit* and identifies attempted moral cooperation with *conatus delicti;* also Luigi Majno, *Commento al Codice penale* (4. ristampa della terza edizione, Torino, 1924), I, 289-290. Roberti, though not considering it under cooperation, agrees with the majority in merely approximating attempted suasion with *conatus delicti*—p. 201.

[23] *Epitome iuris canonici* (2. ed., 3 vols., Mechliniae: Dessain, 1924), III, 195.

[24] Since any antisocial act may be the subject of legislation repressing such act by penalties, attempted suasion may be constituted a delict. By virtue

operation is not considered as cooperation since it is ineffectual.[25] While it is outside the scope of canon 2209, nevertheless, it can conform to the definition of attempted crime as given in canon 2212, § § 1-2, and can, therefore, be considered a crime, when provision is made by law to punish attempts to commit a certain crime.[26] The difference between moral and physical attempted cooperation, as regard imputability, may be said to rest in the requirement that the former must be specified by name in order to be constituted a crime, whereas the latter may be included in a general provision punishing all attempts to commit a certain crime. Such a provision would not include advice or persuasion, since these, as defined by canon 2212, § 3, only approach the nature of attempted crime.

While every kind of attempted physical cooperation may be constituted a crime if it is specifically mentioned in the law as punishable, nevertheless a general provision penalizing attempted crime will include only those acts of physical cooperation, which verify the definition of attempted crime. These acts by their nature must at least conduce to the accomplishment of the crime.[27] Hence, in a general provision against attempts at a certain crime, not every act of attempted physical cooperation can be punished apart from an express specification by law, but only those acts which by their nature are directed to the accomplishment of the crime. Where the acts are described by name all types of attempted cooperation, moral and physical, may be punished; where, in general, attempts to commit a certain crime are punished, only physical acts which by their nature are directed to accomplish the crime, are included.

of canon 2212, § 3, however, it would seem that to penalize attempted suasion, this act must be expressly specified, and not merely contained in a general provision punishing attempts to commit a certain crime.

[25] ". . . quia nullum exercet influxum in exsecutionem . . ."—Roberti, p. 212.

[26] Canon 2212, § 4.

[27] Canon 2212, § § 1-2. Not every effort to effect a crime can be considered as attempted crime. Not preparatory acts, which though indifferent in themselves are directed toward the accomplishment of the crime by the intention of the agent, fulfil the requirement but only executive acts, which by their nature are unequivocally directed to effect the crime—cf. Lega, pp. 26-28; Coronata, *Institutiones*, IV, 22.

With regard to cooperation in attempted crime, such cooperation is illegal and punishable only when the attempted crime has been declared a crime by law. Otherwise, there is only cooperation apart from crime.[28] When the attempted crime has been constituted a crime, the general rules of cooperation, as contained in canons 2209 and 2231, may be applied.

In the Code are found the following instances of attempted crimes which have been legally declared crimes. Necessary cooperation [29] in attempted crimes has been legislated into special crimes in the case of conspiracy against the Roman Pontiff, his legate, or one's own ordinary;[30] in the case of provocation and acceptance of a duel;[31] and in the case of attempted marriage involving a person in sacred orders or having solemn vows.[32] There are, furthermore, attempted crimes penalized in the Code in which *de facto* cooperation may occur, such as: the taking away of the Sacred Species for an evil purpose;[33] provocation of subjects to disobedience against certain ecclesiastical superiors;[34] the abduction of a woman for the purpose of lust or of marriage;[35] the presentation or nomination of one unworthy;[36] and the attempted subornation of curial officials, judges, advocates, and procurators.[37]

Article 5. Negligence as a Source of Cooperative Guilt

In the first chapter, it has already been pointed out that a crime essentially consists of three elements, objective, subjective, and juridical. With regard to the subjective element a question arises in con-

[28] Cf. canon 2212, § 4; Roberti, p. 213; Michiels, *De delictis et poenis*, I,317-318.

[29] Cf. *infra*, Chapter ten.

[30] Canon 2331, § 2.

[31] Canon 2351, § 1; Chelodi, *Ius poenale*, p. 112. Provocation alone is also a crime.

[32] Canon 2388, § 1.

[33] Canon 2320.

[34] Canon 2331, § 2; Chelodi, *Ius poenale*, *p*. 90; Wernz-Vidal, *Ius canonicum*, VII, 477.

[35] Canon 2353; Vermeersch-Creusen, *Epitome*, III, 291.

[36] Canon 2391, § 3.

[37] Canon 2407.

nection with cooperation in crime. Ordinarily, this subjective element may be verified in either of two roots—criminal intent (*dolus*) or criminal negligence (*culpa*).[38] Of cooperation motivated by criminal intent there is no doubt; it is rather in relation to concurrence in crime which arises out of negligence that some obscurity as to imputability occurs. Some canonists[39] are of the opinion that the Code does not envisage cooperation in infractions of the law due to negligence because in negligence there is lacking the intention of joining one's own action with the criminal action of another. Others,[40] however in consideration of canon 2199, which notes that juridical imputability for a crime may also be founded in negligence, admit cooperation in such crimes, when the canonical concept of cooperation is verified.[41] The constituents of criminal cooperation as required in relation to crime are readily verified; these are: 1) a penal law; 2) criminal intent, or in this case, the will to produce an act from which, because of negligence, the effect forbidden by law results; and 3) some external action contributed by all cooperators

[38] "Imputabilitas delicti pendet ex dolo delinquentis vel ex eiusdem culpa in ignorantia legis violatae aut in omissione debitae deligentiae . . . "—canon 2199.

[39] Roberti, pp. 212-213; Wernz, n. 42; Wernz-Vidal, *Ius canonicum*, VII, 135; Sole, *De delictis et poenis* (Romae: Pustet, 1920), pp. 318-319. Sole discusses only *dolus* without considering the possibility of complicity arising from *culpa*.

[40] Coronata, *Institutiones*, IV, 44; Chelodi, *Ius poenale*, p. 16; Michiels, *De delictis et poenis*, I, 318-319; Berutti, *Institutiones iuris canonici* (Taurini-Romae: Marietti, 1938), VI, 37.

[41] Concerning the nature of negligence itself, cf. Michiels, *De delictis et poenis*, I, 105-112; Roberti, pp. 91-95; Swoboda, *Ignorance in Relation to the Imputability of Delictis*, The Catholic University of America Canon Law Studies, n. 143 (Washington, D. C.: The Catholic University of America Press, 1941), pp. 102-113. Briefly: "In *culpa* the effect is never directly willed; it is either foreseen and, in consequence, culpably permitted, because of a failure in the duty to prevent a foreseen criminal effect; or it is due to negligence in not foreseeing the violation of a law, whether it be that the law remains unknown to the person or that the effects of his actions are not properly weighed by him. If there is no moral guilt either in not preventing the injurious or anti-juridical effect or in not foreseeing the effect there is *casus* or accident in the juridical sense of the word."—Swoboda, *op. cit.*, p. 105.

and ordained towards this forbidden effect. These elements may be found in all acts of negligence which tend to break the law. There is, however, some doubt to be dispelled in connection with the presence of the requirements pertaining to cooperative unity. The difficulty consists in predicating a common purpose and a common knowledge of this purpose to delinquents acting by way of negligence. But it must be recalled that in negligence the criminal effect is never directly willed. Not the violation of the law, therefore, but the act negligently committed, from which the violation of the law results, may become the object of cooperative purpose. Thus it is possible to have a common purpose and common knowledge of that purpose among cooperators in acts of negligence. The confluence of purpose is directed not to something unwilled, or not jointly willed, which would preclude any cooperation, but to an object of concerted volition from which results the criminal effect.[42] Michiels[43] demonstrates by means of examples that cooperation in crime is possible to participants who act only out of negligence. Thus two friends may with common consent drive a car carelessly through a crowded street and so kill a pedestrian. The same effect can be obtained by a chauffeur who is ordered by his employer to drive too fast in similar circumstances. In these cases all would be guilty of homicide through negligence, because they failed to take the due care required by the situation. All could be held as cooperators because they contributed to the criminal fact by consenting with common intent in the act of negligence, which produced the criminal result. Cooperation is also possible in the case of physical aid, as in the lending of a weapon which, it is known, will be used without due precaution in a dangerous situation, and which, as a matter of fact, causes death.

Beside intentional cooperation, or cooperation in which the crime is directly willed, account must also be taken of negligent cooperation, or cooperation in acts of negligence. But the field of possibility is not yet exhausted. With both these modes of cooperation established, there is no reason to assume that criminal cooperation may not partake of the qualities of both these modes, so as to be, in

[42] Cf. Michiels, *De delictis et poenis*, I, 319.

[43] *Op. cit.*, pp. 318-319.

relation to the same crime, intentional as far as some cooperators are concerned, and negligent as far as others are concerned.[44] Thus the crime may be, on the part of the perpetrator, an act of negligence, whereas, on the part of the *mandans* it is an act of criminal intent, conceived with a view to breaking the law and capitalizing upon another's carelessness to secure that end. The divergence of final purposes does not obviate cooperation as long as there is a common agreement regarding the immediate act from which the imputable criminal result originates.

While the opinions here stated with regard to cooperation involving negligence, as derived from canonical principles, should remain undisturbed in theory, a difficulty must, nevertheless, be admitted concerning the application of these opinions to the penalties of the Code. While negligent cooperation must be admitted, the possibility of its occurrence in regard to canonical delicts is considerably restricted. In the first place, the ambit of negligent delicts, which are those which may be committed by way of negligence as well as by direct intention, is very limited in the penology of the Code.[45] This

[44] Michiels, *op. cit.*, p. 319.

[45] Theoretically, this is subject to dispute. Michiels (*De delictis et poenis*, I, 112-113), Coronata (*Institutiones*, IV, 28), and Swoboda (*Ignorance in Relation to the Imputability of Delicts*, pp. 111-112) hold that if any act forbidden by a penal canon be done out of negligence, the person so acting is subject to *ferendae sententiae* penalties, according to canons 2203, § 1; 2229, § 4. The other opinion, supported by Hollweck (*Die kirchlichen Strafgesetze* [Mainz, 1899], n. 19, note 1), Heimberger (*Die Schuld im Strafrecht des Codex J. C.* [in Festgabe zum 60 Geburtstag von Gustav Aschaffenburg, Heidelberg, 1926], p. 16), and Moersdorf (*Die Rechtssprache des Codex Juris Canonici* [Paderborn: Schoeningh, 1937], p. 376) maintain that certain penal canons by their nature or wording require special *dolus* so as to eliminate negligence as a source of imputability in their regard, at least in cases of *latae sententiae* penalties; this view is in accord with canons 2219, § 3; 2229, § 2; 2228; 2219, § 1. Canon 2229, § 4 should not be quoted in favor of the former opinion since it refers to laws treated in canon 2229, § 3, which do not require special *dolus*. Canon 2203, § 1 must be ruled out as a *petitio principii*, since it is based on the condition *si quis legem violaverit* . . .; the very question here is whether the law has been violated by an act of negligence. Canon 2203 does not supply the answer, and canon 2229, § 4 is not pertinent to the class of delicts here considered, namely, those requiring special *dolus*. Hence it would seem that even in theory the first opinion

limitation occurs in delicts where criminal intent is demanded to the exclusion of negligence. a) Delicts punished only with censures, which require contumacy, are not juridically imputable to those acting with negligence.[46] b) Canons employing the terminology mentioned by canon 2229, § 2 [47] do not operate in cases of negligence. c) Moreover, delicts traditionally interpreted as requiring criminal intent at least to the exclusion of a merely negligent violation of the law [48] must also be eliminated. In the second place, the field is further narrowed by the requisites of the concept of complicity. While cooperation is, as has been shown, possible in cases of negligence, it is not always easily obtained. However, the concept of negligent cooperation may be verified especially in those canons in which vindictive penalties are invoked without any account of special or explicit criminal intent (*dolus*) against those who fail to perform pre-

is without support from the law itself. At any rate, there is in this matter sufficient doubt to render obligatory in practice the more benign interpretation according to canon 2219, § 1, which as Michiels (*Normae generales juris canonici* [Lublin. Universitas Catholica, 1929], p. 445) points out, is to be applied in *dubium quoddam juris vel facti*. Certainly it is difficult to see how there could be a negligent crime or a quasi-delict, when the law requires not negligence but criminal intent.

[46] Cf. Roberti, p. 278. If, however, other penalties besides censures are threatened, as in canon 2344 and 2337, the violation of the law by negligence is punishable—cf. canon 2229, § 3.

[47] " . . . *presumpserit, ausus fuerit, scienter, studiose, temerarie, consulto egerit* aliave similia quae plenam cognitionem ac deliberationem exigunt . . ." To those enumerated may be added *pertinaciter, malitiose, fraude et dolo, de industria*—Chelodi, *Ius poenale*, pp. 98-99; Roberti, p. 277; Wernz-Vidal, *Ius canonicum*, VII, 214; also, *sponte et scienter*—Wernz-Vidal, *ibid.*; Roberti, *ibid.*, note 3. "Verbum *procurare* (c. 2350) requirit dolum sed non plenum dolum; quare tantum delictum culposum excludit."—Roberti, p. 277.

[48] "In this class are the *precurantes abortum*, the *fabricatores* and *falsarii* of papal rescripts and other ecclesiastical documents, the electores who are *sollicitantes immixtionem* of lay power in a canonical election, the *attentantes* of a civil marriage, and the *iniicientes violentas manus* in violation of the *privilegium canonis*."—Swoboda, *Ignorance in Relation to the Imputability of Delicts*, p. 100. "Finally, it seems that *usurpare, conspirare*, and *dolose detrectare* can be included in the classification of expressions which presuppose simple *dolus*. For, it is difficult to understand how one could become guilty of the delicts described and defined by these terms through mere negligence or *culpa*."—Swoboda, *op. cit.*, p. 101.

scribed duties or solemnities. Hence the possible cases of cooperation in negligent crimes in the Code seem restricted to canons 2316;[49] 2324;[50] 2348;[51] 2370;[52] 2373;[53] 2381, n. 1;[54] 2383;[55] 2394, n. 1,

[49] ". . . aut qui communicat in divinis cum haereticis contra praescriptum can. 1258, suspectus de haeresi est."

[50] "Qui deliquerint contra praescriptum can. 827, 828, 840, § 1, ab Ordinario pro gravitate culpae puniantur, non exclusa, si res ferat, suspensione aut beneficii vel officii ecclesiastici privatione, vel, si de laicis agatur, excommunicatione." The penalty here is undertermined. When, however, censures or severe vindictive penalties are invoked, the crime must have proceeded from a criminal intention, not mere negligence.

[51] "Qui legatum vel donationem ad causas pias sive actu inter vivos sive testamento, etiam per fiduciam, obtinuerit et implere negligat, ab Ordinario, etiam per censuram, ad id cogatur." In case of negligence, however, censures could not be applied.

[52] "Episcopus aliquem consecrans in Episcopum, Episcopi vel, loco Episcoporum, presbyteri assistentes, et qui consecrationem recipit sine apostolico mandato contra praescriptum can. 953, ipso iure suspensi sunt, donec Sedes Apostolica eos dispensaverit." This is a vindictive penalty.

[53] "In suspensionem per annum ab ordinum collatione Sedi Apostolicae reservatam ipso facto incurrunt: 1°, Qui contra praescriptum can. 955, alienum subditum sine Ordinarii proprii litteris dimissoriis ordinaverint; 2°, Qui subditum proprium, qui alibi tanto tempore moratus sit ut canonicum impedimentum contrahere ibi potuerit, ordinaverint contra praescriptum can. 993, n. 4, 994; 3°, Qui aliquem ad ordines maiores sine titulo canonico promoverint contra praescriptum can. 974, § 1, n. 7; 4°, Qui, salvo legitimo privilegio, religiosum, ad familiam pertinentem quae sit extra territorium ipsius ordinantis, promoverint etiam cum litteris dimissorialibus proprii Superioris, nisi legitime probatum fuerit aliquem e casibus occurrere, de quibus in can. 966.

[54] "Qui officium, beneficium, dignitatem obtinet cum onere residentiae, si illegitime absit: 1°, Eo ipso privatur omnibus fructibus sui beneficii vel officii pro rata illegitimae absentiae, eosque tradere debet Ordinario, qui ecclesiae vel alicui pio loco vel pauperibus distribuat . . ."

[55] "Parochus qui paroeciales libros diligenter, ad normam iuris, non conscripserit aut servaverit, a proprio Ordinario pro gravitate culpae puniatur."

3;[56] 2398;[57] 2404;[58] 2408;[59] 2411;[60] 2412, n. 2;[61] and 2357 with respect to sexual crimes committed with minors under sixteen years of age.[62] The other delicts of the Code seem to be removed from the possibility of negligent cooperation because they are penalized exclusively by censures, or because by nature or wording they require *dolus* to the exclusion of *culpa*. Yet, even in the case of the crimes mentioned, the qualities of criminal cooperation must be established

[56] "Qui beneficium, officium vel dignitatem ecclesiasticam propria auctoritate occupaverit vel, ad ea electus, praesentatus, nominatus in eorundem possessionem vel regimen seu administrationem sese ingesserit, antequam necessarias litteras confirmationis vel institutionis acceperit easque illis ostenderit, quibus de iure debet: 1°, Sit ipso iure ad eadem inhabilis et praeterea ab Ordinario pro gravitate culpae puniatur; 3°, Capitula vero, conventus aliique omnes ad quos spectat, huiusmodi electos, praesentatos vel nominatos ante litterarum exhibitionem admittentes, ipso facto a iure eligendi, nominandi vel praesentandi suspensi maneant ad beneplacitum Sedis Apostolicae."

[57] "Si quis ad episcopatum promotus, contra praescriptum can. 333 intra tres menses consecrationem suscipere neglexerit, fructus non facit suos, fabricae ecclesiae cathedralis applicandos; et si postea in eadem negligentia per totidem menses perstiterit, episcopatu privatus ipso iure manet."

[58] "Abusus potestatis ecclesiasticae, prudenti legitimi Superioris arbitrio, pro gravitate culpae puniatur, salvo praescripto canonum qui certam poenam in aliquos abusus statuunt."

[59] "Taxas consuetas et legitime approbatas ad normam can. 1507, augentes aut ultra eas aliquid exigentes, gravi mulcta pecuniaria coerceantur, et recidivi ab officio suspendantur vel removeantur pro culpae gravitate, praeter obligationem restituendi quod iniuste perceperint."

[60] "Superiores religiosi qui candidatum non idoneum contra praescriptum can. 542, aut sine requisitis litteris testimonialibus contra praescriptum can. 544, ad novitiatum receperint, vel ad professionem contra praescriptum can. 571, § 2 admiserint, pro gravitate culpae puniantur, non exclusa officii privatone."

[61] "Religiosarum etiam exemptarum Antistitae pro gravitate culpae, non exclusa, si res ferat, officii privatione, ab Ordinario loci puniantur: 2°, Si contra praescriptum can. 552 omiserint Ordinarium loci certiorem facere de proxima alicuius admissione ad novitiatum vel ad professionem."

[62] Sexual crimes are committed by direct intention, not by negligence; for this reason the other sexual crimes mentioned in the Code are not included in this list of crimes arising from negligence. The possibility of imputable negligence occurs in the crime stated, not from its sexual element, but from the added qualification of a specified age.

in each instance. The list as it stands is merely an enumeration of those canons of the Code which admit the possibility of cooperation in crimes committed through negligence.

Chapter Nine

CO-AGENTS

Canon 2209 § 1. **Qui communi delinquendi consilio simul physice concurrunt in delictum, omnes eodem modo rei habentur, nisi adiuncta alicuius culpabilitatem augeant vel minuant.**

Article 1. The Nature of Complete Participation

The concept of responsibility by way of complicity is achieved most truly in those who acting together with the same intent perform the external deeds which accomplish the crime. This is complete participation. The acts lending themselves to criminal cooperation fall into two chief categories: physical, which represents material contributions of action performed or equipment offered; and moral, which consists of instigation or encouragement leading to crime. Partial participation results when the effort of an accomplice is limited to one category, either physical or moral. The distinction between complete participation and that partial participation without which the crime would not have been committed, is of no moment as regards guilt, damages, and punishment.[1] But the practical importance of the distinction must not on this account be overlooked,[2] insofar that certain cooperators may be subject to canon 2209,§ 1, who would not be held by canon 2209, § 3, and vice versa.

Canon 2209, § 1 deals with complete participation. It is not, therefore, a definition of criminal cooperation with appropriate provisions suitable to each class of cooperators to be made in the succeeding paragraphs of the canon. While the essence of cooperation in crime is found in the words *qui communi delinquendi consilio . . . concurrunt in delicto*, the qualification *simul physice* is too exclusive to embrace all cooperators. This demands a proximity in time and a physical engagement at the commission of the crime which are not to be expected of all the participants in the crime. This special

[1] Canons 2209, § § 1, 2, 3; 2211; 2231; cf. Chelodi; Ius poenale, p. 17.

[2] As Coronata seems to do—*Institutiones*, IV, 49.

group, contemplated by canon 2209, § 1, will be refered to under the term *co-agents.*

These co-agents must not only concur in the crime with the same common intent of breaking the law, as is required for cooperators generally, but they must also take part in the crime physically and at the same time. This physical participation includes any material contribution towards the accomplishment of the crime, within limits to be defined later. But insofar as an identity of time is also required, the material contribution must be made during the actual time of the commission of the crime. Thus the person who brought to the scene of the crime the weapons in advance of the action would not be a co-agent. On the other hand, it is not necessary that all the participants perform their share simultaneously. Each can have a part in a long succession of acts which comprise the accomplishment of the crime. These physical and temporal requirements will have to be determined in particular.

As a basis for understanding the physical element of complete participation, an analysis of the development of a crime will be helpful.[3] A crime is effected through two processes, one psychological, the other physical.[4] The psychological process includes all the internal acts, sensitive, cognitive, and volitional, which determine the person to the criminal act. This process, however, does not come within the competence of the law which looks only toward the external violation of the law.[5] The physical process, on the other hand, comprehends all external acts done with a view to accomplishing the criminal purpose. These may be divided into preparatory acts and executive acts. The preparatory acts prepare the means and remove the obstacles to the criminal act, without making any direct contribution to the criminal act itself. The executive acts directly enter into the commission of the crime.

These two classes are readily admitted but the exact line of demarcation between them is sometimes hard to draw. When does an act

[3] This approach has been adopted by Wernz-Vidal, *Ius Canonicum*, VII, 139-141.

[4] Cf. Michiels, *De delictis et poenis*, I, 247-248.

[5] Canon 2195, § 1; "Cogitationis poenam nemo patitur"— D (48, 19), 18—c. 14, D. 1, de poen.; cf. Roberti, *De delictis et poenis*, p. 53-54.

cease to be preparatory to the crime and really become executive? The distinction cannot rest in the intention of the agent since all these acts are placed with the idea of directly or indirectly accomplishing the crime. The criterion is rather to be found in the nature of the concrete acts themselves considered in relation to the particular crime toward which they are directed. When the relationship of cause and effect is clearly established, the stage of preparatory acts has been passed, and executive acts are considered to be realized. This is true because the preparatory acts, even though in each particular case they are directed by the criminal intent towards the accomplishment of the crime, nevertheless are, viewed in themselves, indifferent with regard to the accomplishment of the crime; this may be seen in the purchases of drugs, weapons, and tools. The executive acts are, however, by their own nature, unequivocally directed to effect the crime. Canonists,[6] therefore, place the mode of differentiation in the lack of objective ambiguity characterizing the executive acts as to their purpose in accomplishing the crime.[7] Thus when the act placed is by its own nature clearly directed toward the accomplishment of a specific crime, it falls within the category of executive acts.

With this analysis of the development of the crime, it is now easy to point out the conditions for complete participation in its physical phase. A person may engage in preparatory acts and still become a cooperator, provided there exist a common intention and a consummated crime. The resulting imputability is to be diagnosed, however, according to canon 2209, § § 3, 4. It must be remembered

[6] Lega, *De delictis et poenis*, pp. 26-28; Coronata, *Institutiones*, IV, 58-59; Latini, *Iuris criminalis philosophici summa lineamenta*, pp. 142-143; Michiels, *De delictis et poenis*, I, 249-250; Roberti, *De delictis et poenis*, pp. 198-200; Wernz, *Ius decretalium*, VI, 42.

[7] This examination of the genesis of the crime is usually made in connection with attempted crime, *conatus delicti*. Preparatory acts, though they may be defined as crimes in themselves by express legislation, nevertheless are not considered attempted crimes—canon 2212, § 1; Lega, *op. cit.* p. 26; Roberti, *op. cit.* p. 200; Coronata, *op. cit.*, p. 58. Executive acts, however, when destitute of consummation, present the nature of attempted crimes—canon 2212, § 1; Lega, *loc. cit.*; Coronata, *op. cit.*, p. 59; Michiels, *op. cit.*, pp. 262, 268.

that these preparatory acts are indifferent in themselves, and are directed to the accomplishment of the crime by the intention of the agent. Hence, to offer the physical participation required in a co-agent, one must engage at least in executive acts.[8] For these acts, which by their nature tend to effect the crime, present the physical participation required by canon 2209, § 1. Otherwise, the words *physice concurrunt* are scarcely realized in acts which are directed to the crime only by intention. Such preparatory acts are not even considered attempted crime,[9] but, of course, when joined to a consummated crime intentionally through cooperation, they become punishable as partial physical participation. Hence it is seen that the physical constituent of complete participation is not verified in acts which are embraced into the cooperative ensemble of criminal acts principally through a moral, not a physical bond. Merely external acts do not fulfill the meaning of *physice,* which is opposed to the term *moral.* The physical deficiency of an external act, therefore, cannot be compensated by moral participation. Thus it is here stated that a person who gave sufficient moral cooperation to be held by canon 2209, § 3, and in addition, gave some slight external aid, would not be considered as physically concurring in the crime according to canon 2209, § 1. In other words, the executive act of the co-agent must itself be physical, and not merely joined to external aid such as is properly considered by canon 2209, § 4.[10] Therefore, only they concur physically in the crime, who while co-

[8] Wernz-Vidal require consummating acts, those executive acts which effect the crime as defined in law—*Ius canonicum,* VII, 139. Michiels, *De delictis et poenis,* I, 309, note 1. This seems excessive in so far that if one co-agent anticipated another, the latter would be relieved of his proper responsibility.

[9] Canon 2212, § 1 ". . . ad executionem delicti natura sua conducunt . . ."

[10] Wernz-Vidal, to the contrary, allow completely moral participation to characterize a co-agent. Rightly, however, they point out that sometimes mere words will constitute the element of physical participation, when they have effect not only on the will but also in the deed; e.g., when according to plan a person persuades another to walk by a place where murderers lie in wait for him.—*Ius Canonicum,* VII, 139-140; also, Latini in reference to latter point, p. 161.

operating with others place executive or consummating physical acts.[11]

The distinction between executive and preparatory acts does not coincide with the distinction between effective and facilitating cooperation made by canon 2209 § § 3, 4. The former considers the objective nature of the participation, whereas the latter looks to the actual effect the act has on the crime. It is possible to conceive of executive acts without which the crime would, nevertheless, have been committed. It should also be noted that, while the executive acts thus far considered are acts of physical cooperation as opposed to moral cooperation, the concept of preparatory and executive acts can readily be applied to moral participation. Thus directions on the procedure in mixing drugs, in aiming firearms, are preparatory acts; the command or the instigation to poison or to shoot belong to the class of executive acts.

A further note is to be made to the effect that *physice concurrunt* is not to be understood in an ontological sense, as though it included all the cooperators who were responsible for the existence of the crime. Otherwise moral cooperators could be brought into the concept of co-agents, in so far as they also bring the crime into existence. Canon 2209, § 3 makes separate provision for such moral cooperators, so as to make their inclusion under canon 2209, § 1 without meaning.

The norm of the physical participation required of co-agents is now fully established. To examine in particular its operation, the case of procuring an abortion is both apt and practical. With the *dolus*, as previously adverted to, required by this crime granted in each instance, there may be considered as being involved in this regard the following persons: the mother, the persons advising the operation, including the physician consulted, the official granting admission to the hospital, nurses, physicians making general health examinations or making preparations required of any serious operation, the sur-

[11] Latin agrees with this conclusion—p. 158. This he refers to all physical cooperation, but it must be remembered that he does not distinguish between complete participation and partial cooperation by physical aid, as is to be done by virtue of canon 2209, § § 1 and 3—p. 161.

geon and his assistants at the operation.[12] Only the mother and the surgeon perform physical executive acts so as to be held under canon 2209, § 1 as co-agentes. The others, with the exception of those advising the operation who perform moral executive acts, carry out merely routine hospital duties pertinent to any operation.[13] This is true even of those assisting at the operation, as by administering the anesthetic or passing the instruments,[14] unless they should, at the surgeon's direction, perform an action specifically directed to the abortion.

The requisite of simultaneous activity in complete participation must now be examined. In denoting it, the canon uses the word *simul.* It has been suggested that this word be interpreted in a merely temporal sense, so that all co-agents must act at the same time.[15] But this perfect simultaneity would impose limits so narrow that all cases of complete participation would not be included. On the other hand, a modified concept of simultaneity, including actions placed within an arbitrarily fixed time-limit, would be difficult to determine and be too indefinite for practical purposes. The word *simul,* however, may also be understood in the sense of concerted action. This is usually expressed in English by the word *together.* Such an interpretation accords fully with the idea of complete participation. The co-agents must be considered as working together for the accom-

[12] To incur the penalty, it is necessary that the offense be not craniotomy but true abortion, the ejection of a living fetus which cannot live outside the uterus; cf. Chelodi, *Ius poenale,* p. 110.

[13] Delinquunt procurantes, . . . actione physica vel morali, sed de se efficaci, et consulto. Non tales sunt qui abortum permittunt, etiam praevidentes ex propria actione illicita indirecte secuturum."—Chelodi, *Ius poenale,* p. 110.

[14] ". . . la cooperazione, agli effetti della censura, deve essere diretta, efficace, e immediata rispetto al fine voluto, anche se si compie per mezzo di altri. Cosi non sono cooperatori il farmacista, che somministra le medicine; la persona che va in cerca del medico; chi perpara il bagno, l'ago, le pozioni, ecc. ecc."—Salucci, *Il Diritto Penale secondo il Codice di Diritto Canonico* (2 vols., Subiaco: Tipografia dei Monasteri, 1926-1930), II, 224; cf. Cipollini, *De censuris latae sententiae iuxta codicem iuris canonici* (Taurini: *Marietti,* 1925), p. 145.

[15] Heimberger, *Aus dem Strafrecht des Codex J. C.* (Sonderdruck aus der Bonner Festgabe fuer Ernst Zitelmann, Muenchen und Leipzig, 1923), pp. 65-66.

plishment of their common purpose. Thus the contribution of each is part of the general execution of the deed. This is said with regard to objective causality, because juridically each co-agent is responsible for the complete crime. As regards guilt, each is *exsecutor delitci;* it just happens that circumstances direct a division of labor as regards the physics of the crime. Unity of action is, therefore, the proper sense of the word *simul.*[16]

How is this unity of action constituted? Often it will result from careful planning which integrates the many steps required in a complicated enterprise; but it may just as well come about through a desire for cooperative action which springs up almost spontaneously without formal planning, but not, of course, without a common purpose mutually known. It is not the degree of planning which is decisive, but rather the result of the planning, the integration of the efforts of the various cooperators. This integration must be such that the accomplices, whether operating with simultaneity or operating in succession, nevertheless fulfil the concept of acting together. Accordingly, the efforts of the cooperators must be actually [17] united by intention and effect. By the intention of the co-agents they are to be directed toward the accomplishment of the crime, and as regards effect, they are to be such as by their natural effect would, at least, cumulatively accomplish the crime. This actual unity of cooperative effort is sufficient to bear out the meaning of *simul;* for then the work of each cooperator conspires to attain the common end, and each cooperator is, moreover, a principal agent in the matter, and not merely an assistant to another. The integration of effort,

[16] "Opinor significationem temporalem vocis *simul* non esse nimis urgendam. Vocabulum istud ad nullum alium scopum videtur adhibitum, nisi ad indicandum quod ambo seu omnes debent concurrere in actus ipsius facti delictuosi consummativos. De facto sane concursus iste est regulariter simultaneus; nihil tamen obstare videtur, quominus actus ab uno positus actum alterius tempore praecedat, dummodo amborum actus natura sua sint inter se conjuncti et simul sumpti facti delictuosi consummativi."—Michiels, *De delictis et poenis,* I, 309, note 1.

[17] Michiels, as quoted *supra,* in note 16, requires the efforts to be united by their nature. Such acts are difficult to conceive outside of necessary cooperation, and there seems to be no reason in law or jurisprudence to suppose them in this case.

or concerted action, is constituted by two elements, intention and effect. If a person should contribute to the commission of a crime accidentally or independentally of the general plan, he cannot be accorded the status of a co-agent, of one who commits the crime neither singly nor subordinately, but in conjunction with other principal agents. Hence the co-agent must act with the explicit intention of effecting the crime with the aid of the other principal agents. On the other hand, the act, itself, of the co-agent must help to effect the crime; it should not merely assist the perpetrators but actually contribute to the constitution of the crime. Thus the cumulative effect of all the acts of the co-agents is the crime. The question now arises: what acts can be considered as cumulatively effecting the crime? Since the effect of the act is here to be examined, and not the intention of the cooperators, the conclusion must be drawn that, not preparatory acts, but executive or consummating acts, which by nature tend toward the accomplishing of the crime, are required. In this latter aspect the temporal and physical requirements of complete participation overlap; both demand executive acts. Concerted action, therefore, as denoted by *simul,* arises from executive acts which are performed with the intention of achieving the common purpose. Accordingly, there is no extrinsic time-limit with regard to complete participation but only an intrinsic limit insofar as the specific crime and the particular mode of operation selected are capable of united action. Either simultaneous action or successive action can be concerted in the sense of *simul.* In the case of simultaneity, however, the unity of intention and effect is more readily discerned. Nevertheless, even in successive action the integration of cooperative effort may be observed in the convergence of the various acts in the constitution of the crime. Hence a distinction must be drawn between the origin of concerted action and the recognition of concerted action. The former is found in the intention of the cooperator and in the effect of the act; the latter is indicated in the combined objective efficacy of the various acts to constitute the crime.

This investigation has shown that the physical element of complete participation as considered by canon 2209, § 1 consists of executive acts which contribute directly to the crime, and so are physical, not moral, in character. The temporal element, on the other hand, is established by the concept of concerted action, which is verified in executive acts directed by the intention to the common purpose. In accordance with what has been thus established one may readily understand the expression employed by the canon—*simul physice concurrunt*. It designates the placing of physical executive acts with the intention of contributing with others to the commission of the crime—or, more simply, physical executive acts in concerted action.

The commentators of the Code have not, as a rule, explored this concept in great detail. Many simply state the need of physical participation, action, or personal intervention.[18] General statements of this kind leave the notion of physical participation undefined. Roberti,[19] with Wernz-Vidal [20] concurring, however, maintains that there is no special mode by which the co-agents participate in the material execution of the crime. Accordingly, when several persons intend by common intent to kill, all are guilty of homicide, even though only one grave the lethal stroke, and the others merely watched or stood by. This view leads to correct conclusions with regard to concurrent action, but when the acts of the co-agents are not simultaneous, but successive, difficulties arise. In the latter situation, how is the operation of co-agents to be distinguished from physical cooperation as considered in canon 2209, § § 3-4? [21] But if the pro-

[18] Ayrinhac-Lydon, *Penal Legislation*, p. 18; Augustine, *Commentary*, VIII, 48; Cappello, *De censuris*, p. 31; Chelodi, *Ius poenale*, p. 17; Sole, *De delictis et poenis*, p. 34; but it would seem that this last author also required that the physical action be such that without it the crime would not be committed, *op. cit.*, p. 33—cf. Coronata, *Institutiones*, IV, 47, note 5; Vermeersch-Creusen (*Epitome*, III, 193): "simul et actione;" Blat (*Commentarium*, V, 30): "simul in illius [communis consilii] consequentiam atque *physice*, opera nempe manuum, verborum, scriptorum, etc." Michiels, (*De delictis et poenis*, I, 309): ". . . hoc propositum de facto simul exsequuntur per concurrentem actionem . . . "—this author's note on *simul* has been already quoted, *supra*, note 15.

[19] *De delictis et poenis*, p. 218.

[20] *Ius canonicum*, VII, 143. Latini also considers all concomitant aid as complete participation—p. 161. Similarly, Heimberger, *Aus dem Strafrecht des Codex Juris Canonici*, pp. 69-70.

[21] Roberti in effect says there is no difference: "Quin immo, post consummationem, imputantur ad conreitatem etiam actus praeparatorii, qui ad finem pravum, communi consilio, peracti sunt."—p. 218.

visions of canon 2209, § § 3-4 are not to be confused with § 1, some way must be found to distinguish co-agents from other physical participants in successive cooperation. This distinction is adequately made by requiring physical executive acts in concert, as previously explained, for complete participation. As regards concurrent action, it will be seen upon closer inspection that this norm holds true there also. In the case related of several standing by while the lethal blow was given by another, it would appear at first that since many of those concerned contributed nothing palpably to the physical constitution of the crime, they should at the most be considered as moral participants. The correct view is, however, that their presence in such circumstances correlated with their determination must be accepted as a physical executive act, which would accomplish the crime, if not anticipated by the act of another.[22] Conversely, this is not a frustrated or attempted crime because the criminal purpose has really been accomplished through the instrumentality of others who share the same intent; [23] nor is it necessary that an executive act be a consummating act. What has been said of those merely present, applies, *a fortiori*, to those who in addition to presence contribute even facilitating acts to the commission of the crime. This is not merely a teleological interpretation; it considers the objective nature of the concrete act—presence—with its circumstances, and not merely the intention of those present. Though presence is usually an indifferent act, in this case, the companions in crime are not present as mere spectators, but as potential agents; their presence is itself a physical act of aggression against the victim and of support and sometimes of assistance to their co-delinquents. This kind of presence is by its concrete nature ordained to the commission of the crime. A note is here to be added in reference to the case of abortion already discussed. Certain persons, though present, were considered as not presenting executive acts; this was because they were present in their ordinary capacity for the performance of routine

[22] *Glossa ordinaria* ad c. 5, *de poenis*, V, 9 in VI°, v. *Socius*: "Cum enim comitetur per facinus, pari poena punitur."

[23] "Qui facit per alium, est perinde, ac si faciat per se ipsum."—Reg. 72, R. J.

hospital tasks, and were not there prepared or willing to effect the abortion personally.

It has now been shown that, according to the more practical and consistent view, the complete participation of canon 2209, § 1 is verified in physical executive acts placed in concerted action.

Article 2. The Guilt of Complete Participation

Each co-agent, no matter how small his part in the crime has been, is equally guilty with all the others—*omnes eodem modo rei habentur.* This is a matter of objective responsibility, which, as has been pointed out, is one and indivisible.[24] The words of the canon clearly express this equality of guilt.[25] Nor is there any need to say as in canon 2209, § 3 that the guilt is not less than that of the perpetrator of the crime, since from the nature of his participation each co-agent is considered to be in the same position as the perpetrator of the crime.[26] What is thus understood is also made clear from the words of the canon; for if the guilt of each is equal, then each is guilty of the whole crime. It has already been remarked that the objective responsibility is one and indivisible in the sense that the criminal fact with all its circumstances is communicable to all co-agents. What therefore is done by each co-agent is juridically attributable to all, provided, of course, it is contained within the common intent.[27] It is clear from what has just been said concerning the principle of objectivity [28] and the nature of complete participation, that co-agents are not merely compared to each other, but are implicitly made responsible for the whole crime. Accordingly, they must answer not only for the actions of all other co-agents but also for the actions of all other cooperators, provided, once again, that these actions are contained within the common intent.

[24] Michiels, *De delictis et poenis,* I. 321; cf. *supra,* chapter 8, article 3.

[25] Roberti, *De delictis et poenis,* p. 218.

[26] ". . . ita ut *unicuique* co-auctori *totum et totaliter* imputetur delictum, ac si unusquisque illud commisisset solus . . . "—Michiels, *loc. cit.* Cf. Roberti, *loc. cit.;* Vermeersch-Creusen, *Epitome,* III, 193.

[27] Cf. Latini, p. 159.

[28] Cf. *supra,* chapter 8, article 5.

Hence, all real circumstances, which refer to the nature of the crime, are brought within the orbit of objective responsibility and are communicable to all co-agents.[29] Such are, for example, the dignity of the person offended,[30] the place and time of the crime, and the means by which it is effected.[31] Thus if any of these circumstances should involve a sacrilege, this graver guilt would be common to all participants. A question arises, however, in connection with a circumstance personal to the agent which, nevertheless, affects the nature of the crime. Is such a circumstance communicable to others, as in the murder of a man by several co-agents, one of whom is his son? Roberti is of the opinion that the guilt of patricide is communicated to all participants.[32] The opposite view is held by Wernz-Vidal.[33] And this would seem preferable inasmuch as such circumstances, since they refer directly to the agent and not to the nature of the crime, should appertain to the subjective guilt and hence be incommunicable. For if they change the nature of the crime at all, it is only because of the subject and hence in relation to the subject. Thus if several men, one of whom was a cleric bound to celibacy, should engage in an act of rape, there would be no sharing in the sacrilege by those not bound to celibacy. If, however, the crime were committed with special advertence to this personal circumstance, and this should enter into the common motive, then all would be guilty of the sacrilege properly imputable to one.[34]

The canon also takes account of any modification of the invariable objective guilt realized in an individual by personal circumstances—*nisi adiuncta alicuius culpabilitatem augeant vel minuant.* A matter of subjective imputability is personal and not communicable to others.[35] The individual co-agent, therefore, is responsible only for as much of the criminal fact with its attendant circumstances as is contained in his intention or is due to his criminal negligence in

[29] Coronata, *Institutiones,* IV, 50; Michiels, *De delictis et poenis,* I, 316.
[30] Canon 2207, n. 1.
[31] Coronata, *loc cit.;* Roberti, *De delictis et poenis,* p. 214.
[32] Roberti, *ibid.,* p. 215.
[33] *Ius canonicum,* III, 143.
[34] Cf. Roberti, *ibid.,* p. 214, note 1. Latini, pp. 159-160.
[35] Michiels, *De delicitis et poenis* I, 322; Roberti, p. 214.

accord with the personal circumstances which qualify imputability.[36] It may be assumed with canon 2209, § 1 that imputability by reason of criminal intent or negligence exists; otherwise, there would be no co-agents. Yet advertence may be made to the fact that when some cooperators operate in accordance with their own special purpose, the others are responsible only for what has been done according to the common intent.[37] The subjective responsibility is, however, obtained only after consideration has been made of the circumstances modifying guilt. These personal circumstances are listed in canons 2201, 2202, 2203, 2204, 2205, 2206, 2207, 2208, and include insanity, drunkenness, mental weakness, ignorance, inadvertence, error, carelessness (omissio debitae diligentiae), chance, minor age, violence, fear, self-defense, passion, personal dignity, abuse of authority, repeated offenses.[38]

According to the Code, the guilt of co-agents in a concrete case is derived from the interaction of objective imputability and subjective imputability. The principle of objectivity determines the responsibility of all co-agents for having engaged in a specific crime. The principle of subjectivity modifies this responsibility, which, as objective, is the same for all, in accord with the dispositions of the individual. Thus is established the concrete guilt of each cooperator for canonical purposes.

Scholion. The Status of a Single Perpetrator Acting in Cooperation.

In the case of cooperation where only one person performs the forbidden act and the others concur merely by aid or moral participation, is the perpetrator held by canon 2209, § 1, or only by the canon penalizing the specific delict? Of all the provisions of canon 2209, only the first and second paragraphs deal with those who directly effect the crime. Yet it must be pointed out these paragraphs are concerned only with action in concert, not with singular action.

[36] Canon 2199; Michiels, *op. cit.*, pp. 317, 321-322, 324; Coronata, *op. cit.*, p. 49; Ayrinhac-Lydon, *op. cit.*, p. 18.

[37] Michiels, *op. cit.*, p. 317.

[38] For a full treatment of these causes, cf. Coronata, *op. cit.*, pp. 26-44; Roberti, pp. 91-181; Michiels, *op. cit.*, I, 138-240; Chelodi, *Ius poenale*, pp. 8-15; Swoboda, *Ignorance in Relation to the Imputability of Delicts, in toto.*

On the other hand, it is absurd to consider the perpetrator of the crime as a cooperator when he is joined by other co-agents, but not when he acts in conjunction with moral participants. The answer to the difficulty lies in the fact that canon 2209 merely gives the norms for deciding the guilt of certain cooperators, and is not a full treatment of cooperation. Hence the perpetrator aided only by the moral cooperation of others may be considered a cooperator and treated according to the jurisprudence of cooperation.

Chapter Ten

NECESSARY COOPERATORS

Canon 2209, § 2. **In delicto quod sua natura complicem postulat, unaquaeque pars est eodem modo culpabilis, nisi ex adiunctis aliud appareat.**

This paragraph of canon 2209 deals with the guilt of those who engage in a crime which by its very nature requires an accomplice. The nature of such necessary cooperation has already been explained in chapter one. Its distinguishing characteristic is the fact that the crime cannot be completed according to its nature except by the intervention of several persons; accomplices are thus necessary to its existence. Without settling the controversy concerning its classification as true or analogous cooperation, the legislator here takes up the question of the juridical responsibility of necessary cooperators as a matter of convenience in canon 2209.

The necessary cooperators are placed after co-agents in the enumeration of cooperators because the equality of their guilt is as readily established as that of the co-agents. This equal guilt is due to the fact that these necessary cooperators, being indispensable to the crime, have the status of perpetrators of the crime.[1] The words used in canon 2209, § 2 to indicate such equality of guilt are substantially equivalent to the expression employed in relation to co-agents.[2] Accordingly the concrete guilt of each necessary cooperator is to be measured on the basis of objective and subjective responsibility, as has been explained in connection with co-agents. In cases of necessary cooperation, it is evident that according to the principle of objectivity each cooperator is responsible for the whole crime.[3]

[1] Sole, *De delictis et poenis*, p. 34; Michiels, *De delictis et poenis*, I, 321; Wernz-Vidal, *Ius canonicum*, VII, 144; Pistocchi, "Concorso di più persone in uno stesso delitto"—*Il Monitore Ecclesiastico*, XLVII (1935), 228; Salucci, *Il Diritto Penale*, I, 37.

[2] Michiels, *op. cit.*, pp. 321-322.

[3] Michiels, *op. cit.*, p. 321.

Yet even in crimes demanding reciprocity of action, the dispositions of individuals vary through the operation of personal circumstances; hence, the principle of subjectivity is to be applied.[4] Necessary cooperators, therefore, are held guilty of the whole crime, but in the concrete case, this objective guilt may be modified by subjective dispositions which increase or diminish guilt.

While the Code gives this norm for determining the guilt of necessary cooperators, nevertheless, in many particular crimes, such cooperators are treated individually by canonical legislation. In express provision of law, the separate members in crimes which ordinarily postulate necessary cooperation are referred to by name, or at least specifically, so that one may come to the conclusion that what were once parts of necessary cooperation, are now made by legislation into separate crimes. At any rate, because of the definite quality of the law itself, there is no need for recourse to canon 2209, § 2 to discover the guilt, or to canon 2231 to determine the penalty.

This legislation will now be considered. In canon 2347, n. 3, all who give or receive alienated church property, when the requisite permission of the Holy See has been knowingly been omitted, incur a *latae sententiae* excommunication. By canon 2351, § 1, those who provoke others to a duel, or accept a duel, as well as the actual duellers themselves, are all automatically subjected to excommunication simply reserved to the Holy See. In the crime of episcopal consecration without apostolic mandate as considered by canon 2370, on one hand, the bishop consecrating and his assisting bishops or priests, and on the other, the one receiving consecration, are all suspended until the Holy See dispenses. According to canon 2371, all, bishops included, who knowingly confer or receive orders, or who knowingly administer or receive other sacraments through simony incur suspicion of heresy; clerics moreover are punished by suspension. Canon 2388, § 1 states that clerics in sacred orders or religious having the solemn vow of chastity, and their partners, who presume to attempt marriage, even civilly, incur a *latae sententiae* excommunication simply reserved to the Holy See; in canon 2388, § 2,

[4] Coronata, *Institutiones*, IV, 49; Ayrinhac-Lydon, *Penal Legislation*, p. 18; Michiels, *op. cit.*, *pp.* 321-322; Salucci, *loc. cit.*

when one party to the forbidden marriage is a religious having simple vows, both partners fall under excommunication reserved to the Ordinary. In all these laws, it may be noticed, the various members of the crime requiring necessary cooperation are specified as liable to punishment. In view of these express provisions there is no need to apply the general norms of canon 2209, § 2 and canon 2231.

On the other hand, the canons sometimes penalize only one person concerned in what would naturally be a case of necessary cooperation. Accordingly, the unmentioned party, from the viewpoint of canon 2209, § 2, presents only material cooperation, since he is not considered by the law which merely describes the action of his partner. The situation would be different if the canon described the crime involving necessary cooperation. But the law merely adverts to the action of one partner, which then becomes a simple crime involving no complicity as contemplated by canon 2209, § 2. Thus among the offenses regarding false relics listed in canon 2326, selling, but not buying, is mentioned. In canon 2338, § 2, clerics who knowingly and willingly communicate with an excommunicated cleric who is *vitandus,* by performing any divine office with him, or who permit him to exercise any divine office, automatically incur excommunication simply reserved to the Holy See; in this penalty, the excommunicated, *vitandus* cleric is not included.[5] Canon 2354, § 1 considers only the crime of selling a human being into slavery or for some other evil purpose, without referring to the complemental act of purchasing. Canon 2372 punishes only those who presume to receive orders from one who has by sentence been pronounced excommunicated, suspended or interdicted, or from a notorious apostate, heretic, or schismatic; the minister of the ordination is not considered. In canon 2395 those who knowingly accept an office, benefice, or dignity not legally vacant, and allow themselves to be put in possession of one of these ecclesiastical positions, are punished by being made permanently ineligible for this position, and by other discretionary penalties—the one who confers the position, or who installs another in it is not penalized. Likewise, in canon 2400 only

[5] Cf. Chelodi, *Ius poenale,* p. 97; Coronata, *Institutiones,* IV, 393; canon 2256, n. 1.

the cleric who resigns an ecclesiastical office, benefice, or dignity to a lay person is punished by suspension *a divinis*; no punishment is stated for the layman who receives these ecclesiastical rights. Canon 646, § 1, n. 2 punitively singles out, to the exclusion of the guilty partner, those religious who take flight with a member of the opposite sex.[6] This is a catalog of simple crimes, which do not juridically postulate necessary cooperation. The phraseology employed in these canons precludes the application of canon 2209, § 2 insofar as there is described for punitive purposes not a crime implying necessary cooperation but rather the action of certain persons, with no reference to the mutually requisite action of their partners. When, however, these crimes are committed, cooperation must be present; hence, there is no reason why, *ceteris paribus*, canon 2209, § 3 should not be applied to those cooperators who are necessary to the crime. Whereupon the cooperators become, according to canon 2231, liable to the penalty as stated in the pertinent canon, provided the person cooperating is capable of suffering the specified penalty.

The force of canon 2209, § 2, nevertheless, finds full scope in following cases; in these, crimes requiring necessary cooperation are described. Canon 2319, § 1, nn. 1, 2 subjects to excommunication reserved to the ordinary, Catholics[7] who enter marriage before a non-Catholic minister in disregard of canon 1063, § 1, and likewise Catholics who marry with a pact to educate any of their children outside the Catholic Church. Those who conspire against the authority of the Roman Pontiff, his legate, or their own ordinary, or against the legitimate commands of these superiors, are, by virtue of canon 2331, § 2, to be corrected by discretionary penalties; moreover, if clerics, they are to be deprived of dignities, benefices, and other offices; if religious, they are to be deprived of active and passive voice, and of their office. According to canon 2357, §§ 1, 2, lay

[6] Cf. Goyeneche, "Consultationes,"—CpRM, XVII (1936), 343-345.

[7] Beste excludes Catholics who have become apostates, heretics, or schismatics, but not negligent Catholics—*Introductio in codicem*, canon 2319. Moreover, it must be noted that canon 2819 is considered here only in the case when both delinquents are Catholics since only they come under the sanction of the canon. Accordingly, the cooperation of persons not comprehended within the meaning of the term *Catholics* is only material; cf. *supra*, p. 5.

persons legally convicted of sodomy and incest,[8] incur infamy of law[9] besides discretionary punishments; those who commit public adultery or concubinage,[10] or who are legally convicted of other crimes against the Sixth Commandment,[11] which, for the purpose of the present discussion, imply necessary cooperation, are to be excluded from legitimate ecclesiastical acts[12] until they have given signs of true repentance. Canons 2358 and 2359 describe the special penalties for clerics in these matters; their lay accomplices remain subject to canon 2357. While the penalties differ for laymen and clerics, there is no reason to exclude the rule of canon 2209, § 2 regarding the equality of objective guilt of necessary cooperators, although that guilt may be modified by subjective factors. In canon 2392, those committing simony with regard to any ecclesiastical office, benefice, or dignity fall into excommunication simply reserved to the Holy See; they are deprived perpetually of the right of election, presentation, nomina-

[8] These and other crimes against the Sixth Commandment are to be understood in accord with the notions of the law of the state; this is true even in the case of clerics, when the concept of the law of the state is not opposed to the Code—Coronata, *Institutiones*, IV, 491; Chelodi, *Ius poenale*, p. 117; *Eichmann, Das Strafrecht des Codex iuris canonici* (Paderborn, 1920), p. 189. It is for this reason that *stuprum*, though mentioned in this canon, is not included in the above list, since, being restricted to rape in accord with the law of the state, it is not a crime postulating necessary cooperation—Chelodi, *Ius poenale*, p. 118; Coronata, *Institutiones*, IV, 493.

[9] Canons 2293, § 2; 2294, § 1.

[10] Legal conviction by the state is not required in the case of adultery and concubinage—Chelodi, *Ius poenale*, p. 119; Eichmann, *Das Strafrecht des Codex iuris canonici*, p. 192; Coronata, *Institutiones*, IV, 496.

[11] Among these are not to be included *lenocinium* and acts of impurity with minors not yet sixteen years of age; the former, because juridically, by the term, *procuring*, only the act of the procurer is considered, notwithstanding the fact that this crime is not effected without cooperation; and the latter because the phraseology of canon 2357, §§ 1, 2, excludes the minors from the punishment.

[12] Canon 2256, n. 2. This penalty is a *ferendae* sententiae penalty according to Augustine (*Commentary*, VIII, 416), Coronata (*Institutiones*, IV, 496), Wernz-Vidal (*Ius canonicum*, VII, 548), and also, presumably, Ayrinhac-Lydon (*Penal Legislation*, p. 253). Blat (*Commentarium*, V, 264) considers it a *latae sententiae* penalty—"nulla sententia ecclesiastica expectata."

tion, and if clerics they are also suspended: all members of the simoniacal pact are evidently included.[13]

This catalog is small; but it cannot be augmented by including crimes in which the intervention of several people is non-essential. Blat[14] classifies with crimes postulating necessary cooperation the publication of a book, when the editor is distinct from the printer. But in this instance, the nature of the crime does not necessarily require cooperation for its existence. As a matter of fact, in consideration of canon 2318, § 1, which in this regard refers only to the editor, the others cooperating would come only within the scope of canon 2209, § 3 or § 4.

If the true concept of necessary cooperation is to be retained, only those cases will be considered as coming within this category in which the cooperation is not something contingent, but is really required by the nature of the crime. Attention is also to be drawn to the peculiar viewpoint of the legal system which may sometimes find it fitting to coerce only one member of several mutual cooperators. A review of the crimes of the Code conducted in accord with these two norms will, it is believed, disclose only the crimes mentioned in the foregoing list as being dependent upon necessary cooperation. To them, then, is restricted the scope of canon 2209, § 2, in reference to the Code.

[13] Chelodi, *Ius poenale,* pp. 146-147.
[14] *Commentarium,* V, 30.

Chapter Eleven

EFFECTIVE COOPERATORS

Canon 2209, § 3. **Non solum mandans qui est principalis delicti auctor, sed etiam qui ad delicti consummationem inducunt vel in hanc quoquo modo concurrunt, non minorem, ceteris paribus, imputabilitatem contrahunt, quam ipse delicti exsecutor, si delictum sine eorum opera commissum non fuisset.**

Article 1. The Forms of Partial Cooperation.

Canon 2209, § 1 and § 2 treats of complete cooperation, either in crimes, which could be freely committed by one or more persons, or in crimes which necessarily require an accomplice. In both cases the cooperators participate morally and physically because of their mutual encouragement and action. But in canon 2209, § 3 consideration is made of partial cooperation, according to which the cooperator enters the crime either morally or physically by external action which is a true, though partial, cause either of the criminal intent conceived by another, or of the execution performed by another, whereby in either case the crime is effected.[1] Thus he may be responsible for the crime either by moral participation because he influenced the will of the actual perpetrator, or by physical participation because he gave material aid or supplies.[2] In canon 2209, § 3, moreover, the cooperation considered is effective in the sense that without it the crime would not have been effected. This section of canon 2209, therefore, treats of effective partial cooperation, and those cooperators so involved are designated in this treatise as effective cooperators. Hence, with regard to formal cooperation, effective partial participation is to be distinguished from complete participation and from facilitating partial participation. The various types of effective cooperation will now be considered.

[1] Michiels, *De delictis et poenis*, I, 309.

[2] Beste, *Introductio in codicem*, p. 883. There are, moreover, other modes of partial cooperation, as will be seen in section C of this article.

A. The *Mandans*.

First mentioned is the *mandans*, who is called the principal author of the crime; hence if anyone should be held responsible for the crime, it is the *mandans*.[3] This is clear from the definition. Traditionally, as may be seen in the Roman Law concept,[4] mandate requires that the crime be done in favor of the *mandans* and that the mandate be accepted by the mandatary, who is otherwise unwilling to commit the crime.[5] Canonists, however, include within the notion of mandate, the command of a superior who orders his subject to commit a crime,[6] and the contract of hire by which one is paid to perform an illicit action.[7] In all these amplifications of the original Roman contract of mandate [8] as applied to criminal law,[9] the basic idea is retained—the commission of something to another to be done in favor of the *mandans*, and the acceptance by the mandatary. Hence the word *mandans* is to be understood as one who by persuasion, threats, command, hire, or other means short of violence [10]

[3] Cf. c. 6, X, *de sententia excommunicationis*, v. 39.

[4] Bartolus a Saxoferrato (1357): "Mandator dicitur ille, qui mandat delictum committi propter seipsum mandantem et ad satisfactionem voluntatis suae, nulla data pecunia."—*Digestum Novum* ad D (47, 10) 11, 3, n. 2, v. *Si mandato meo*—*Omnia quae extant opera* (10 vols., Sexta Editio Iuntarum, Venetiis, 1590), VI, 128.

[5] Wernz: ". . . pactum sceleris constans ex propositione delicti in favorem mandantis patrandi et ex acceptatione mandatarii"—*Ius decretalium*, VI, 61.

[6] D'Annibale, *Summula theologiae moralis*, I, 178; also, *In constitutionem apostolicae sedis commentarii* (4. ed., Prati, 1894), p. 12; Roberti: "mandatum cum circumstantia aggravante abusus auctoritatis:" *De delictis et poenis*, pp. 216-217; Michiels, *De delictis et poenis*, I, 311-312.

[7] Vermeersch-Creusen, *Epitome*, III, 193; Blat, *Commentarium*, V, 33; Roberti: "praemiis"—*op. cit.*, p. 215; Michiels: "conventione de praemiis"—*op. cit.*, p. 311; Latini, p. 153.

[8] *Mandatum* was an institute of private, not criminal, law. "A mandate was a contract by which one person (mandatarius) gratuitously undertook to do some service at the request of another."—Leage-Ziegler, *Roman Private Law*, p. 336.

[9] This application was made originally in Roman Law—cf., D. (47, 10) 11, 3.

[10] "Non interest qua ratione determinatio acciderit . . ."—Roberti, p. 215; Michiels, *De delictis et poenis*, I, 311.

succeeds in getting another to execute [11] a crime exclusively in his own favor.[12]

The *mandans* is termed *principalis delicti auctor.* Nor is this difficult to understand since he induces the perpetrator to act, and such action is undertaken by the latter, not for his own sake, but for the *mandans.* Truly it can be said that without the *mandans* the crime would not exist.[13] He is, therefore, the primary cause, in the moral, not the physical, genesis of the delict.[14] This, then, is the sense of the words applied by the Code to the *mandans,* who is the primary moral cause of the crime—*principalis delicti auctor.* He is, however, only a partial cause, and does not detract from the effectiveness of the complete cause, the perpetrator, or from the latter's responsibility.

While the guilt of all effective cooperators will be discussed later, it is well to make several observations here pertinent to the *mandans.* As Roberti [15] points out, the *mandans* is held responsible for the crime and all the circumstances which were explicitly or implicitly contained in the mandate. Furthermore, if the mandatary exceeds the limits of the mandate, he solely is responsible, unless the *mandans* also may share the responsibility because of negligence, for failure to take proper precautions or to foresee what would ordinarily happen.[16] One who misuses his authority to command the com-

[11] "Consummatio delicti semper requiritur ad perfectam responsabilitatem mandantis, nisi ipsum mandatum crimen per se stans constitutum sit, independenter ab exsecutione."—Roberti, pp. 215-216.

[12] Cf. Latini, p. 153; Lega, p. 75, note 1.

[13] Hence in the very nature of the mandate is contained the condition of canon 2209, §3: "si delictum sine eorum opera commissum non fuisset." It is clear, moreover, that when a person has already determined upon a crime, there is no place for a *mandans.*

[14] Wernz-Vidal, *Ius canonicum,* VII, 138; cf. Pistocchi, "Il Concorso"—*Mon. Eccl.* XLVII (1935), 230.

[15] *De delictis et poenis,* p. 216.

[16] Roberti, p. 216. Coronata, distinguishing between exceeding of mandate as regards limits and as regards means, holds the *mandans* responsible for the latter; a small excess in executing the mandate is also imputed to the *mandans*-*Institutiones,* IV, 55. This may occasionally be true in particular cases because of negligence, but it cannot be given as a general rule. With respect to

mission of a crime, incurs the added guilt of abuse of authority.[17]

What has been thus far said concerning the guilt of the *mandans* presupposes that the crime as contained in the mandate has been effected. When the mandate has not been brought into execution, the *mandans* is in the position, already discussed, of a person giving attempted moral cooperation. The guilt of one who gives an unfulfilled mandate is, therefore, to be regulated by laws specifically coercing attempted suasion.[18] When no such laws exist, the author of the ineffectual mandate is not even held to attempted crime; nor can he be held to the status of a cooperator, since the definition of *mandans,* requiring an executed mandate, is unsatisfied. Roberti,[19] however, claims that if the mandatary commits a lesser crime comprehended within the greater mandated crime, as, for example, mutilation in place of homicide, the *mandans* is guilty of the lesser crime. This does not seem to be altogether evident because of the need of restrictive interpretation in penal matters.[20] The rule is that the *mandans* is responsible for the total crime with all its circumstances after its consummation.[21] If, moreover, the crime has been partially executed, the *mandans* is a cooperator in attempted crime and incurs the guilt of attempted crime.[22] However, a distinction must be recognized between the partial execution of a crime and the substitution of a lesser crime for the greater crime in which this lesser crime may be comprehended. Any substitution of this sort is made not only without the authority of the *mandans* but also against his will. Briefly, the person giving the original mandate cannot be considered the *mandans* in case of substitution. Whatever responsibility he has in this case rests on other bases. He may be

dolus, the *mandans* is responsible only for what was contained in the mandate, provided the crime was effected—cf. canons 2199 and 2200, § 1.

[17] Canon 2207, n. 2; Roberti, p. 217.

[18] Cf. canon 2212, § 3; also *supra,* chapter 8, article 4.

[19] *De delictis et poenis,* p. 215.

[20] Canons 19; 2219, § 1.

[21] Roberti, pp. 215-216.

[22] Cf. *supra,* chapter 8, article 4. Only if the attempted crime is itself made a crime, will the *mandans* in this case, be guilty of a crime and liable to punishment—canon 2212, § 4.

subject to canon 2209, § 3 or § 4, because of moral cooperation other than mandate, or be held responsible because of negligence. When, however, the mandate directs the commission of two independent crimes, or specifies the commission of several crimes in order to each other, and only one of these is effected, the *mandans* is responsible for the crime committed.

B. *Moral Cooperators Other Than the Mandans.*

All other forms of moral participation, exclusive of mandate, are expressed by the phrase *sed etiam qui ad delicti consummationem inducunt.* The concept detailed by this phrase is verified in all forms of moral participation, since the only requisite is that the influence exerted by the accomplice on the perpetrator or his assistants be directed towards the consummation of the crime.[24] It is important to note the unrestricted sense of *inducunt.* Some canonists [25] in describing the modes of moral cooperation other than mandate consider only the converse of mandate—counsel—wherein a person persuades another, otherwise unwilling, to commit some crime in the latter's behalf. If the crime were to be for the benefit of the one persuading, the moral cooperator would be classified as a *mandans.* However, by this restriction of the remaining forms of moral cooperation to counsel, an undue limit would be placed upon the word *inducunt,* since there is nothing in the canon to indicate that in the remaining forms of moral cooperation the perpetrator or his assistants must be persuaded to act only in their own behalf. Every means of influencing another's will, other than by way of mandate, is to be included in the meaning of *inducunt.* Mandate itself could be so included, if it were not considered separately by the canon. Moral cooperation, exclusive of mandate, therefore, may be directed to the

[24] ". . . quicumque modus a mandato (de quo prius separatim agitur) diversus quo quis efficaciter movetur 'ad delicti consummationem' "—Michiels, *De delictis et poenis,* I, 312.

[25] Wernz, *Ius decretalium,* VI, 61; D'Annibale, *Summula,* I, n. 301; Lega, *De delictis et poenis,* p. 75, note 1—these authors wrote before the Code and offered no interpretation of canon 2209, § 3, but only of the modes of cooperation—the following authors take the same position after the Code: Roberti, p. 217; Wernz-Vidal, *Ius canonicum,* VII, 138; Latini, p. 156.

benefit of the perpetrator, or of the perpetrator and the moral accomplice together,[26] or of a third party.[27] Furthermore, it makes no difference how this influence to crime is exerted, whether by persuasion, petition, threats, or coercion.[28]

While counsel or advice is not to be accepted as the single type of moral cooperation exclusive of mandate, nevertheless the traditional concept of counsel is to be retained, when a criminal law mentions counsel by name.[29] In penal matters three kinds of counsel are distinguished: doctrinal counsel, which merely gives instruction referring to the crime without influencing the will; hortative counsel, which influences the will by encouraging one to commit a crime; and cooperative counsel, which influences the will and instructs the intellect in regard to the commission of the crime.[30] Doctrinal counsel, since it does not influence the will to commit crime, is not included under the meaning of the term *counsel* in penal laws.[31] Roberti [32] admits both hortative and cooperative counsel as fulfilling the canonical concept of counsel. Michiels,[33] however, regards only cooperative counsel as satisfying the requirements of this form of complicity. In this he adopts the Roman notion of counsel [34] as accepted traditionally by pre-Code canonists.[35] There can be no doubt that hortative counsel is contained within the notion of moral cooperation, and this, possibly, may have been the consideration which influenced Roberti's position. When, however, the word

[26] This latter type is known as *societas*—cf. Wernz-Vidal, *Ius canonicum*, VII, 139; Roberti, p. 217; Lega, *loc. cit.*

[27] Michiels, *De delictis et poenis*, I, 312.

[28] Michiels, *loc. cit.*

[29] Cf. canon 6. However, the penal canons of the Code avoid the use of the word *consilium*.

[30] *Consilium doctrinale, hortativum, cooperativum*, respectively—cf. Roberti, p. 217; Michiels, *De delictis et poenis*, I, 312-313; Wernz-Vidal, *Ius canonicum*, VII, 138; Latini, p. 156.

[31] Roberti, p. 217.

[32] *De delictis et poenis*, p. 217.

[33] *De delictis et poenis*, I, 313.

[34] "Consilium autem dare uidetur, qui persuadet et impellit atque instruit consilio ad furtum faciendum"—D. (47, 2) 50, 3.

[35] Wernz, p. 61; D'Annibale, *Summula theologiae moralis*, I, 178-179.

counsel is used in penal laws it is to be accepted in the traditional sense of cooperative counsel, as Michiels declares.

C. *All Other Partial Cooperators.*

With mandate and other moral cooperation thus indicated, the canon next refers to all remaining types of partial cooperation under the general formula *vel in hanc* [*delicti consummationem*] [36] *quoquo modo concurrunt*. Because of the unrestricted sense of these words, no limit can be placed on the extension of this phrase, except as it is expressly limited by the foregoing words of the canon. All partial cooperation outside of mandate and other moral cooperation is to be here included.[37] These residual types of partial cooperation comprise physical cooperation, and under certain conditions, intellectual aid, negative and subsequent cooperation. Intellectual aid, which is the same as doctrinal counsel, cannot be listed under the forms of moral cooperation since it supplies information to the intellect without moving the will toward the commission of the crime. Nevertheless, when this information is essential or helpful to the commission of the crime, it must be considered as positive assistance. Those offering this intellectual aid will then be placed in the class of those who in any way concur in the consummation of the crime. Ordinarily, acts of subsequent and negative cooperation are not regarded as true cooperation in crime.[38] When, however, these acts are performed in virtue of a previous agreement made with the criminal before the

[36] Cf. Blat, *Commentarium*, V, 33.

[37] "Abbraccia questa categoria concorso entitativamente fisico o morale, e vi sono compresi con i citati, coloro che promettono o danno aiuto, tolgono ostacoli, esaltano il fine dell'opera delittuosa, prestano nascondiglio, preparano *alibi*, ecc."—Pistocchi, "Concorso di pìu persone in uno stesso delitto"—*Mon. Eccl.*, XLVII (1935), 230. Blat: ". . . *quoquo modo*, physice . . . vel moraliter . . ."—*Commentarium*, V, 33. Beste: "Agitur in his verbis de qualibet cooperatione, sive morali sive physica, positiva vel negativa, quam concurrentes actu praestant sive praevia inita conventione, conspiratione aut communi delinquendi consilio, puta, auxilia vel opem pecuniariam ferendo, obstacula removendo, excubias agendo, officium negligendo, actionem delictuosam extollendo, etc."—*Introductio*, p. 884.

[38] Cf. *supra*, chapter I, article I.

crime, they assume the nature of true cooperation.[39] To these forms of cooperation Salucci adds physico-moral complicity.[40] However, it seems that one who participates in a crime both morally and physically should be classified under canon 2209, § 1, since he offers complete cooperation, rather than the partial cooperation which is the subject of canon 2209, § 3. Such a person would, in effect, plan as well as execute the crime. It is, of course, possible that the same person may offer several kinds of partial cooperation in the same crime. Thus, without intending to participate further, a person may give advice in the commission of a crime; later, upon request, he may also act as sentinel for the criminal. But these two acts of partial cooperation remain separate since the person did not give encouragement in virtue of his later participation. Hence these two acts cannot be regarded as physico-moral cooperation.

But the principal form indicated by the general formula under discussion is physical cooperation. This is defined as intervention in a crime by way of material assistance.[41] Such cooperation is verified when one, being aware of another's criminal intent and wishing to further that intent, performs an act which is efficaciously ordained to the consummation of the other person's crime.[42] Thus physical participation is indirect, exercised through another, and partial in contradistinction to the complete participation of co-agents. It may, at times, be difficult to make this distinction in practice. Allusion has previously been made to this difficulty.[43] According to Heimberger,[44] the kind of cooperation is determined by the intention of the cooperator: if he has the intention of a co-agent, he is a co-agent; if he has the intention of a physical cooperator, he is a physical cooperator. Michiels,[45] however, recurs to the presence of connivance (*conniventia*), which he defines as a common intent of perpetrating a

[39] Cf. canon 2209, § 7.

[40] "Concorso fisico o morale oppure fisico-morale"—Salucci, *Il Diritto Penale*, I, 38.

[41] Roberti, p. 219.

[42] Michiels, *De delictis et poenis*, I, 313.

[43] Chapter 9, article 1.

[44] *Aus dem Strafrecht des Codex J. C.*, p. 70.

[45] *De delictis et poenis*, I, 314-315.

crime (*commune deliquendi consilium*) to distinguish co-agents from physical cooperators. There is much truth in Heimberger's opinion, but it is incomplete since it furnishes only the subjective, not the objective, guilt—if the latter is dismissed, canon 2209 loses its value. Michiels' theory is also insufficient, insofar as connivance or common criminal intent is requisite in all true cooperation;[46] nor can connivance be satisfactorily distinguished from common intent by any standard based on length of time or degree of explicitness.[47] The criterion must be objective and definite. This is found for reasons already indicated [48] in physical executive acts performed in concerted action, which constitute the norm for complete participation. All physical acts not included in this concept can be referred to the physical participation treated in canon 2209, § 3. These may be executive or preparatory acts if done independently of concerted action.[49] However, it will be rare to find executive acts placed outside concerted action by one who is, nevertheless, operating with the common intent requisite in a cooperator. This could happen only when the cooperator placed such acts mistakenly or unintentionally, while still desiring to cooperate in other ways; for concerted action has been defined as executive acts directed by intent to the common purpose; or, finally, it could happen if the cooperator acted according to the common intent but not according to the common plan. Since these cases are difficult to verify, practically, physical cooperation is reduced to preparatory acts. Accordingly, physical cooperation may be differentiated from complete participation insofar as the latter is fulfilled in physical executive acts performed in concerted action, whereas physical cooperation, which is a form of partial participation, usually consists of physical preparatory acts. Thus

[46] Cf. Michiels, *De delictis et poenis*, I, 307.

[47] Beste seems to hold Michiels' view: ". . . [cooperationem] concurrentes actu praestant sive praevia inita conventione, aut communi delinquendi consilio . . ."—*Introductio*, p. 884. Yet for formal cooperation he requires that the accomplice "malum eius alterius intentionem seu propositium deliberatum delinquendi participat"—*op. cit.*, p. 883.

[48] Cf. *supra*, chapter 9, article 1.

[49] It may be recalled that presence at the scene of the crime may change such preparatory acts to executive acts.

it is apparent that physical cooperation is rightly termed material assistance since those offering it merely aid in a material way the perpetrators of the crime.

Subsequent cooperation, such as that given by one receiving stolen goods, offering refuge, and preparing alibis or defenses, may also be considered as embraced in the general formula under discussion, provided that agreement has been reached concerning this aid before the crime.[50] Michiels considers such cooperation in reference to its status before the crime as moral cooperation, even though it should be physical in execution after the crime.[51] Thus the effect of this cooperation upon the commission of the crime is not by way of the physical execution, but by influence on the will of the delinquent. Yet it is not quite certain whether such subsequent cooperation should be listed as a mode of moral cooperation, or rather as being simply within the all-embracing scope of the formula *in hanc quoquo modo concurrunt,* since this phrase easily covers pre-arranged subsequent cooperation. This latter classification seems preferable since it is adequate and lacks the complication of reducing subsequent cooperation to moral effectiveness before the crime and physical effectiveness after the crime. What has been said here is also true of negative cooperation when it has been agreed upon antecedently to the crime. In any case, pre-arranged subsequent and negative cooperation are amenable to the dispositions of canon 2209, § 3, as forms of true partial cooperation.

The various kinds of partial cooperation described in this chapter have been discussed in general terms, and, with the exception of mandate, are equally referable to canon 2209, § 3 or § 4. Mandate, of course, is always effective cooperation and comes under canon 2209, § 3 exclusively. The other forms of partial cooperation are subject to the provision of canon 2209, § 3 only when the condition *si delictum sine eorum opera commissum non fuisset* is fulfilled. This condition will be discussed later.

[50] Canon 2209, § 7.
[51] *De delictis et poenis,* I, 313-314.

Article 2. The Guilt of Effective Cooperators.

The juridical responsibility due effective cooperation is likened to the guilt of the perpetrator of the crime—*non minorem, ceteris paribus, imputabilitatem contrahunt, quam ipse delicti exsecutor.* The canon does not say that all effective cooperators are equally guilty, as has been done in the case of co-agents, though what it does say amounts to this. In the case of co-agents and necessary cooperators, however, where each was considered a perpetrator of the crime, it was sufficient to indicate the equality of guilt. But in order to be explicit, the canon now compares the guilt contracted by effective cooperation to the guilt of the perpetrator of the crime. There can be no doubt, then, that canonically, the effective cooperators are responsible for the whole crime with all its circumstances.[52] This is because such cooperators constitute a true, though partial cause of the indivisible delict.[53] Since their act was necessary to the completion of the crime, equally with the act of the perpetrator, their objective responsibility is also equal, since a quantitative measuring and division is juridically repugnant when the concurrence of many separate causes produces one, not a multiple, crime.[54] The subjective responsibility, which varies according to the individual's disposition, is indicated in the words *ceteris paribus.*[55] The nature and operation of the objective and the subjective aspects of guilt have already been described in chapter eight, article three and chapter nine, article two. It need only be emphasized that good faith or excusing causes on the part of the perpetrator in no way helps the other cooperators, since these qualities are incommunicable.

Article 3. The Essential Characteristic of Effective Cooperators

But this objective guilt, equal to the guilt of the perpetrator of the crime, is contracted only if the work of the cooperator was necessary to the crime—*si delictum sine eorum opera commissum non fuisset.*

[52] Cf. Roberti, p. 219.

[53] Wernz-Vidal, *Ius canonicum,* VII, 144.

[54] Michiels, *De delictis et poenis,* I, 324.

[55] Augustine, *Commentary,* VIII, 50; Roberti, p. 219; Michiels, *loc. cit.*

It is clear that *delictum* in this context does not refer to the crime in general, but rather to the concrete crime which has been committed, so that consideration must be made of attending circumstances.[56] This condition is not properly applied if the work of the cooperator is considered merely in reference to the specific nature of a crime, and not to the concrete crime itself. The effect of the cooperation must be weighed in relation to the crime, as it was committed, with all its surrounding details. The condition is a *post-factum* judgment, as is shown from the tense used—the pluperfect of the subjunctive, indicating completed action. But even after consummation of the crime, cooperation can be judged effective, in the sense of the condition, only if the cooperation is considered in relation to the concrete crime, as it was committed, not merely in relation to the specific crime, e. g., the crime of abortion. Hence account must be taken of all circumstances of persons, time, and place, in connection with the individual crime which has been committed, e. g., this abortion.

As to the interpretation of the condition, nearly all commentators,[57]

[56] Michiels: "in casu concreto"—*De delictis et poenis,* I, 323; Wernz-Vidal: "eorum opera in facto fuit eodem modo necessaria, ac opera seu actus exsecutoris delicti"—*Ius canonicum,* VII, 144; Pistocchi: "*senza la loro opera realmente il delitto non si sarebbe commesso.* Questa condizione richiama il concetto che solo nel fatto unito alla intenzione . . . si ha il delitto che la legge perseque."—"Concorso di più persone in uno stesso delitto"—*Mon. Eccl.,* XLVII (1935), 231; Blat: "si delictum hoc vel illud singulariter"—*Commentarium,* V, 33; Cappello: "qui *ita* induxerint aut in eam quoquo modo *ita* concurrerint, *ut* sine tali mandato vel concursu *delictum non fuisset patratum.*"—*De censuris,* pp. 30-31; Cerato uses practically the same words as Cappello—*Censurae vigentes* (2. ed., Patavii, Typis Seminarii, 1921), pp. 22-23; Roberti: "Contra multum interest cognoscere utrum sine hoc auxilio crimen identidem fuisset perfectum vel minus, e.g. in casu quo impossible fuisset in loco invenire veneum."—*De delictis et poenis,* p. 219.

[57] Augustine, *Commentary,* VIII, 50; Ayrinhac-Lydon, *Penal Legislation,* p. 18; Beste, *Introductio,* p. 884; Blat, *Commentarium,* V, 33; Cappello, *De censuris,* pp. 30-31; Cerato, *Censurae vigentes,* pp. 22-23; Chelodi, *Ius poenale,* p. 17; Cipollini, *De censuris latae sententiae,* p. 26; Coronata, *Institutiones,* IV, 49; Ferreres, *Institutiones canonicae* (2. ed., Barcinone, 1920), p. 404; Pistocchi, "Concorso di più persone in uno stesso delitto"—*Mon. Eccl.,* XLVII (1935), p. 231; Sole, *De delictis et poenis,* p. 34.

taking the expression of the Code at its face value, understand it in a factual sense—if without their work the crime would not have been committed. Heimberger,[58] however, whom Michiels [59] follows, suggests an interpretation based, not on fact, but on possibility, so that the condition would be understood thus: if without their work, the crime could not have been committed.[60] But Wernz-Vidal [61] taking cognizance of this interpretation, state that the condition refers, not to the impossibility of the crime, but to the fact of non-commission in the absence of cooperation; hence the sense of the law is "without whose work (*de facto*) the crime would not have been committed," not, "could not have been committed." Of all the commentators consulted, only Wernz-Vidal advert to the new interpretation and reject it. The older view is, then, espoused principally by authors who, at the moment of writing, were not acquainted with the interpretation offered by Heimberger and Michiels. This latter theory, an ingenious attempt to supply an accurate and convenient interpretation of the essential condition of canon 2209, § 3, is now to be examined.

In the first place, it must be noted that this interpretation is not extended to cases of moral cooperation. This kind of cooperation, as Michiels [62] points out, is never so essential to a crime that without it the crime could not have been committed. In respect to moral

[58] *Aus dem Strafrecht des Codex J. C.*, p. 69.

[59] *De delictis et poenis*, I, 322-323.

[60] Roberti could also be understood in this sense: "Si enim crimen sine auxilio minime commissum fuisset, quo auxilium praestat habetur condicio *sine qua non*, seu et ipse auctor principalis criminis efficitur (c. 2209, § 3) . . . Complex sine cuius participatione delictum non potuerit committi, ad expensas et damna tenetur in solidum (c. 2211)."—*De delictis et poenis*, p. 219. The expressions *condicio sine qua non* and *non potuerit* would seem to indicate an indispensability based, not on fact, but on incapability. Whether this is really his meaning may be called into doubt, since neither statement quoted treats *ex professo* of the condition under discussion, but neither does he treat of it elsewhere, or say anything to defend the factual interpretation.

[61] *Ius canonicum*, VII, 144, note 38.

[62] *De delictis et poenis*, I, 322-323. Pre-arranged negative and subsequent cooperation are moral in nature, when considered in relation to their effect upon the perpetrator of the crime.

cooperation, therefore, the factual interpretation of the condition is to be retained. Accordingly, the interpretation based on possibility has reference only to the remaining types of partial participation, namely, to physical assistance and intellectual aid.

In these cases, the condition *si delictum sine eorum opera commissum non fuisset* is to be understood in the sense of possibility, *if without their work the crime could not have been committed.* The arguments offered by Michiel[63] in favor of this interpretation are two, one practical, the other juridical. Practically, there is the difficulty for the judge to decide the *fact* of indispensable cooperation, which is based on internal and subjective dispositions of the perpetrator; on the other hand, if Heimberger's norm is adopted, the judge need consider only the objective nature of the cooperation in relation to the circumstances of the case. In some cases, the factual interpretation is impossible of application; thus, when the perpetrator makes no admissions regarding the influence which the cooperation offered had on his commission of the crime, no reliable norm can be found to indicate whether in the absence of this cooperation the crime would, as a matter of fact, have nevertheless been effected. When, on the other hand, the interpretation based on possibility is employed, the effect of the cooperation on the commission of the crime may be readily determined by considering the objective nature of the cooperation in relation to the concrete crime; thus it may be known if without this work the crime could not have been committed. Since the law must be capable of application, it is to be understood in the sense according to which it can be reduced to practice. The juridical argument may be stated thus. The proximate cause why the cooperation is indispensable rests in the intrinsic nature of the cooperation, as is implied in canon 2209, § 4: "si vero eorum concursus facilius tantum reddidit delictum, quod etiam sine eorundem concursu commissum fuisset"—if the cooperation here described is merely facilitating, then the cooperation mentioned in canon 2209, § 3 must be necessary, so that in the concrete case the crime could not be committed without it. Thus from the parallelism of the conditional clauses in sections three and four of the canon a

[63] *Loc. cit.*

deduction is made concerning the nature of effective cooperation as specified in section three. For if, as the law indicates in section four, facilitating cooperation is the converse of effective cooperation, the latter is not to be judged contingently necessary to the crime in accord with the factual interpretation, but must be essentially necessary to the concrete crime as the interpretation based on possibility proposes. The factual interpretation fails to distinguish effective and facilitating cooperation quite as rigorously as the canon does, since by this interpretation what is properly facilitating cooperation could be classified as effective if it should happen that without it the crime would not have been committed. The canon clearly separates the two kinds of cooperation. Accordingly, a consonant interpretation cannot chose a criterion based on the fact of the aid being contingently necessary to the crime; rather, it must consider the nature of the cooperation in relation to the concrete crime, and thus conclude whether in the absence of the cooperation the crime could have been committed or not. Hence the interpretation based on possibility concords with the canon in making an invariable distinction between effective and facilitating cooperation.

To this development of Michiels' arguments may be added a concordance of this theory with the exclusion of moral cooperation from his interpretation of the condition in the sense of possibility. These remarks will not be applicable to mandate, which, as has been previously stated, is not subject to the condition, but by its very nature constitutes effective cooperation. Moral cooperation is never so necessary to a crime that without it the crime could not have been committed. Hence in respect to this kind of complicity the condition must be interpreted in a factual sense. But this in no way disturbs the validity of the arguments offered for the acceptance of the interpretation based on possibility in cases of partial participation other than moral. With regard to the practical argument it may be pointed out that moral cooperation and non-moral aid have different probative values. Moral cooperation consists of words or signs of instigation and encouragement; non-moral aid is made up of materials, actions, or even information. The former affects only the will of the delinquent; the latter acts as an auxiliary or supplement to his criminal action. By its very nature, then, moral cooperation must be gauged in relation to the subjective dispositions of the perpetrator, whereas the value of non-moral aid is capable of being assessed in reference to the objective nature of the crime. But although the practical argument does not apply to moral cooperation, it must not be supposed that such complicity within the meaning of canon 2209, § 3 is excessively difficult to establish. Dealing with words or signs, moral cooperation has its own evidential solution. The essential value of the encouragement or instigation may be fixed, when the delinquent's previous unwillingness and his subsequent criminal act are established. With regard to the juridical argument it may be stated that since moral cooperation is capable of no further distinction the factual interpretation of the condition will suffice. But this is no reason why the other kinds of cooperation, which act in a different manner upon the commission of the crime, should not present the matter for a new interpretation of the condition in which the words of the law are more completely borne out. Since neither the practical or the juridical argument have then any value in respect to moral cooperation there is no real inconsistency in selecting one interpretation for moral cooperation and another for non-moral aid, especially when the words of the law are thus more completely realized in these different kinds of complicity. Accordingly, the condition should be understood in the case of moral participation as: if without their work the crime would not, in point of fact, have been committed; and in the case of the other kinds of partial participation as: if without their work the crime could not have been committed.

In criticism of the new interpretation in cases of non-moral aid, the following considerations may be offered. The factual interpretation follows the *prima facie* sense of the words of the canon; it avoids the complication of two interpretations, one for moral cooperation, the other for non-moral cooperation; it is accepted by the majority of commentators. The other view, however, is not without probability because of the authority of its proponents and because of the reasons adduced. The words of the canon no longer seem obvious, as was the case to the majority of commentators. Assuredly, the legislator could have made either interpretation more secure by using words like *de facto* or *potuisset*. But, on the other hand, the canonical expression does not exclude either interpretation; the words themselves seem at first to convey the factual sense, yet, considered in their context, they imply an indispensability based on impossibility. In practice, moreover, the latter view had already been implicitly accepted by canonists who hold that doctors or druggists supplying drugs for abortion do not incur the censure of canon 2350, § 1.[64] For unless the druggist gave the drug the concrete crime would not, as a matter of fact, have been committed, but it could have been committed otherwise, because of other sources of supply, or other means at hand.[65] Furthermore, the new interpretation is more consonant with the rules of canons 19 and 2219, § 1, since it is the milder and more restrictive interpretation of a penal matter.[66] While, therefore, both views regarding the interpretation of the condition are theoretically tenable, nevertheless, in practice, the interpretation based on possibility is to be followed in cases of physical and intellectual cooperation.

Article 4. The Application of Canon 2209, § 3.

Canon 2209 operates with regard to every penal canon, even though there be no express mention of complicity. By the mere fact that cooperation in crime has occurred, the provisions of canon 2209 are set in force. Accordingly, when the commission of a crime is accompanied by effective cooperation, the persons who have so cooperated are, by virtue of canon 2209, § 3, regarded equally guilty

[64] Augustine, Commentary, VIII, 401; Cipollini, *De censuris latae sententiae*, p. 175; Salucci, *Il Diritto Penale*, II, 224; cf. Vermeersch-Creusen, *Epitome*, III, 210.

[65] In consideration of this, no doubt, Cappello (*De censuris*, p. 337), Beste (*Introductio*, p. 954), and Genicot-Salsmans (*Institutiones theologiae moralis*, II, n. 607) do not except the druggist from the censure, wishing to retain the factual interpretation.

[66] ". . . 'in poenis benignior est interpretatio facienda;' quo principio non solummodo injungitur stricta seu benigna legis, sed et poenae omniumque factorum antecedenter, concomitanter vel subsequenter cum poena conjunctorum, interpretatio et applicato, ita ut quotiescumque, re diligenter inspecta, permaneat dubium quoddam juris vel facti, semper reo, favendum sit."—Michiels, *Normae generales juris canonici*, p. 445.

as the perpetrator. Nor is there any need that this be expressed in the canon punishing the crime.

When, as a matter of fact, a specific form of cooperation is described in the canon, this is to be interpreted according to its own meaning and context, with no regard to canon 2209, § 3. Examples of this specified complicity are found in the phrase *per se vel per alios,*[67] indicating direct or indirect action, and in other forms of cooperation as mandate,[68] aid or favor,[69] consent,[70] and finally, permission or failure to prohibit.[71] Hence, these are all constituted special crimes by express legislation. It may be noted here, however, that in the absence of any declaration in the law to the contrary, these accessory crimes are not to be punished unless the principal crime has been consummated.[72] Thus these canonized forms of complicity have become separate delicts, so that to incur the guilt and punishment it is not necessary to apply the condition of canon 2209, § 3: *si delictum sine eorum opera commissum non fuisset.* But, on the other hand, cooperation can be admitted in these accessory crimes themselves according to the rules of canon 2209; thus one may give mandate or counsel to a person committing the delict of giving aid according to canons 2338 or 2351, § 1. Since they are separate crimes, they also may be committed by means of cooperation or in conjunction with it.

What has been stated in this article in relation to canon 2209, § 3 is to be applied to the other provisions of canon 2209, with due alterations, of course, to be made in accord with the individual mean-

[67] Canons 2345; 2346; 2363; 2380; 2390, § 1; 2405; 2413;

[68] Canons 2338, § 3; *facientes;* 2339: *mandare seu cogere.*

[69] Canons 2316: *iuvat;* 2338, § 2: *impendentes quodvis auxilium vel favorem;* 2351, §1: *operam vel favorem praebentes;* 2357, § 1: *lenocinium;* 2359, § 2: *lenocinium.*

[70] Canons 2346: *consentiens;* 2347, n. 3: *consensum praebendo.*

[71] Canon 2351, § 1: *illud permittentes; non prohibentes.*

[72] Lega, pp. 78-79; *glossa ordinaria* ad v. *Mandaverit,* c. 1, *de poenis,* V, 8 in Clem: "Nota casum quo punitur solum mandatum et est maleficium perfectum . . . Penitentia et revocatio hoc casui non prodest sed quia hoc durum videtur quem ex solo mandato maleficio non secuto tot poenis involvi, qua regulariter verba cum effectu recipiuntur." Coronata, *Institutiones,* IV, 404.

ings of these provisions. Thus, for example, complete participation by several persons and facilitating cooperation are also to be admitted in accessory crimes.

CHAPTER TWELVE

FACILITATING COOPERATORS

Canon 2209, § 4. **Si vero eorum concursus facilius tantum reddidit delictum, quod etiam sine eorundem concursu commissum fuisset, minorem imputabalitatem secumfert.**

ARTICLE 1. THE NATURE OF FACILITATING COOPERATION.

Thus far directions have been established regarding cooperative forms in which the juridical imputability of the cooperator is that of one who would actually perpetrate the crime himself. In these forms, the objective guilt was not only equated to the guilt of the perpetrator but it was also communicated equally to all the cooperators. In canon 2209, § 4, the cooperation entails guilt with a double difference: the cooperators are no longer as guilty as the perpetrator, nor are the cooperators equally guilty among themselves. Equality of guilt is canonically regarded as dependent upon authorship of the crime. When all concerned are true causes, even though partially, of the crime, all are made juridically responsible for the whole crime; thus all are held responsible in the same measure as the perpetrator, and all are considered equally guilty among themselves. The cooperation described in canon 2209, § 4, however, is not a cause of the crime [1] but only a condition which expedites the crime. Accordingly, the cooperators while incurring canonical responsibility due their antisocial action, nevertheless are not held guilty in the same degree as the perpetrator of the crime, and hence their guilt as considered in relation to themselves lacks a common point of comparison. Their guilt is individual, a matter to be determined in each particular case.

This non-causal cooperation is described in the canon as facilitating—*Si vero eorum concursus facilius tantum reddidit delictum.*

[1] ". . . conrei accessorii . . . non possunt retineri uti vera causa eiusdem delicti, quod etiam sine ipsorum concursu consummatum fuisset"—Sole, *De delictis et poenis*, p. 34.

Accordingly this term has been selected to designate this kind of cooperation. Facilitating cooperation must verify the requirements of formal cooperation.[2] Neither negative nor subsequent cooperation can qualify as facilitating cooperation, unless an arrangement or pact has been made previously to the crime, concerning them.[3] The nature of the particular kind of formal cooperation termed facilitating is expressed in two requisites, one positive, the other negative.

The positive[4] requirement is that this cooperation should have rendered the commission of the crime more easy—*facilius*. This kind of complicity is limited to the expediting of the crime without contributing causally to the crime's existence.[5] Accordingly, this cooperation, comprehended within the bounds of formal cooperation, yet exclusive of causal efficacy,[6] must make a positive contribution to the commission of the crime. This contribution may be either moral, intellectual, or physical. In the foregoing chapter, such moral, intellectual, and physical forms have been described. There was offered an exposition of the nature of partial participation and a review of its various forms: physical, moral, and intellectual aid, and prearranged negative and subsequent cooperation. At that time, however, these types of partial participation were considered as causes of the crime, insofar as they were indispensable to its commission. But what has been said in general to determine the nature of these causes, may be also understood here as applying to facilitating conditions. Thus physical, moral, and intellectual aid, and prearranged negative and subsequent cooperation may assume the qualities of facilitating cooperation. Mandate, which is always a cause of the crime, is, of course, excluded. But all remaining types of moral cooperation and all other forms of partial participation, which do not, in fact, act as causes of the crime, are pertinent here, provided they facilitate the crime.

It is not to be assumed, however, that all the usual forms of complicity when applied to a specific crime, render that crime more easy.

[2] Coronata, *Institutiones*, IV, 52.

[3] Cf. *supra*, chapter 1, article 1.

[4] Cf. Coronata, *loc. cit.*

[5] Salucci, *Il Diritto Penale*, I, 38.

[6] Such as characterizes the cooperation described in canon 2209, § § 1-3.

This problem must be examined in connection with the nature of the crime and its circumstances. Doctrinal counsel may be given to a person who disregards it, but nevertheless commits the crime in his own way. In this case, the cooperation was not efficacious and made no contribution to the commission of the crime. Accordingly, the cooperator is guilty only of criminal intent manifested by his attempted cooperation. Hence, the imputability established by canon 2209, § 4 is not contracted, since the crime has not actually been rendered more easy by the contribution of doctrinal counsel, which was, in this case, completely unavailing.[7] From this may be seen the importance of determining the juridical nature of acts performed with the intention of participating partially in the crime. If the acts are efficacious, i. e., if they really help in the commission of the crime, facilitating cooperation is verified; otherwise, only attempted cooperation in crime may be present.[8]

What, then, constitutes the specific acts of facilitation? Here must be understood all positive acts of assistance, whether physical, moral, or intellectual, which are not necessary to the commission of the crime. Positive acts are required at least by the nature of formal cooperation. However, the promise of a negative act, as neglect of a certain duty, may be a positive form of assistance.[9] Mere inactivity or omission, of itself, does not constitute true cooperation, as will be revealed from a consideration of canon 2209, § 6. But the promise of such dereliction of duty may positively aid the perpetrator. Moreover, the nature of formal cooperation requires that acts be antecedent to the crime, or at least concommitant with it. Subsequent

[7] Such attempted cooperation may, however, be punitively repressed by express legislation; cf. c. 5, *de poenis,* V, 9, in VI°: "Illud autem non duximus omittendum, quod si quis fuerit in praemissis nudo consilio aut simplici favore culpabilis iudex in talem poenam metiatur ex culpa, ut secundum quod excessus exegerit vindicta procedat." In explanation of the terms here employed, the following is quoted: "Nudum consilium vel simplex favor intelligitur illius qui ad maleficium faciendum nihil adjicit"—*glossa* ad c. 5, de poenis, V, 9, in VI°, v. *Simplici favori.*

[8] The nature, guilt, and punishment of attempted cooperation in crime has been discussed in chapter 8, article 4.

[9] Coronata, *Institutiones,* IV, 52; Roberti, p. 222; Michiels, *De delictis et poenis,* I, 328.

cooperation cannot be classified as facilitating cooperation, as may be seen from canon 2209, § 7, unless the promise of subsequent aid actually helps in the commission of the crime. The various types of facilitating cooperation will now be considered in particular.

Heimberger [10] denies the possibility of facilitating moral cooperation, because such cooperation will merely be an attempt, and so only attempted crime, if the perpetrator had independently determined upon the crime; any guilt at all will arise only according to canon 2213, § 3. Hence this author admits moral cooperation only within the meaning of canon 2209, § 3. This view, however, fails to consider the influence exerted by moral cooperation, even when the crime would have been committed despite it. When a person is already determined upon a crime, his purpose can be strengthened, or more quickly activated by another's encouragement. Accordingly, moral cooperation, which merely facilitates the crime must be admitted.[11]

With regard to intellectual aid, it need only be stated that any contribution towards the crime by way of information may qualify as facilitating cooperation when the crime could be committed without such aid, but when, nevertheless, the information has actually helped in the commission of the crime. The same rule holds for prearranged negative and subsequent cooperation.

The limits of physical cooperation have been fixed by what has already been established regarding the distinction between co-agents and effective cooperators.[12] Co-agents present physical executive acts performed in concerted action, whereas effective cooperators by way of physical participation offer physical executive acts performed outside of concerted action, or physical preparatory acts, provided both the executive acts and the preparatory acts are such that without them the concrete crime could not have been committed. The same kind of cooperation—physical executive acts performed outside of concerted action and also physical preparatory

[10] *Aus dem Strafrecht des Codex J. C.*, p. 69.

[11] Cf. Michiels, *De delictis et poenis*, I, 323-324; Coronata, *Institutiones*, IV, 52.

[12] Cf. *supra*, chapter 11, article 1, section C.

acts—may supply the matter for physical facilitating cooperation provided that these acts are not essential to the concrete crime but merely make easier the commission of this crime. It will be generally found that such acts only remotely influence the criminal effect, which they in no way cause. Their contribution is by way of making easier the crime that even in their absence would have been committed.

Thus the positive requisite of facilitating cooperation is found in those acts, whether physical, moral, intellectual, negative, or subsequent, by which the commission of the crime was expedited but without which the crime would have been committed. If these acts do not in fact make the commission of the crime more expeditious, the word *facilius* is not fulfilled. Hence, it is not enough for the imputation of guilt that the effort, though placed with cooperative intent, should neither add nor detract from the criminal purpose or action of another. Whether this requirement of facilitation actually exists, is to be determined in each case from an inspection of the facts. This also is a *post-factum* judgment, to be made in reference to the concrete crime.

The category of cooperative facilitation is, moreover, made definite in canon 2209, § 4 by a negative requirement.[13] This provides explicitly that the cooperation be such that even without it the crime would have been committed—*quod etiam sine eorundem concursu commissum fuisset.* This characteristic was implicitly made by the foregoing provisions of canon 2209, but the phrase is here advantageous in making clear the meanings of canon 2209, § 3 and § 4. There is no need to debate at this juncture whether fact or potentiality is meant, since this is a negative requirement which merely excludes, the meaning of which is to be understood by contrast with its opposed condition in canon 2209, § 3. The purpose of the negative requirement is to distinguish facilitating cooperation from the cooperation described in canon 2209, § 3.[14] This is clear from the

[13] Coronata, *Institutiones,* IV, 52.

[14] ". . . ob defectum conditionis postremae paragraphi praecedentis sunt conrei proprie accessorii . . ."—Blat, *Commentarium,* V, 34; cf. Coronata, *Institutiones,* IV, 52.

parallelism of the two clauses: *si delictum sine eorum opera commissum non fuisset* in canon 2209, § 3, and *quod etiam sine eorundem concursu commissum fuisset* in canon 2209, § 4. The latter clause, indeed, is affirmative in its grammatical form, but its whole sense is negative since its force rests not in its own meaning but rather in the exclusion of the foregoing condition in canon 2209, § 3. If, therefore, the condition as interpreted in the preceding chapter is not verified, the cooperation may be classified as facilitating, since it is distinct from canon 2209, § 3. Whether, in point of fact, this cooperation will actually come within the meaning of canon 2209, § 4 depends upon the fulfillment of the positive requirement already discussed.

Article 2. The Guilt of Facilitating Cooperation.

Facilitating cooperation results in the imputation not of the same guilt as that ascribed to the perpetrator of the crime, but of a lesser guilt—*minorem imputabilitatem secumfert.*[15] The only point definitely determined here is the maximum limit of responsibility which is thus placed below complete responsibilty for the crime. Since nothing is clearly determined by law, facilitating cooperators are affected only by an indefinite minor guilt, until this is defined by judicial pronouncement.[16]

In arriving at this verdict, the judge will consider in relation to the gravity of the law violated, both the objective nature [17]

[15] Blat, *Commentarium*, V, 34; Coronata, *Institutiones*, IV, 52; Sole, *De delictis et poenis*, p. 34.

[16] Michiels, *De delictis et poenis*, I, 325; Coronata, *Institutiones*, IV, 53; Wernz-Vidal, *Ius canonicum*, VII, 145.

[17] Cf. Roberti, p. 284. Contrarily, Salucci: ". . . quasi exclusivemente nella mala voluntas in se di violare la legge, più che negli effetti che dalla violazione derivano."—*Il Dirritto Penale*, I, 38. Such a subjective norm cannot be acceptable to the legal system of a society which is concerned with externals—cf. canon 2200, § 2. The external action, which alone disturbs the juridical order, is the basic source in estimating the amount of guilt; the will to violate the law may fluctuate in intensity without any corresponding change in the external violation.

of the cooperation in connection with its effect upon the crime[18] and the subjective factors modifying this objective guilt in the individual.[19] The subjective element is well understood. It is necessary, however, to discuss the objective element. If all facilitating cooperators would give the same kind of aid, as, for example, if all would encourage equally or give the same amount of financial assistance, then all would, according to the principle of objectivity, incur the same objective guilt. Usually, however, the cooperators will concur in diverse fashions. There is, then, no common basis for predicating guilt. Each case of cooperation must be considered individually, with a view to establishing the relative gravity of its effect upon the crime.

Facilitating cooperation entails a guilt to be estimated objectively as proportional to the efficacy with which it expedites the commission of the crime. Thus without ever attaining the full responsibility of the perpetrator, the facilitating cooperator will approach that guilt, the more he contributes to the facilitation of the crime.[20] Conversely, the less aid given the crime, the less is his responsibility. This rule is not explicit in canon 2209, §4, but is agreeable with the canonical principle of estimating the *quantitas* or gravity of a crime as stated in canon 2196. Here among several other norms, which are not pertinent to this discussion,[21] is listed the harm or damage brought on by the crime. This refers not only to damage to an injured per-

[18] Wernz-Vidal, *Ius canonicum*, VII, 144-145.

[19] Roberti, p. 219; Coronata, *Institutiones*, IV, 53.

[20] "Hi sunt cooperatores *accessorii* quibus proportionata respondet imputabilitas pro ratione influxus, quem in existentiam delicti suo externo actu exercuerunt, ex quorum iuvamine usi sunt delicti executores tametsi non necessario"—Wernz-Vidal, *Ius canonicum*, VII, 144.

[21] These are (1) the gravity of the law violated, which remains the same for all cooperators, and (2) the degree of imputability. Coronata interpretes the latter subjectively as all the causes which increase or diminish subjective guilt—*Institutiones*, IV, 12. Chelodi, on the other hand, regards it objectively as the degree of *dolus* presumed by the law as attaching to the offense—*Ius poenale*, p. 5. In neither case is it pertinent here; for the subjective guilt is not now under discussion, and the objective *dolus* presumed by the law would affect all cooperators equally.

son but also to the social order.[22] The work of facilitating cooperators harms the social order in proportion to the degree to which it makes the commission of the crime more easy.[23] Hence, the more the facilitating cooperation aids the commission of the crime, the greater will be the guilt entailed, always considered, of course, in relation to the gravity of the crime itself.

[22] Chelodi, *Ius poenale*, p. 5; Sole, *De delictis et poenis*, p. 6; Roberti, p. 58.

[23] Once it is accepted, as in the foregoing article of this chapter, that facilitating cooperation positively aids in the commission of the crime, then corresponding damage to the social order must be admitted. If the commission of a crime disturbs the social order, aiding the crime will have the same effect, provided, at least, that the crime itself is actually consummated. *Accessorium naturam sequi congruit principalis*—Reg. 42, R. J., in VI°.

Chapter Thirteen

THE WITHDRAWAL OF COOPERATION

Canon 2209, § 5. **Qui suum influxum in delictum patrandum opportuna retractatione abduxerit plene, ab omni imputabilitate liberatur, etiamsi executor delictum ob alias causas sibi proprias nihilominus patraverit; si non abduxerit plene, retractatio minuit, sed non aufert culpabilitatem.**

Article 1. The Complete Withdrawal of Cooperation.

Cooperation in crime may be reduced to two elements, one voluntary, the other external. It may happen that the intention from which the cooperation originated does not remain in force up to the time of the completion of the crime. Such repentance may provide cause for diminishing the penalty but does not lessen or remove the guilt,[1] insofar as repentance alone in no way withdraws the fact of cooperation. In order to effect a lessened or canceled guilt, the cooperator must not only change his criminal intent but must also prevent his illegal action from being reduced to its effect.[2] Such nullified cooperation has no influence on the crime, and brings no responsibility. Canon 2209, § 5 lays down the canonical provisions in regard to withdrawal of cooperation.

All voiding of guilt is based on actual subtraction of cooperation —*Qui suum influxum in delictum patrandum opportuna retractatione abduxerit plene*. One is held only for his own effect or influence on the crime. If that effect or influence is removed, the former cooperator is liberated from responsibility for the crime, despite the commission of the crime by others independently of his cooperation.

It is required that the cooperator withdraw his influence or effect —*influxum suum*—from the crime. The words of the law, being

[1] Michiels, *De delictis et poenis*, I, 325.

[2] "Retractatio influxus' in delictum habetur cum tollitur relatio casualitatis inter participationem 'et effectum criminosum, si forte secutus sit."—Roberti, p. 220.

unrestricted, include whatever effect one may have had on the crime by way of cooperation. Hence, the law itself admits the withdrawal of any form of cooperation.[3] It is, then, only a question of fact whether in a certain case the cooperation has been withdrawn. However, the force of the word *influxum* rests in the fact that it means an actual effect on the commission of the crime. Hence, withdrawal of cooperation is signified, not of cooperative intent. This withdrawal of cooperation is accomplished when the efficacy of the cooperation is neutralized or removed.[4] Mere notice of changed intention to one's fellow accomplices is not, of itself, sufficient, but rather the influence, which the repentant cooperator might have had on the crime by reason of his antecedent cooperation, must be prevented from operating, so that if the crime should be accomplished, it will be ascribed to the other accomplices, and in no way to the repentant cooperator.[5]

The various kinds of cooperation will now be considered insofar as they are capable of being withdrawn.

Physical cooperation is removed, when it no longer has efficacy with regard to the crime.[6] Thus materials and instruments previously

[3] Blat, *Commentarium,* V, 34; Coronata, *Institutiones,* IV, 55; Michiels, *De delictis et poenis,* I, 326; Pistocchi, "Concorso di più persone in uno stesso delitto"—*Mon. Eccl.* XLVII (1935), 233. Wernz-Vidal consider explicitly the withdrawal of moral cooperation only—*Ius canonicum,* VII, 141.

[4] Michiels, *De delictis et poenis,* I, 326. But Bouuaert-Simenon are not so stringent: "Codex etiam declarat: 1. plenam et opportunam, etsi non efficacem retractationem concursus omnem imputabilitatem tollere."—*Manuale juris canonici* (3 vols., Gandae et Leodii: Prostat apud auctores in Seminariis Gandavensi et Leodiensi, Vols. I et III, 3. ed., 1930-1931; Vol. II, 1931), III, 320. But this view cannot be reconciled with the force of the words *abduxerit plene* which imply a complete and effective removal of the cooperation. Certainly, an ineffective withdrawal of cooperation would not fulfill the meaning of *abduxerit plene.* Sole, moreover, makes *opportuna retractatione* equivalent to *efficaci retractatione*—*De delictis et poenis,* p. 35.

[5] Michiels, *De delictis et poenis,* I, 326; Roberti, p. 220.

[6] Blat merely requires that further aid be denied—"auxilii denegatione ulterioris"—*Commentarium,* V, 34. To withdraw cooperation, however, it is not enough to refuse cooperation in the future, but all the cooperation already given must be removed.

given in aid of the crime may be repossessed or destroyed. With regard to actions, it is more difficult to arrest their effect, except, perhaps, by counteractions, such as informing the authorities, warning the victim.[7]

Moral cooperation is likewise withdrawn when it no longer influences the perpetrator in favor of the crime. With regard to mandate, this is done by giving notice to the mandatary before the commission of the crime concerning the revoked mandate, since the crime is to be done at the behest of the *mandans* and in favor of *him*.[8] The withdrawal of hortative and cooperative counsel is, however, more difficult, since the crime urged is for the benefit of the perpetrator, and not of the one giving counsel. Simple notice of the counsel being disavowed is not enough, but rather the influence previously exerted in favor of the crime must now be counteracted, at least, by arguments or persuasion against the crime[9] so that the commission of the crime can in no way be ascribed to the influence of the repentant cooperator.[10] Intellectual aid or doctrinal counsel cannot be removed directly. The information once given remains. But it must be prevented from attaining its effect, possibly by an appeal to the perpetrator or by counteractions.[11]

Prearranged negative and subsequent cooperation are not withdrawn simply by failure to perform the negative or subsequent aid

[7] In this case, Roberti makes those who counteract their own cooperative efforts liable to attempted crime, and the other cooperators liable to frustrated crime—*De delictis et poenis*, p. 221. But it seems that, according to canon 2209, § 5, the former are to be absolved of all blame since they have rendered their cooperation, and incidentally, the cooperation of everyone else, inoperative. Coronata holds that even in the case of full withdrawal of cooperation, one who had induced another to commit a crime is guilty of attempted crime—*Institutiones*, IV, 54. This, however, is a loose interpretation of canon 2212, § 3, which by its context—*studuerit sed inefficaciter*—demonstrates that frustration, not voluntary withdrawal of effort, is meant, as is clear from canon 2213, § 3.

[8] ". . . debet revocare mandatum et de revocatione facere mandatarium." —Roberti, p. 220; Michiels, *De delictis et poenis*, I, 326.

[9] Roberti, p. 220; Blat, *Commentarium*, V, 34; Michiels, *De delictis et poenis*, I, 326; Ayrinhac-Lydon, *Penal Legislation*, p. 19.

[10] Michiels, *loc. cit.*

[11] Coronata, *Institutiones*, IV, 54.

promised. The negative and subsequent acts do not, in themselves, constitute true cooperation, but rather it is the promise or pact to perform such acts that encourages the perpetrator to proceed with his criminal design. Hence, notice must be given to the perpetrator before the consummation of the crime that the acts promised will not be performed.

For co-agents and necessary cooperators, there is ordinarily no opportunity to withdraw their cooperation, which is part of the actual execution of the crime. Those co-agents, however, who have performed their portion of the deed in advance of the crime's consummation may still have the opportunity of persuading their accomplices to abandon their criminal intent, of counteracting their previous cooperation, or of frustrating the crime by appropriate measures. Since the co-agents enter fully into the counsel and the action, they must withdraw both; this may be done either by frustrating the entire crime, or by removing both physical and moral cooperation. Thus, a co-agent who canceled his material effect upon the crime without persuading his associates to desist from their efforts would be held guilty of moral cooperation, since his counsel has not been removed.

In all this is seen the general notion of cooperative withdrawal, which consists in removing or canceling whatever effect one may have had on the crime. Thus the withdrawal of cooperation must actually render the cooperation inoperative. But insofar as the process of committing a crime is not static, the opportunity of nullifying the cooperation does not remain open indefinitely. At what point in the commission of the crime is it impossible to withdraw cooperation?

Withdrawal of cooperation presupposes that the crime is as yet incomplete—*in delictum patrandum.*[12] The exact point up to which withdrawal is possible must be determined from a consideration of the cooperation and of the crime to be committed. The withdrawal of cooperation must occur before the cooperation has had its effect upon the completed crime—*opportuna retractatione.*[13] It is obvious

[12] Salucci, *Il Diritto Penale*, I, 38.

[13] Cf. Michiels, *De delictis et poenis*, I, 325-326; Wernz-Vidal, *Ius canonicum*, VII, 145.

that withdrawal of cooperation cannot be considered opportune which takes place after the crime is completed; at this stage, only repentance is possible, which may provide cause for a reduction of punishment but not for the extinction or diminution of guilt.[14] What is the terminus of opportune withdrawal of cooperation? It is the point just before the crime is consummated.[15] The cooperation may have been complete and in fact have operated with final efficacy, but as long as the crime itself has not yet been consummated, the cooperation can be withdrawn.[16] Theoretically, then, cooperation can be withdrawn until the point of the consummation of the crime. In practice, however, the opportunity will be limited by circumstances. Hence, the special force of the word *opportuna;* this requires that the withdrawal of cooperation be done not only in due time but also in such circumstances that the whole effect of the cooperator upon the crime be excluded.[17] It is necessary to emphasize here a point previously made; viz., withdrawal of cooperation or *retractatio* is verified when the cooperation is prevented from obtaining its effect in the commission of the crime.[18] Accordingly, by opportune withdrawal or *retractatio* is meant that the cooperation be removed in due time and in such circumstances before the consummation of the crime that the whole effect of the cooperator upon the crime be excluded.

Whether the withdrawal of cooperation has actually been made is a question of fact. It may be pointed out that the words of the canon do not express a command, but merely give an objective norm stating the fact of complete or partial withdrawal. There is no account to be made of the difficulties or, perhaps, even of the impossibility of removing the cooperation. If the cause or facilitation once given with canonical responsibility is not removed, the guilt

[14] Michiels, *De delictis et poenis*, I, 325.

[15] Michiels, *De delictis et poenis*, I, 326.

[16] ". . . in ordine al delitto non ancora in via di consumazione, e cioè, re integra"—Pistocchi, "Concorso di più persone in uno stesso delitto"—*Mon. Eccl.* XLVII (1935), 233.

[17] Coronata, *Institutiones*, IV, 54, note 2.

[18] Roberti, p. 220: Coronata, *Institutiones*, IV, 54, note 2; Michiels, *De delictis et poenis*, I, 326.

due cooperation is incurred. All decisions in this matter with respect to guilt are to be based on fact. The case would be different if there were a law obliging the cooperator to remove the effect of his cooperation. It would then be possible to consider impossibility, grave inconvenience, and all the circumstances which diminish guilt. Since, however, the canonical norm simply expresses a fact, guilt will be extinguished if the cooperation is fully withdrawn, or guilt will be diminished but not taken away if the cooperation is only partially withdrawn.

The rule for complete withdrawal of cooperation is given first—*abduxerit plene*. If the crime were completely frustrated, there is no difficulty, since there is then no crime to be ascribed to anyone. When, however, the crime has nevertheless been committed, it must be ascertained if the crime is to be attributed to the perpetrator independently of the repentant cooperator—*etiamsi exsecutor delictum ob alias causas sibi proprias nihilominus patraverit.* In this case, great care must be taken to establish the inefficacy of the withdrawn cooperation on the crime. Good intentions, of themselves, apart from effective withdrawal, are of no avail. The law requires that the cause or facilitating condition embodied in the cooperation be prevented from operating with regard to the crime. Only if it is demonstrated that this cooperation has had no influence on the crime, is the withdrawal complete. It may be said here, but also with reference to partial withdrawal of cooperation, that once cooperation to crime is established, withdrawal of cooperation must be proved in the external forum.[19] This is true not only of the fact of withdrawal, but also of its extent, whether full or partial.

Complete withdrawal of cooperation releases from all guilt—*ab omni imputabilitate liberatur.* This is a clear application of the principle of causality. Since the nullified cooperation has had no effect upon the crime, the repentant cooperator after making complete withdrawal of cooperation incurs no responsibility for the crime.[20] One is not held for the acts of another.

[19] Roberti, p. 323.

[20] Pistocchi, "Concorso di più persone in uno stesso delitto"—*Mon. Eccl.* XLVII (1935), 233; Michiels, *De delictis et poenis*, I, 326.

Article 2. The Incomplete Withdrawal of Cooperation

When, however, the withdrawal of cooperation is not complete—*si non abduxerit plene*—the cooperation once given still exerts some influence upon the commission of the crime. After an incomplete withdrawal of cooperation, the residual cooperation must again be scrutinized and reclassified. What had previously been effective cooperation may now be merely facilitating. It is even possible that only the material element is withdrawn, so that the cooperation may become moral instead of physical. These factors must be noted in order to determine the degree of diminution of responsibility. Of great practical importance is, moreover, the fact of diminished guilt itself. This diminished guilt may arise, according to the canon, from incomplete withdrawal of cooperation.

Incomplete withdrawal of cooperation, which is not defined in the canon, must be delimited by the concept of complete withdrawal—*si non abduxerit plene.* Hence, if the effort to remove the efficacy of the cooperation is not fully successful, the withdrawal is only partial, and not complete. Incomplete withdrawal of cooperation itself must consist in some removal of the previously given cooperation—*retractatio* [*influxus*]. It is this latter requirement wherein the exact concept of incomplete withdrawal is blurred.[21] Only a few of the canonical authors have expressed opinions in this regard. But since the word *retractatio,* and not *poenitentia,* is used at least some positive withdrawal in fact seems to be indicated, and not a mere change of intent. At least some external effort to overcome the former cooperation must be made. This is consonant with the views and exemplifications offered by those authors who are articulate on this subject. Vermeersch-Creusen give as examples of incomplete withdrawal of cooperation, the vain attempt to heal a mortal wound previously inflicted, and the inefficacious removal of doctrinal counsel regarding abortion.[22] Augustine mentions the dilution of an abor-

[21] Thus Pistocchi: "Si *non abduxerit plene.* Se reste cioè in essere alcunche della causalità morale o fisica posta col concorso."—"Concorso di più persone in uno stesso delitto"—*Mon. Eccl.* XLVII (1935), 234.

[22] *Epitome,* III, 193.

tional drug from which, nevertheless, the abortion results.[23] Coronata holds that notice of withdrawal is probably sufficient even for complete withdrawal of counsel in the internal forum; in the external forum, the superior is to decide if this has been sufficient.[24] Sole concurs in this last opinion.[25] It is to be noted that in these cases, the cooperation once given operates fully, and has, as regards its effect on the crime, full efficacy. There has, therefore, been only an effort at counteraction, not success, or even reduction of efficacy. Accordingly, to constitute incomplete withdrawal, it does not seem necessary that the influence of the cooperation be quantitatively reduced, but merely that an external effort be made, how successfully does not matter, to nullify one's previous action. In brief, then, it seems that any external effort, short of complete withdrawal, to render the cooperation inefficacious may be considered incomplete withdrawal of cooperation in the sense of canon 2209, §5.

Cooperation partially withdrawn, at least, by an external effort, diminishes but does not take away guilt—*retractatio minuit sed non aufert culpabilitatem*. Once again the principle of causality is invoked; the cooperator is held responsible only for that cooperation which has influenced the commission of the crime. Hence his former responsibility, proper to fully efficacious cooperation, while not cancelled, is reduced. The quantity of this reduced guilt is to be estimated from the effect which the cooperation has in fact had on the crime.[26] This judgment is to be made along the lines indicated when the lesser guilt of canon 2209, § 4 was discussed. Here, too, there is a definite starting point—the guilt which would have been incurred by the original cooperation. The responsibility remaining because of the partially withdrawn cooperation must be less than this former responsibility. Thus if one had participated in a crime according to canon 2209, § 1, § 2, or § 3, and later made an effort to withdraw his cooperation before the consummation of the crime,

[23] *Commentary*, VIII, 51.

[24] *Institutiones*, IV, 118.

[25] *De delictis et poenis*, p. 35.

[26] " . . . minuit scilicet pro gradu quo minuitur ipse causalis influxus."—Michiels, *De delictis et poenis*, I, 326.

his guilt would remain but would be lessened in proportion to the efficacy of his effort.

The difficulty may occur that certain cooperation once placed is intrinsically incapable of being reduced in effectiveness, or that, extrinsically, the opportunity, the means, or the personal ability to withdraw it may not exist in certain circumstances. This does not seem to make any difference according to the explanation just given. In speaking of complete withdrawal of cooperation, the Code specifies that it should be opportune, or, in other words, that the withdrawal be made in due time and in such circumstances so as to be capable of counteracting the cooperation.[27] No such demand is made for incomplete withdrawal of cooperation. The only temporal requirement is that the effort be made before the consummation of the crime. Hence it seems that even in cases where withdrawal is impossible, if the repentant cooperator makes an earnest external effort to withdraw the cooperation, this effort fulfills the canonical notion of incomplete withdrawal of cooperation and brings about a lessening of imputability.[28] It is evident that the mere outward pretense of withdrawing cooperation cannot be included in the concept of incomplete withdrawal of cooperation since the canon is treating of a lessening of imputability. Hence the external effort must be earnest, not fraudulent.

Article 3. The Application of Penalties in Cases of Withdrawn Cooperation

Thus far account has been taken of the guilt resulting upon withdrawal of cooperation, but although penalties have not as yet been discussed, it seems opportune to review here the special problems of applying penalties in cases withdrawn cooperation. By way of preface, it may be pointed out that excuse and diminution with regard to guilt are different from excuse and diminution regarding

[27] Coronata, *Institutiones*, IV, 54, note 2; Sole, *De delictis et poenis*, pp. 35-36.

[28] Cf. Vermeersch-Creusen, *Epitome*, III, 193; Pistocchi, "Corcorso di più persone in uno stesso delitto"—*Mon. Eccl.* XLVII (1935), 234; Augustine, *Commentary*, VIII, 51.

penalties.[29] The distinction may be observed in canon 2230 which excuses children below the age of puberty from *latae sententiae* penalties, no account being made of their guilt.[30] The purpose of this animadversion is to indicate that the rules governing the presence of guilt and of penalty do not necessarily coincide, and although according to canon 2218, § 2 whatever excuses from grave responsibility also excuses from all punishment, nevertheless, it cannot be said that whatever excuses from the penalty, also excuses from the guilt.

In canon 2231 it is stated that unless the law provides otherwise cooperators according to canon 2209, § 1, §2, or § 3, are held to the penalty of the law; the others are not so held, but they are to be punished according to the prudent judgment of the superior, unless the law lays down a special penalty. According to the restrictive and benign interpretation of this canon, the other cooperators here mentioned would include all others referred to in canon 2209 except in sections 1, 2, 3. Thus all who have either completely or partially withdrawn their cooperation, as described in canon 2209, § 5, would be exempted from the penalty of the law.[31] Hence, anyone who had

[29] Cf. canons 2199-2209; 2227, § 2; 2229; 2230. The difference is particularly noted in canon 2218, § 2: "Non solum quae ab omni imputabilitate excusant, sed etiam quae a gravi, excusant pariter a qualibet poena tum latae tum ferendae sententiae etiam in foro externo, si pro foro externo excusatio evincatur." Here it is evident that excuse from guilt and excuse from punishment are two distinct legal concepts, and that one may exist without the other.

[30] Sole, *De delictis et poenis*, pp. 83-84.

[31] Cerato makes this comparison between canons 2209 and 2231 with regard to censures: "*non illi*, qui suum influxum *plene* aut etiam *non plene* abduxerint;"—*Censurae vigentes*, p. 23; Augustine: "Others mentioned under can. 2209 are to be punished proportionately, according to the prudent discretion of the superior unless the law provides a special penalty."—*Commentary*, VIII, 102; Vermeersch-Creusen: "Alii cooperatores poenis f. s. subiacent, nisi lex peculiarem poenam in ipsos constituat."—*Epitome, III*, 210; Blat: "*ceteri vero* conrei, nempe sub seqq. paragraphis eiusdem cit. canonis considerati *non item*, seu non veniunt implicite sub poenali lege, *sed* canonis huius praescripto, uti participes delicti, alia iusta poena . . . *puniendi sunt*"—*Commentarium*, V, 76; Chelodi: "*Retractatio* unius complicis, si imperfecta, liberat a poena delicti sed non ab alia minore."—*Ius poenale*.

cooperated in crime in the sense of canon 2209, §§ 1, 2, or 3, would, according to a probable interpretation of canon 2231, be excused from the penalty as stated in the law, provided he had at least made an external effort to withdraw his cooperation before the consummation of the crime. Probably, therefore, both complete and incomplete withdrawal of cooperation excuses from the penalty of the law, though the delinquent is still liable, according to his guilt, to discretionary penalties of the superior in cases of incomplete withdrawal of cooperation.

There can be no question that complete withdrawal of cooperation excuses from penalties since it also liberates from guilt. However, it must be admitted from a comparison of canons 2231 and 2209 that even incomplete withdrawal of cooperation excuses from the penalty of the law, even though it does not remove all guilt. Incomplete withdrawal is constituted at least by an external effort to render the cooperation inefficacious. Hence, any slight earnest effort to neutralize the antecedent cooperation will excuse from the penalty of the law, though it will reduce the guilt only in proportion to its success in canceling the cooperation.

This conclusion is reasonable when it is considered that only the minimum external requisite of partial withdrawal of cooperation is here stated. The effort must be an earnest attempt to withdraw the cooperation, and accordingly, if the effort is ineffectual or only partially successful, this must be due to external circumstances, not as far as can be determined, to the will of the cooperator. Fraudulent or fictitious withdrawal of cooperation is of no help. There are, however, many situations in which only extrinsic circumstances prevent complete cooperative withdrawal. These are most easily recognized in unforeseen events, physical violence, grave fear, especially if inflicted by one's former associates, and finally inconvenience which, in consideration of the gravity of the crime to be effected, is nevertheless serious beyond the degree ordinarily occasioned by

p. 17. This interpretation is not followed by Cappello (*De censuris*, p. 31), Roberti (*De delictis et poenis*, pp. 275-276), Coronata (*Institutiones*, IV, 118), Sole (*De delictis et poenis*, p. 85), and probably, Wernz-Vidal (*Ius canonicum*, VIII, 211).

withdrawal of cooperation.[32] Besides these, there may also be admitted, according to the definition given of partial withdrawal of cooperation, the intrinsic impossibility of halting the operation of the cooperation, and the personal incapacity of the repentant cooperator to halt it. In the presence of such circumstances, it is easy to see why withdrawal of cooperation may be sincere, yet cannot be complete.[33]

The norms thus far detailed may be applied more exactly in the internal forum. The cooperator himself knows whether he has made an earnest external effort to withdraw his cooperation. It is probable that such a person would incur no *latae sententiae* penalty. In the external forum, once cooperation is established, the fact of withdrawal of cooperation must be proved, and also, it seems, the degree of effort possible under the circumstances.[34]

The solution indicated with regard to all penalties stated in the law has special pertinence to penalties *latae sententiae* in crimes which require special *dolus*.[35] In these crimes any diminution of guilt excuses from the penalty stated in the law.[36]

In all these cases of partially withdrawn cooperation, however, in which the penalty of the law is not incurred or imposed, the Superior may punish the repentant cooperator with some other just penalty according to his prudent judgment, unless the law specifies a determinate penalty for him.[37]

The solution proposed here with regard to all penalties stated in the law, as probable, is certain in practice with regard to censures. While authors disagree speculatively, the practical disposition of the

[32] Cf. Van Hove, *De legibus ecclesiasticis* (Mechliniae-Romae: H. Dessain, 1930), pp. 198-199; Roberti, p. 157; Michiels, *De delictis et poenis*, I, 206-207.

[33] Blat seems to imply that account is to be taken of these circumstances: "*non abduxerit plene* quia retractavit minus quam necesse fuerat secundum prudens iudicium, attentis influxus dati adiunctis"—*Commentarium*, V, 34-35.

[34] Cf. canon 2218, § 1; Roberti, p. 323.

[35] Canon 2229, § 2; Chelodi, *Ius poenale*, pp. 98-99; Roberti, p. 277; Wernz-Vidal, Ius canonicum, VII, 214.

[36] Canon 2229, § 2.

[37] Canon 2231. This will be discussed in chapter 16, article 2, section B.

matter favors the exemption from censures in accordance with canon 2219, § 1.[38]

Thus censures are not incurred unless the crime is committed with contumacy, nor until the crime is consummated.[39] Accordingly, it may happen that cooperation, or indeed any action, which, of itself, is subject to a censure, will not immediately bring on the punishment, but only after the crime has been consummated. In that interval between the placing of the cause and the consummation of the crime, during which, it is universally admitted, no censure is incurred, the delinquent may repent of his action, and thereby purge himself of contumacy before the censure is contracted. An earnest repentance will include the effort to impede the illegal effect. When, however, this effort is impossible or ineffectual, the question arises: is repentance alone sufficient to excuse from the censure? In other words, is it enough to recede from contumacy, or must the cooperation be at least partially withdrawn in order to avoid the censure? Beste,[40] Noldin-Schoeneggar,[41] Pistocchi,[42] Vermeersch-Creusen,[43] and Wernz-Vidal,[44] hold that since contumacy was present at the time when the action was performed, and since the effect of this action was not removed in accordance to canon 2209, § 5, the censure is nevertheless incurred at the time when the crime is consummated. On the other hand, Cerato,[45] Cavigioli,[46] Chelodi,[47] and Coronata [48] maintain that the censure is not contracted in the ab-

[38] Cappello, *De censuris*, p. 33.

[39] Canon 2242, § 1.

[40] *Introductio*, p. 884.

[41] *De poenis ecclesiasticis*, p. 21.

[42] *I Canoni Penali del Codice Ecclesiastico* (Torino-Roma: Marietti, 1925), p. 172.

[43] *Epitome*, III, 288-289; 289, note 1.

[44] *Ius canonicum*, VII, 516-517.

[45] *Censurae vigentes*, pp. 100-101. Cerato admits this only in cases contemplated by canon 2229, § 2.

[46] *De censuris latae sententiae quae in Codice Iuris Canonici continentur commentarium* (Torino: Libreria Editrice Internazionale, 1918), p. 133.

[47] *Ius poenale*, pp. 110-111. This author allows not only freedom from the penalty but also from imputability.

[48] *Institutiones*, IV, 461.

sence of contumacy. Because this is the more benign interpretation, which, according to canon 2219, § 1, is to be followed in penal matters, Cappello,[49] Ayrinhac-Lydon,[50] Roberti,[51] and Salucci[52] contend that in practice the censure is not incurred. The view, therefore, that repentance alone, which takes away contumacy, suffices to exempt from censures is probable in theory and certain in practice. This repentance, however, must be correctly understood. Canon 2242, § 3 remarks: "Contumaciam desiise dicendum est, cum reum vere delicti commissi poenituerit et simul ipse congruam satisfactionem pro damnis et scandalo dederit aut saltem serio promiserit . . . " Hence, the repentance is not to be an empty regret, but must include all possible effort repair the damage. Canon 2242, § 3 contemplates a consummated crime, but, from its sense, canonical jurisprudence clearly requires all possible effort to prevent the act done with criminal intent from attaining its effect. Accordingly, repentance implicitly includes complete and partial withdrawal of cooperation, but makes the further provision that where no external effort to cancel or reduce the efficacy of the former cooperation is possible, a sincere regret with at least the sincere intent of repairing the damage and scandal exempts from censures. In this connection, however, the dualism of the two fora must be observed. While in the internal forum the inward repentance may obviate the censure, yet if in the external forum the cooperation be imputed as a delict, then the repentance must be proved, or the observance of the censure in the external forum may be urged by the superior.[53]

This matter of the effect of repentance upon the incurring of censures is usually discussed by the canonical writers in connection with impeding a cause placed to secure an abortion, though sometimes also with reference to censures in general. There can, however, be no doubt that the application of this principle to censures aris-

[49] *De censuris*, pp. 32-33; 336-337.

[50] *Penal Legislation*, p. 242.

[51] *De delictis et poenis*, pp. 322-323.

[52] *Il Diritto Penale*, II, 229.

[53] Cf. canons 2232, § 1; 2242, § 2; 2251. "Notamus tamen nec poenitentiam nec remotionem effectuum praesumi sed debet probari."—Roberti, p. 323.

ing from cooperation is perfectly appropriate. As long as the cooperation has not yet had its effect upon the consummated crime, the principle has validity, since contumacy is removed before the censure would be incurred. The application of the conclusion based on the cessation of contumacy to all censures arising from cooperation is original in the foregoing pages but not unwarranted.

Thus with regard to censures, repentance will excuse the former cooperator from censures provided the repentance occur before the crime is consummated. In crimes which require special *dolus*, any diminution of guilt before the consummation of the crime, either by repentance or even partial withdrawal of cooperation, will excuse the former cooperator from all *latae sententiae* penalties, according to canon 2229, § 2. Finally, with regard to all penalties stated in the law, a probable interpretation of canon 2231, supported by many authors, would excuse from these penalties those cooperators who have made at least an external effort to arrest the effects of cooperation before the consummation of the crime.

Chapter Fourteen

NEGATIVE COOPERATORS

Canon 2209, § 6. **Qui in delictum concurrit suum dumtaxat officium negligendo, imputabilitate tenetur proportionata obligationi qua adigebatur ad delictum suo officio impediendum.**

It occasionally happens that crimes could be prevented by persons who are not directly concerned therein. In a wide sense, these people have cooperated with the delinquent by not preventing the crime. With regard to canonical guilt, however, only those are held responsible who are obliged by their office to prevent the crime. This is made clear by the phrase, *qui in delictum concurrit suum dumtaxat officium negligendo,* which is to be interpreted not in the sense of the general duties of charity, but rather of a strict duty of justice.[1]

Article 1. Neglect of Office in Relation to Negative Cooperation

Officium is here to be understood of a specific duty or position to which is attached the legal obligation of positively impeding certain definite crimes.[2] There is nothing to indicate that this term signifies an ecclesiastical office in the strict sense according to canon 145, § 1.[3] Of use in determining the office in particular is the characterization given by Michiels[4] that the office should have been constituted, at least, partially to impede certain crimes. As an example may be cited the duty of guarding the tabernacle entrusted to pastors in order to

[1] Pistocchi, "Concorso di più persone in uno stesso delitto"—*Mon. Eccl.* XLVII (1935)), 235; Sole, *De delictis et poenis,* p. 35.

[2] Michiels, *De delictis et poenis,* I, 327; Salucci, *Il Diritto Penale,* I, 40; D'Annibale, *In constitutionem apostolicae sedis commentarii,* p. 12; Berutti, *Institutiones,* VI, 37.

[3] Cf. Chelodi, *Ius de personis* (2. ed., Tridenti: Libr. Editr. Tridentum, 1927), p. 225.

[4] *Loc. cit.*

prevent the crime of sacrilege. Accordingly, the office considered in relation to negative cooperation is any position or duty in virtue of which one is obliged by law to prevent certain crimes. This is indicated in the canon itself which declares that there must be attached to the office the obligation of impeding the crime.[5]

The neglect of office may be either intentional or negligent.[6] The former arises from *dolus;* the latter, from *culpa.* Thus one may fail to fulfill a duty either deliberately, or through the omission of due diligence. Both intentional and negligent dereliction of duty may constitute negative cooperation; however, the negligent type is considered delictual only when juridically imputable.[7] Furthermore, intentional neglect of office may give rise to formal cooperation as considered in canon 2209, §§3, 4, as well as to the negative cooperation of canon 2209, § 6. Hence, with regard to the intentional neglect of office, a distinction must be drawn between formal and negative cooperation. The act of neglect, when promised previously to the crime, becomes formal cooperation [8] arising from a common intent and producing a positive effect, either morally, by encouraging the delinquent,[9] or physically, since the omission would be equivalent to aid given by physical cooperation. Such formal cooperation is positively excluded from the concept of negative cooperation in the law by the foregoing provisions of canon 2209, and implicitly, at least, in canon 2209, § 6 by the word, *dumtaxat,* which limits the neglect to an act of omission without cooperation. The intentional neglect, then, may be placed voluntarily and with the hope of having the crime realized by the act of another, but as long as the criminal intent is not made manifest to all concerned, there is only negative cooperation.[10] Negligent neglect, on the other hand, is not due to a

[5] " . . . obligationi qua adigebatur ad delictum suo officio impediendum." —canon 2209, § 6.

[6] Cf. Swoboda, *Ignorance in Relation to the Imputability of Delicts,* p. 104; Latini, p. 81; Michiels, *De delictis et poenis,* I, 67.

[7] Cf. p. 66, note 1; canons 2199-2206.

[8] Roberti, p. 220; Latini, p. 161; Wernz-Vidal, *Ius canonicum,* VII, 145-146.

[9] This is the view preferred by Michiels—*De delictis et poenis,* I, 327.

[10] Roberti, p. 220.

deliberate omission of duty, but merely to a failure to exercise the proper care in fulfilling the duty.

A further requirement of negative cooperation is found in the fact that the violation of the law must be attributable to some extent to the neglect—*Qui in delictum concurrit.* Since there is here no formal cooperation, the only way in which negative cooperators enter into the crime is by the actual advantage which their dereliction of duty gives to the commission of the crime. Hence it is not sufficient that there be a concurrent neglect on the one hand, and the commission of the crime on the other, but a relation must exist between the crime and the neglect. How is this relation to be determined? Insofar as the duty or office has been defined as one which, properly exercised, will impede the crime,[11] it is reasonable to assume that only that neglect is here contemplated, which if eliminated would have given no advantage to the criminal. Insistence cannot be made in favor of an absolute prevention of the crime, since many crimes will occur even when the pertinent office is exercised with due care. If, therefore, any advantage is given the perpetrator by the neglect, the remiss official is guilty of negative cooperation. This advantage may be either subjective, in the sense that the neglect being known, the delinquent is encouraged to commit the crime; or it may be objective, insofar as it actually aids in the commission of the crime, whether it be known to the delinquent or not.[12] Moreover, this advantageous neglect of office is to be clearly established and not merely presumed. Hence, neglect within the scope of canon 2209, § 6 is not to be assumed merely because of the co-existence of a crime and concomitant neglect, since this provision of the canon definitely requires neglect by which one concurs in the crime. Thus, even if the key to the tabernacle were carelessly guarded, this neglect of office could not be construed as beneficial to a burglar who used tools to break open the tabernacle.

[11] " . . . adigebatur ad delictum impediendum."—canon 2209, § 6.

[12] Pistocchi, "Concorso di più persone in uno stesso delitto"—*Mon. Eccl.* XLVII (1935), 234: " . . . deve positivemente influire nella consumazione del delitto." Berutti, *Institutiones,* VI, 37: " . . . quae causa fit ut quis vel delictum committere possit quod secus non commisset, vel saltem facilius ipsum delictum committat."

Finally, neglect of office, as considered by canon 2209, § 6, must be distinguished from crimes of omission. The latter are constituted by transgressions of laws which command under penalty the performance of some duty.[13] In this case the infraction of the law proceeds directly from the omission. With regard to the neglect of office mentioned in canon 2209, § 6, the guilt arises not from the omission, but from the advantage given to the crime of another by one's own neglect of office. This, however, is not to be understood in the sense of formal cooperation in crime, as though the delinquent and the remiss official both commit and share in the same crime. Each transgresses separately, although the guilt of the remiss official is constituted when the crime of another occurs upon the occasion and with the material help of his dereliction of duty. Crimes of omission are individual delicts, explicitly defined in the law. Negative cooperation, on the other hand, exists when a legal obligation, designed to impede certain crimes, is left unfulfilled, and when the pertinent crimes are realized with some assistance from the neglect of office. In all this, there is to be no pact or promise as to constitute formal cooperation, but the assistance is to be actual, yet apart from all arrangement between the remiss official and the delinquent.[14]

Article 2. The Various Offices, the Neglect of Which Can Lead to Negative Cooperation

A. *The General Obligation of Preventing All Crime.*

Besides offices which entail the obligation of preventing certain crimes, there are also offices which have the general obligation of

[13] Cf. Roberti, p. 67.

[14] Various crimes of omission mentioned in the Code of Canon Law are: the failure of civil authorities to forbid duels—canon 2351, § 1; the failure of a penitent to denounce a confessor guilty of solicitation—canon 2368, § 2; non-residence in the place required on the part of those who hold an office, a benefice, or a dignity—canon 2381; neglect of the pastor to care for the church, the Blessed Sacrament, and the sacred oils—canon 2382; the failure of the pastor to keep the parish books—canon 2383. These are all delicts in themselves and may be punished without reference to canon 2209, § 6.

preventing all crimes. This general obligation is incumbent upon ecclesiastical superiors. By the mere fact that the superior has the duty of maintaining discipline he is obliged to prevent all crimes on the part of his subjects.[15] If, therefore, a crime should be committed upon the occasion of the superior's remissness and with some advantage derived from this fact, the superior would be accounted guilty of negative cooperation. The superior's obligation to prevent the crime, however, holds only to the extent to which it is possible,

A distinction, made by the law itself in virtue of canon 2209, § 6, exists between these crimes of omission and negative cooperation, which is constituted, not by simple neglect of office, but by neglect of office that, without formal cooperation, nevertheless lends some aid to the commission of another's crime.

[15] "Ut enim finis socialis obtineatur, necessarium est procurare, etiam vi physica, si oportuerit, adhibita, ut tum singulorum tum socialia iura serventur, omnesque subditi in officio suo contineantur et ordo socialis, ubi laesus fuerit, prompte restauretur.

"Profecto, ad talem iuris et ordinis proportionatam tutelam habendam, oportet:

'1. praevenire, quantum fieri potest, iuris laesiones, homines continendo in officio suo, cogendo eos qui renuunt oboedire, ut ex invitis fiant volentes, seu ad id faciendum vi adigantur quod sponte facere nolint: en *coactio* stricto sensu, idest *ius cogendi invitos;*"—Ottaviani, *Institutiones iuris publici ecclesiastici* (2. ed., 2 vols., Romae: Typis Polyglottis Vaticanis, 1935-1936), I, 126.

" . . . potestas coactiva exercenda sit: nimirum in omnes a quibus socialis ordo laeditur, aut in discrimen vocatur, proindeque:

"III. In eos *de quibus*, certitudine quadam morali, *iudicari aut praesumi* potest socialem ordinem ab iis turbatum iri, ut sunt otiosi, delinquentes, praeiudicati, etc."—Ottaviani, *op. cit.*, I, 133-134.

" . . . although the ecclesiastical superior possesses the power to inflict coercive measures, he must be ever mindful of his duty to prevent transgressions of the law and to eliminate disturbances of the established order whenever possible."—Esswein, *The Extrajudicial Coercive Powers of Ecclesiastical Superiors*, The Catholic University of America Canon Law Studies, n. 127 (Washington, D. C.: The Catholic University of America Press, 1941), p. 102.

These quotations refer to perfect societies. The doctrine, however, may also be applied to imperfect societies in the church, in which the members are bound by contract or vow to accept the will of the superior—cf. Schaefer, *De religiosis* (3. ed., Romae: S. A. L. E. R., 1940), pp. 68-69.

by a prudent exercise of the office, to prevent the crime. Extraordinary care is not required since only the omission of due diligence is enumerated among the roots of canonical guilt.[16] But certainly when definite methods to maintain order and to repress crime are prescribed by law and not merely suggested, failure to employ these means will be an indication of neglected office.

Among the first who hold an office in the sense of canon 2209, § 6, are those who with ordinary power are commissioned to maintain ecclesiastical order. These superiors are enumerated in canon 198, § 1. Here are listed, besides the Roman Pontiff, the following in respect to their own territory: the residential bishop, the abbot or prelate *nullius*, and their vicars general, also the administrator apostolic, the vicar apostolic, the prefect apostolic, together with the lawful successors of the foregoing; and finally, in respect to their subjects, the major superiors [17] in clerical exempt religious societies.[18] The religious superiors will be considered later. What is said now in regard to the residential bishop may be applied to the other territorial rulers, as they are all made similar in regard to their obligations by law.[19]

The bishop has the supreme administrative or executive power in the diocese; accordingly, it is part of his duty to urge the observance of ecclesiastical law and to watch that abuses do not creep into ecclesiastical discipline,[20] to supervise and direct the inferior magistrates in fulfilling their office, to correct the negligent, to dismiss clerics, to execute pontifical mandates and rescripts, and to favor and promote all that is necessary or useful to the advancement of the

[16] Canon 2199; cf. Roberti, p. 93-94. " . . . ex culpabili negligentia illud non impedivit."—Berutti, *Institutiones*, VI, 37.

[17] Canon 488, n. 8.

[18] Canon 488, nn. 2, 4.

[19] Metropolitans, canon 273; apostolic vicars, and prefects, canon 294, § 1; administrators apostolic, canon 315, §§ 1-2, n. 1; abbots and prelates *nullius*, canon 323, § 1; vicars general, canon 368, § 1; the cathedral chapter, canon 431; vicars capitular, canon 431; the diocesan consultors, canon 427.

[20] Canons 336, §§ 1-2; 1261, § 1; 1279, § 3; 1478; 1519.

spiritual interests of the faithful.[21] Particularly noteworthy here are the urging of the observance of ecclesiastical law, the vigilance against abuses, and the correction of the negligent.[22] Special measures are prescribed by law for the maintenance of ecclesiastical discipline. Thus the bishop is bound to the law of residence by canon 338, and is under obligation to see that no harm results to the diocese from his absence.[23] Moreover, the diocesan visitation is imposed on him in order that he may observe and correct abuses and defects, and preserve and restore by due means the observance of obligations.[24] Besides, the Code specifically enjoins upon the bishop the use of penal remedies [25] the purpose of which is principally the prevention of crimes.[26] These are to be invoked according to the gravity of the situation whenever a subject is in the proximate occasion of committing a crime.[27] In fact there is actually a command placed by law on the ordinary to proceed in this manner by canon 2307. There are also at the disposal of the bishop, several other legal measures

[21] Chelodi, *Ius de personis*, pp. 311-312. These are not merely priveleges but also duties—"Haec sunt simul ius et officium Episcoporum quae proinde non solum facere possunt, sed et debent."—Coronata, *Institutiones*, I, 475.

[22] With regard to clerics, cf. S. C. P. F., Instructio "Cum Magnopere" 1884: "ordinarius pro suo pastorali munere tenetur disciplinam correptionemque clericorum ita diligentur curare, ut circa eorum mores assidue vigilet, ac remedia a canonibus statuta sive praecavendis, sive tollendis abusibus in clerum aliquando irrepentibus provide adhibeat." This instruction together with a commentary is found in Smith, *The New Procedure in Criminal and Disciplinary Causes of Ecclesiastics* (2. ed., New York-Cincinnati, 1888). "This article indicates two principles: one, that it is the bishop's right and duty to watch over the conduct of his clergy, and to prevent or punish crime and abuses among them. . . . "—Smith, *op. cit.*, p. 25.

[23] Chelodi, *Ius de personis*, p. 313.

[24] Canon 343, § 1; Chelodi, *Ius de personis*, p. 217; Slafkosky, *The Canonical Episcopal Visitation of the Diocese*, The Catholic University of America Canon Law Studies, n. 142 (Washington, D. C.: The Catholic University of America Press, 1941), pp. 73-74.

[25] Canons 2306-2311.

[26] Wernz-Vidal, *Ius canonicum*, VII, 397: Bouuaert-Simenon, *Manuale juris canonici*, III, 366.

[27] Canons 2307-2311.

to forestall crimes, especially on the part of clerics: the procedure against *concubinarii,*[28] the procedure against non-resident clerics,[29] the procedure against negligent pastors,[30] and the power of dismissal[31] and of transfer.[32] Specifically then, neglect of office could arise from these headings: failure of vigilance, non-observance of the rules of residence or of visitation, failure to take preventive measures. From the first and second headings comes the occasion for crimes which could have been discouraged except for the culpable ignorance of the superior; from the third heading comes the occasion for crimes which could have been impeded if penal remedies or administrative measures had been put in use. These duties of vigilance, residence, visitation and repression are in themselves grave; the crimes that may be committed because of their non-observance do not increase or decrease the guilt, which is measured according to the gravity of the neglected obligation; but rather such crimes may be considered as pointers or indications of neglect when it is clear that observance of the law would have decreased the likelihood of the crime being committed.[33]

A special note is to be made in regard to the vicar general. His power is limited by the law, which in certain cases requires the mandate of the bishop; and may be further limited by the bishop, who may reserve certain acts to himself.[34] Thus without a special mandate, the vicar general can not inflict a penalty[35] or remove parochial vicars.[36] Because of their penal connotation, the vicar general cannot employ, without the bishop's mandate, the processes referred to above.[37] Apart from these limitations, the vicar general seems to have

[28] Canons 2176-2181.

[29] Canons 2168-2175.

[30] Canons 2182-2185.

[31] Canons 192, § 3; 2299, § 1; Chelodi, *Ius de personis,* p. 253.

[32] Canon 193; Chelodi, *Ius de personis,* pp. 253-254.

[33] Canon 2209, § 6.

[34] Canon 368, § 1.

[35] Canon 2220, § 2.

[36] Canon 477, § 1.

[37] Canons 2170; 2173; 2176; 2183. Cf. Meier, *Penal Administrative Procedure against Negligent Pastors,* The Catholic University of America Canon Law Studies n. 140 (Washington, D. C.: The Catholic University

the right and duty, enjoined upon ordinaries, of employing penal remedies,[38] except the penal precept, by which a penalty threatened would be inflicted if the precept were disregarded.[39] He may, however, in virtue of his ordinary power, give precepts to which no penalty is attached.[40] Incidentally, it may be noted that these simple precepts, which have as their direct purpose the prevention of crime[41] may be given by all superiors possessing either jurisdiction or dominative power.[42] With these modifications, however, the vicar general has the duty, commensurate with his equal executive power, of providing, with the bishop, for the observance of ecclesiastical discipline. Since the vicar general is to help the bishop in ruling the diocese,[43] he will fulfill his obligation to impede crimes either by taking the opportune means within his power, or, at least, by informing the bishop if time affords. It can be definitely stated that any connivance at crime would be neglect of office. In the face of the probability of a crime being committed, his failure to take appropriate action would be gravely reprehensible.

Religious superiors, next to be considered, also have the duty of enforcing ecclesiastical discipline in relation to their subjects; nor

of America Press: 1941), pp. 95-97. Although not stated explicitly by the Code, it is probable that the vicar general cannot, without a special mandate, employ the administrative processes in removing pastors, since both processes contemplate action by the ordinary who can appoint to another office —canons 2154; 2155; 2161, § 2. The vicar general lacks this power without a special mandate according to canon 152. Moreover, without the mandate he cannot transfer those holding ecclesiastical offices, since he does not have the power of appointing to office, as required by canon 193, § 1.

[38] Canons 2306-2311.

[39] Coronata, *Institutiones*, IV, 84; Salucci, *Il Diritto Penale*, I, 98; Blat, *Commentarium*, V, 56-57.

[40] Canon 24; Cicognani, *Canon Law*, p. 645; Esswein, *The Extrajudicial Coercive Powers of Ecclesiastical Superiors*, p. 70; Van Hove: "Possunt tamen dari praecepta forma solemni, quae contineant iussionem mere obligantem in conscientia. Haec non cessant, amoto praecipiente."—*De legibus ecclesiasticis*, p. 367.

[41] Chelodi, *Ius de personis*, p. 125; esp. p. 125, note 1.

[42] Chelodi, *Ius de personis*, p. 124.

[43] Canon 366, § 1.

does it matter from the standpoint of the obligation whether their power be ordinary or dominative.[44] With regard to the religious superior, it must be noted that, for the purpose of canon 2209, § 6, neglect is considered only in reference to crimes as defined by canon 2195, § 1, and not in reference to mere infractions of the rule.[45] All religious superiors are obliged to the law of residence according to their own constitutions,[46] and major superiors as designated by the constitutions have the duty of visiting personally or through a deputy all their subject houses.[47] Besides, the religious superiors are expected to exercise surveillance over their subjects as dictated by common prudence,[48] and to take appropriate measures against incipient crimes.[49] Schaefer [50] permits the use of the penal remedies of canon 2306 to religious superiors in virtue of their dominative power.[51] The Code itself, however, mentions the use of penal remedies only in connection with ordinaries.[52] Other superiors can, nevertheless,

[44] Cf. canon 501, § 1;; Chelodi, *Ius de personis*, pp. 418-419; Beste, *Introductio*, p. 327; Schaefer, *De religiosis*, pp. 227-229.

[45] However, notable violations of the law of common life as prescribed in the constitutions, after admonition without improvement, may constitute a delict—canon 2389.

[46] Canon 508.

[47] Canon 511.

[48] This is contained within the office of superior. Schaefer implies that living *sub vigilantia Superioris* is the ordinary state of religious—*De religiosis*, p. 633. With regards to delinquents in exempt clerical religious societies, the superior is bound to remove them to a place where surveillance is easier—canon 661, § 2; Schaefer, *De religiosis*, p. 1016; cf. canons 605; 607.

[49] Cf. canon 661, §§ 1-2.

[50] *De religiosis*, p. 228.

[51] Just how this statement is to be understood is not clear in view of the author's note: "Intelligitur hoc in sensu stricto uti remedia poenalia canonica, secundum Codicem, quia ad hoc requiritur iurisdictio in foro externo."—*De religiosis*, p. 228, note 75. Here the author would seem to indicate that only those superiors who are ordinaries can use the penal remedies, without obtaining delegation.

[52] This restriction is made explicitly in canons 2307, 2308, 2311; implicitly in canon 2310, which is limited to those having complete iurisdiction; cf. canon 2220, §§ 1-2.

in virtue of their office, accomplish similar results by giving simple precepts,[53] warnings, or corrections.[54]

B. *Particular Obligations of Preventing Certain Crimes.*

The obligations now to be considered do not have the general purpose of impeding all crime; they are intended to maintain order only in certain respects.

1. *The Care of the Cloister and the Exploration of Will in Candidates to Religious Societies of Women.* The care of the cloister and the exploration of will are two separate obligations here considered together because they devolve upon the same superiors. Both the bishop and the proper religious superior have special duties in connection with the care of the cloister[55] and with the exploration of the will of candidates in religious societies of women before novitiate and first profession.[56] Neglect in the first case may be the occasion of the crime of violation of the cloister,[57] or, in the second case, of the crime of forcing one to accept the religious state.[58]

2. *The Duties of the Metropolitan in His Suffragan Dioceses.* The metropolitan has the right to practice vigilance in his suffragan dioceses with regard to faith and ecclesiastical discipline and also the right to inform the Roman Pontiff concerning abuses;[59] he is to

[53] Chelodi, *Ius de personis*, pp. 124, 415.

[54] "Possunt vero Superiores et Capitula praecepta et ordinationes emittere: poenitentias salutares imponere aliaque omnia quae ad bonum communitatis necessaria sunt: proprie dictas poenas ecclesiasticas imponere tamen nequeunt."—Coronata, *Institutiones*, I, 647. Beste admits the use of penal remedies by religious superiors without distinction, but makes no reference to canon 2305—*Introductio*, p. 327.

[55] Canons 603, §§ 1-2; 604, § 3; 605; 606; S. C. de Rel., Instructio, 6 feb. 1924—AAS, XVI (1924), 96; Bouscaren, *The Canon Law Digest* (2 vols. and Supplement—1941, Milwaukee: Bruce, 1934-1941), I, 314-320.

[56] Canons 544; 552, §§ 1-2.

[57] Canon 2342. Also to be considered here are the cognate crimes of apostasy from religion (canon 2385), temporary desertion from religion (canon 2386), flight by a religious with a member of the opposite sex (canon 646, § 1 n. 2), and marriage or attempted marriage of religious (canon 2388).

[58] Canon 2352.

[59] Canons 338, § 4; 343, § 3; 429, § 5; 785, § 1.

make the canonical visitation in these dioceses with the approbation of the Holy See, if this duty has been neglected by the suffragan.[60] But, because of the phraseology employed, it is doubtful whether these powers of the metropolitan are to be considered as obligations.[61] The one exception to this is his duty of informing the Holy See if a suffragan bishop should fall into excommunication, interdict, or suspension.[62] It is, then, only in regard to this point that the metropolitan can be accused of neglect with reference to his duties in the suffragan dioceses.

3. *The Custody of the Diocesan Archives.* The bishop, the vicar general, the chancellor, the vicar capitular, the first dignitary of the chapter or the consultor senior by appointment, the two selected canons or diocesan consultors, and the priest to whom the bishop has confided the key, all have specific duties in regard to guarding the diocesan archives.[63] The purpose of these obligations is to prevent the crimes of removal, destruction, concealment, or alteration of curial documents.[64]

4. *Vigilance as Practised by the Vicar Forane.* The vicar forane, according to the common law, has the duty of vigilance and visitation in his district.[65]

[60] Canon 274, nn. 4-5.

[61] Canon 274; cf. canons 338, § 4; 343, § 3; 785, § 1 in relation to canon 274. Coronata does not consider these powers as obligations, because of the word *potest*—*Institutiones,* I, 433. Beste looks upon canon 274 as a restrictive enumeration of rights—*Introductio,* p. 252. Chelodi: "Administrativa [potestas] . . . limitatur ad munus *vigilandi*"—*Ius de personis,* p. 296. Vermeersch-Creusen show that the purpose of the terminology was a limitation of the obligations to cases expressed in the Code—*Epitome,* I, 219. Canon 429, § 5 makes no reference to canon 274, and so remains an exception to these considerations. But in connection with his other powers here related, the metropolitan cannot be accused of neglect because of the strict interpretation of the word *potest,* until authentic interpretation declares otherwise.

[62] Canon 429, § 5. If the metropolitan should incur these penalties, this duty of informing the Holy See would devolve upon the senior suffragan.

[63] Canons 375, § 1; 377, §§ 1-2; 378; 379, §§ 1-3; 380; 381, § 1 nn. 1-2, § 2; 382, §§ 1-2.

[64] Canon 2405.

[65] Canon 447. Chelodi, *Ius de personis,* p. 366.

5. *The Custody of the Blessed Sacrament and of the Holy Oils; the Care of the Church.* The pastor is responsible for the custody of the Blessed Sacrament, together with the priest who has the care of the church.[66] Failure in this duty may give occasion to the crime of sacrilege against the Holy Eucharist.[67] Further obligations are imposed upon the pastor with regard to the custody of the holy oils [68] and the care of the church.[69] The fulfillment of these duties will impede the crime of sacrilege as penalized in canon 2325.[70]

6. *The Pre-Nuptial Investigation.* The pastor also has the duty of investigating, according to the rules prescribed by law, the free state of those about to marry.[71] Coupled with this is the duty of making the required notations in the parish baptismal and matrimonial books,[72] and of transmitting the pertinent knowledge to those requesting it.[73] His neglect of these duties may be the occasion of the crimes of bigamy,[74] of incest,[75] of public adultery, of public concubinage,[76] of failure to obtain the needed dispensation from the impedement of mixed religion,[77] of attempted marriage by clerics in sacred orders or by religious in solemn vows, and of illicit marriage by religious in perpetual simple vows.[78]

66 Canons 1269; 2382; S. C. de Sacr., Instructio, 26 maii, 1938—AAS, XXX (1938), 198; Bouscaren, *Canon Law Digest, Supplement*—1941, pp. 151-163.

67 Canon 2320.

68 Canons 735; 946; 2382.

69 Canons 1178; 2382.

70 With regard to the care of the church, the pastor is specifically enjoined by law to keep out of church all commercial transactions and fairs—canon 1178.

71 Canons 1020-1032; S. C. de Sacr., Instructio, 29 iunii, 1941—AAS, XXII (1941), 539 sqq.; *The Jurist* II (1942), n. 1, *Supplement*.

72 Canons 470, 2383; S. C. de Sacr., Instructio, 29 iunii, 1941, § 11, e, b, c—The Jurist, *loc. cit.*

73 Canons 1103, 778; S. C. de Sacr., Instructio, 29 iunii, 1941, § 11, d, b, c—The Jurist, *loc. cit.*

74 Canon 2356.

75 Canon 2357, § 1.

76 Canon 2357, § 2.

77 Canon 2375.

78 Canon 2388.

7. *The Obligation of the Porter.* The violation of the cloister, as previously noted, may also be occasioned by the neglect of the porter.[79]

8. *The Authentication of Relics.* Those having the faculty of authenticating relics [80] must not permit the crime of manufacturing, distributing, selling, or exposing for public veneration false relics to occur because of their failure to exercise their office with due care.[81]

Article 3. The Guilt Attaching to Negative Cooperation

Neglect of office, as explained, entails guilt in proportion to the obligation attached to the office of impeding the crime—*imputabilitate proportionata obligationi qua adigebatur ad delictum suo officio impediendum.*[82] The ensuing guilt is not, therefore, absolute but relative to the obligation of preventing the crime. Accordingly, the more serious the obligation, the graver the responsibility. This is the objective guilt of negative cooperation. As such, it is subject to modification in the individual by the subjective factors as discussed in chapter eight. In this connection, it may be pointed out that intentional neglect is more reprehensible than negligent neglect of office, insofar as the former is motivated by the intention of vio-

[79] Canon 2342, *admittentes.* Canon 2342 punishes both the *introducentes* and the *admittentes* of externs into the cloister. The first term refers to all those who in any way bring an extern into the cloister; the latter to those who, having power as superiors or porters, permit externs to enter, or do not attempt to expel them when already inside—Sole, *De delictis et poenis,* p. 289; D'Annibale, *In constitutionem apostolicae sedis commentarii,* p. 83; Schaefer, *De religiosis,* p. 725; Cipollini, *De censuris,* pp. 143-144; Chelodi, *Ius poenale,* p. 104; Ayrinhac-Lydon, *Penal Legislation,* p. 220; Gibolinus, *Disquisitiones canonicae de clausura regulari* (Lugduni, 1648), p. 51. Other authors extend the meaning of *admittentes* to include all religious who can easily prevent an unlawful entrance—Hollweck, *Die kirchlichen Strafgesetze,* p. 225, note 12; Pennacchi, *Commentaria in constitutionem apostolicae sedis,* I, 742; Cappello, *De censuris,* p. 284. The restrictive interpretation is to be followed in view of canons 19 and 2219, § 1.

[80] Canon 1283.

[81] Canon 2326.

[82] Canon 2209, § 6; Roberti, p. 220.

lating the law whereas the latter is due to failure to observe proper diligence and and lacks all contempt of law.

It is to be noted that canon 2209, § 6 is not limited to crimes which can be committed through negligence as well as by criminal intent. Canon 2209, § 6 considers neglect in regard to all offices which have the obligation of preventing crime. It establishes, therefore, a new mode of guilt by way of neglect. As will be seen later,[83] this guilt in virtue of the indeterminate penalty added to it by canon 2231 becomes in each separate case a new canonical delict. Hence, one must include among the crimes of the Fifth Book neglect of those offices described in article 2 of this chapter when a canonical crime is committed both upon the occasion of this neglect and with some advantage deriving from the neglect. Such neglect, moreover, can occur either through intent or negligence.

[83] *Infra*, chapter 16, article 2, section B.

Chapter Fifteen

SUBSEQUENT COOPERATORS

Canon 2209, § 7. **Delicti patrati laudatio, fructuum participatio, delinquentis occultatio et receptatio aliive actus delictum iam plene absolutum subsequentes, nova delicta constituere possunt, si nempe poena in lege plectantur; sed, nisi cum delinquente de illis actibus ante delictum conventum fuerit, non secumferunt delicti patrati imputabilitatem.**

When aid is given the delinquent in view of a crime already committed, this is termed subsequent cooperation, although, as a matter of fact, there has been no formal cooperation in the crime itself. Since this aid has no influence on the crime,[1] the guilt entailed cannot be estimated from the crime already committed. Accordingly, it is stated in canon 2209, § 7 that the guilt will be dependent upon specific legislation creating new crimes, unless the aid rendered subsequently to the crime should become true cooperation by previous arrangement with the delinquent prior to the commission of the crime. Usually, however, in connection with acts committed subsequently to the crime there will be lacking this previous agreement whereby the subsequent acts would become formal cooperation. In the lack of the previous agreement, the guilt attaching to such acts is to be estimated solely from specific legislation which constitutes any such act a separate crime by stating its proper penalty.

The canon lists the common forms of subsequent cooperation. These are praise of the crime committed, participation in the fruits of the crime, concealing and receiving the delinquent. The determination of these acts is not of great importance, since the legislator includes also any other similar act—*aliive actus delictum iam plene absolutum subsequentes*. The enumeration of specific forms has as its purpose illustration rather than specification. These forms are,

[1] Sole, *De delictis et poenis*, p. 135.

moreover, easily understood without further explanation. As a matter of fact, since these and other forms of cooperation may be offered before, during, or after the crime,[2] it is necessary to the concept of subsequent cooperation that they actually be given after the crime, as the phrase following the enumeration of the forms directs.

This phrase—*aliive actus delictum iam plene absolutum subsequentes*—is of more importance than the enumeration of examples as it characterizes subsequent cooperation. The essence of subsequent cooperation rests in the fact that all aid rendered has been given after the completion of the crime. This refers not only to the actual presentation of aid but even to all intimation of it. For if the delinquent were led to believe he could rely upon some assistance to be offered after the crime, such encouragement could constitute true moral cooperation, as contemplated by canon 2209, §§ 3-4.[3] Moreover, as is stated in the phrase, it is necessary to the concept of subsequent cooperation that before the aid is rendered the crime be complete, requiring no further activity—*plene absolutum*. This has special reference to crimes which are not brought to an immediate close, but which continue in a complete state during a period of time. In the case of these crimes cooperation given at any moment before the conclusion of the crime would be true cooperation, to be ruled by canon 2209, §§ 3-4.[4] This idea of a prolonged crime is not found in a habitual crime, or in a crime of many repetitions, but in a crime which continues to exist in its individual nature.[5]

In the category of permanent crimes are heresy, schism, apostasy;[6] the rearing of children in a non-Catholic religion;[7] pertinacious dis-

[2] Roberti, p. 221.

[3] Sole, *De delictis et poenis*, p. 35; Coronata, *Institutiones*, IV, 53; Roberti, p. 222.

[4] Coronata, *Institutiones*, IV, 53; Roberti, pp. 213, 222; Wernz-Vidal, *Ius canonicum*, VII, 142.

[5] "Delictum permanens inde a primo actu perficitur, sed crimen prosequitur in sua exsecutione, e. g. raptus et servitus eo usque perdurant quo protrahitur coarctatio libertatis."—Roberti, p. 227.

[6] Canon 2314.

[7] Canon 2319, § 1, n. 4.

obedience to the Pope or to one's own ordinary;[8] the offering of aid or favor to a *vitandus* excommunicate in the permanent crime for which he has been excommunicated;[9] the crime of remaining under censure;[10]the refusal to take the examination required by canon 130;[11] public concubinage;[12] not wearing the clerical garb;[13] the conducting of business by clerics;[14] non-residence in the required place on the part of those who hold an office, a benefice, or a dignity;[15] neglect in keeping the parochial books;[16] both apostasy and flight from religion;[17] the refusal to transcribe, send, or exhibit curial or parochial documents;[18] the refusal to make the legitimate offerings according to canons 463, § 1 and 1507;[19] simony;[20] and various crimes of retention: the retention of condemned books;[21] the retention of the sacred species for an evil purpose;[22] the retention of the goods or rights of the Roman Church;[23] the retention of ecclesiastical property for one's own uses;[24] the crime of rape insofar as women are retained for the purpose of marriage or lust;[25] the retention of bene-

[8] Canon 2331, § 1.

[9] Canon 2338, § 2. Cf. Coronata, *Institutiones*, IV, 390-392.

[10] Canon 2340.

[11] Canon 2376.

[12] Canons 2357, § 2; 2359, § 1. Note that adultery, fornication being acts could, if recurring over a period of time, be crimes of repetition, whereas concubinage is essentially a state, hence a permanent crime.

[13] Canon 2379.

[14] Canon 2380.

[15] Canon 2381.

[16] Canon 2383.

[17] Canons 644, §§ 1, 3; 646, § 1, n. 1; 2385; 2386.

[18] Canon 2406, § 2.

[19] Canon 2349.

[20] Canons 729; 2371; 2392. Regarding cooperation *post factum*, cf. Ryder, *Simony*, The Catholic University of America Canon Law Studies, n. 65 (Washington, D. C.: The Catholic University of America, 1931), pp. 91-93.

[21] Canon 2318, § 1.

[22] Canon 2320.

[23] Canon 2345.

[24] Canons 2346; 2347.

[25] Canon 2353.

fices, offices, or dignities after lawful privation or removal.[26]

Once these crimes are initially completed, true cooperation may be rendered, insofar as the nature of the crime permits, as long as the crime is continued.[27] Accordingly, there is no subsequent cooperation possible in reference to permanent crimes, until the crime itself has been brought to a definite conclusion.

One type of concurrence in crime, not mentioned by name in canon 2209, § 7, but certainly to be included in the concept of subsequent cooperation is *ratihabitio,* which might well be expressed in English by the term ratification. It is verified in the approval one gives to the criminal act of others which has been done in one's own name. Its requisites, as stated by canonical authors,[28] are: 1) that the crime to which ratification is given could be performed through the agency of another;[29] 2) that the person giving approval was legally capable of committing the crime at the time when it was actually committed;[30] 3) that he should approve the crime as being done in his name.[31] According to these requirements, ratification is precluded from attaining the status of formal cooperation,[32] since the approval, coming after the completion of the crime, can have no influence upon its commission. This was recognized before the

[26] Canon 2401. Cf. Roberti, p. 227. This list is not authoritative and can be modified by divergent interpretations of the various penal canons. Thus Pistocchi includes the reception of a *vitandus* excommunicate in divine offices (canon 2338, § 2) and the giving of favor to duellers (canon 2351, § 1)—"Concorso di più persone in uno stesso delitto"—*Mon. Eccl.* XLVII (1935), 238.

[27] D'Annibale, *In constitutionem apostolicae sedis commentarii,* p. 13.

[28] Michiels, *De delictis et poenis,* I, 329; Blat, *Commentarium,* V, 35; Lega, *De delictis et poenis,* p. 80; Roberti, p. 222; Wernz-Vidal, *Ius canonicum,* VII, 143; Suarez, *De censuris,* dis. 21, sec. 2, n. 27.

[29] Thus adultery or blasphemy would be excluded—Wernz-Vidal, *ibid.,* note 35; Lega, *loc. cit.*

[30] Habitual use of reason, not actual use, is required—Wernz-Vidal, *ibid.,* note 36; Roberti, *loc. cit.*

[31] "Ratum quis habere non potest quod suo nomine non est gestum."—Reg. 9, R. J., in VI°.

[32] Michiels, *De delictis et poenis,* I, 328; Pistocchi, *art. cit.*—*Mon. Eccl.* XLVII (1935), 237.

Code.[33] In that period, nevertheless, by express legislation ratification was, in several of the more atrocious crimes, given a status equivalent to mandate.[34]

Only when ratification is given to a permanent crime, as in simony, does it become true cooperation, but in that case the crime is not *plene absolutum*. The ratification thus given will then have to be considered according to the rule of canon 2209, §§ 3-4.[35] But even in this case the guilt and consequently also any *latae sententiae* punishment become operative *ex nunc*, from the moment of ratification, and not *ex tunc*, from the inception of the crime;[36] for fiction of law has no place in penal matters.[37]

Various types of subsequent cooperation have been reviewed. It must now be noted that in all types, the aid or support rendered must be explicit. In other words, it must be given in view of the crime already committed, so that the cooperator acts knowingly and willingly. This is sometimes contained in the nature of the action, as in praise of the crime or in ratification. But this is not true of participation in the fruits or of sheltering the criminal. Hence the

[33] Wernz, *Ius poenale*, p. 64.

[34] "Quum quis absque tuo mandato manus iniicit in clericum tuo nomine violentas si hoc ratum habueris: excommunicationem a canone incunctanter incurris, quum ratihabitio retrotrahatur, et mandato debeat comparari."—c. 23, *de sententia excommunicationis, suspensionis, et interdicti*, V, 11, in VI°. Cf. c. 5, *de poenis*, V, 9, in VI° (ratification of violence or constraint imposed on cardinals); c. 1, *de poenis*, V, 8, in Clem. (ratification of violence or constraint imposed on bishops). Although Boniface VIII quoted *regula iuris* 10 with regard to retroaction, which properly has regard to civil, not criminal, affairs (Roberti, p. 222), this rule was not applied in full rigor—"Et ratihabitione praedicta. Dico ergo eum excommunicatum ex nunc, scilicit ex quo ratum habuit, non ex tunc quo fuit facta iniectio [manuum], licet jure dicatur ratihabitionem retrotrahi: quia satis trahitur ad tempus anterius cum ex facto anteriori ligat, licet ex nunc: nec enim sententia excommunicationis trahitur retro, sicut aliae sententiae."—Ioannes Andreae, *glossa* ad c. 23, *de sententia excommunicationis, suspensionis, et interdicti*, V, 11, in VI°, v. *Incurris*.

[35] Roberti, p. 223.

[36] Cf. Michiels, *De delictis et poenis*, I, 328- 329; Wernz, *Ius poenale*, p. 64; Wernz-Vidal, *Ius canonicum*, VII, 143.

[37] Wernz, *loc. cit.*; Wernz-Vidal, *loc. cit.*

person must know that he is accepting the fruits of a crime, or that he is sheltering the criminal as an ecclesiastical delinquent, not as a relative, a friend, or a criminal of the state.[38]

All types of subsequent cooperation may be made separate crimes in themselves if punished with a penalty by law—*nova delicta constituere possunt, si nempe poena in lege plectantur.*[39] This provision is inserted by the legislator more for the sake of clarity than for reasons of legislation. It is by no means necessary to state by statute that subsequent cooperation presents matter for legislation. All types of cooperation and, in fact, all anti-social actions may be specifically repressed by legal sanctions. There is no need of a statement in the law itself concerning their liability to punishment. But such a statement here points to the one possible basis of canonical guilt with regard to subsequent cooperation. Outside of specific legislation,[40] there is no responsibility before the law for acts done in favor of the delinquent after the crime has been committed.

This is made clear in the canon itself. Such acts impose no legal

[38] D'Annibale, *In constitutionem apostolicae sedis commentarii*, p. 13; cf. Latini, pp. 160-161; Lega, *De delictis et poenis*, p. 80; Blat, *Commentarium*, V, 35.

[39] Salucci holds the opinion that even when there is a law penalizing a certain form of subsequent cooperation no act should be considered as coming under the law unless the act was agreed upon before the commission of the principal crime—*Il Diritto Penale*, I, 42. According to this view, subsequent cooperation would, in every case, be formal cooperation. Canon 2209, § 7 distinguishes between the two. It is, of course, possible that the same act may contract a multiple guilt from several different sources—because it is at once an act of formal cooperation, agreed upon previously to the crime, and an act of subsequent aid, forbidden under penalty by specific legislation. But according to the canon cited it is not necessary that subsequent cooperation be formal cooperation—Coronata, *Institutiones*, IV, 53, note 7.

[40] Instances of acts of subsequent cooperation which have been made special crimes by specific legislation are: the defense of certain forbidden books, as outlined in canon 2318, § 1; the knowing admission by clerics of a *vitandus* excommunicate to divine offices, as considered in canon 2338, § 2; the absolution of an accomplice in a sin of impurity, described by canon 2367; the knowing omission of denunciation of a confessor guilty of solicitation, as treated in canon 2368, § 2.

responsibility — *non secumferunt delicti patrati imputabilitatem.*[41] Insofar as the subsequent cooperator has had neither the intention of cooperating in the delict nor any influence upon the effect, he cannot be held guilty of the crime, even though he has given aid after the criminal action was completely finished.

The phrase—*nisi cum delinquente de illis actibus ante delictum conventum fuerit*—emphasizes that freedom from guilt is obtained only in subsequent cooperation because when an arrangement, antecedent to the crime, has been made for aid to be given after the crime, this aid, as promised, has evident influence in the commission of the crime and becomes formal cooperation.[42] This has already been discussed. It is sufficient here to point out that a previous arrangement brings aid given after the crime within the category of true cooperation, and the ensuing guilt is to be estimated accordingly.

[41] Roberti, p. 222; Wernz-Vidal, *Ius canonicum*, VII, 142.

[42] Coronata, *Institutiones*, IV, 53; Eichmann, *Das Strafrecht des Codex iuris canonici*, pp. 47-48.

Chapter Sixteen

THE CONSEQUENCES OF GUILT DERIVING FROM COOPERATION IN CRIME

From the fact of responsibility for a criminal act, as this is determined by law in the case of cooperation in crime, arises a double juridical burden: liability for damages and subjection to punishment.[1]

Article 1. Damages

> Canon 2211. **Omnes qui in delictum concurrunt ad norman can. 2209, §§ 1-3 obligatione tenentur in solidum expensas et damna resarciendi quae ex delicto quibuslibet personis obvenerint, licet a iudice pro rata damnati.**

According to this canon only those who cooperate in the sense of canon 2209, § 1-3 are held for damages. This excludes facilitating cooperators, those who completely or partially withdraw their cooperation, negative cooperators, and subsequent cooperators.[2] But co-agents, necessary cooperators, and effective cooperators are declared liable for damages, because they are all true causes of the crime, and so each is equally responsible for the whole crime. The liability of those in canon 2209, §4-7, however, cannot be thus readily determined, since there is no general criterion by which their responsibility can be fixed. In any case, moreover, they would not be responsible for the whole crime. According to canon 2211, therefore, they escape all liability; hence, if they are held to any damages,

[1] Cf. canon 2210.

[2] Canon 2209, § 4-7; cf. Bouuaert-Simenon, *Manuale juris canonici*, III, 320; Chelodi, *Ius poenale*, p. 17; Augustine, *Commentary*, VIII, 53; Ayrinhac-Lydon, *Penal Legislation*, p. 20; Michiels, *De delictis et poenis*, I, 347; Beste, *Introductio*, pp. 886, 895; Roberti, however, would seem to include those who, in spite of partial withdrawal of cooperation, still contribute to the effectiveness of the crime according to canon 2209, § 1-3—*De delictis et poenis*, p. 241.

it will be by judicial decree. The silence of canon 2211 does not liberate such cooperators from liability for damages; insofar as they have committed a crime, their responsibility can be defined by the judge and a corresponding amount of damages fixed. But these damages will remain unaffected by the provision of canon 2211.

The liability attributed by canon 2211 is termed *in solidum*. This means that each cooperator held to damages by this canon is liable for the whole amount or any part of the whole amount which is not paid by the other cooperators.[3] This norm of canon 2211 derogates any judicial decree by which the payment of damages is apportioned among the cooperators, so that each one cooperating according to canon 2209, §§ 1-3 has the obligation of making full compensation as if he were the sole cause of the crime, whenever the others fail to pay their share.[4] As reason for this, it may be noted that all persons held to this liability are guilty of the whole crime.[5] When, however, one cooperator has made complete indemnification according to this rule, he still has the right to institute a contentious action against the other cooperators to recover the amount for which they individually had been condemned.[6]

Canon 2211 describes the recompense to be made as adequate to the expenses and the damages occasioned by the crime. The expenses to which reference is made are those incurred through the process of litigation, as the cost of conducting the trial and the counsel fees.[7] The damages arise from the destructive or despoiling effect of the unlawful action. These damages may be repaired by natural reparation when that which has been removed or injured is restored to its original state; or by pecuniary reparation, when natural restoration is impossible and a just pecuniary compensation, determined accord-

[3] Michiels, *De delictis et poenis*, I, 347-348; Sole, *De delictis et poenis*, pp. 36-37; Augustine, *Commentary*, VIII, 53-54; Ayrinhac-Lydon, Penal Legislation, p. 20; Blat, *Commentarium*, V, 39; Coronata, *Institutiones*, IV, 56; Salucci, *Il Diritto Penale*, I, 42.

[4] Michiels, *loc. cit.;* Coronata, *loc. cit.* Salucci, *Il Diritto Penale*, I, 43.

[5] Vermeersch-Creusen, *Epitome*, III, 194; Beste, *Introductio*, p. 886.

[6] Augustine, *Commentary*, VIII, 54; Cocchi, *Commentarium*, VIII, 30; cf. Genicot-Salsmans, *Institutiones theologiae moralis*, I, 468.

[7] Coronata, *Institutiones*, IV, 55.

ing to the loss inflicted and the cessation of profits, is substituted; or finally, by honorary reparation, when honor is restored by the retraction of calumny or by the offering of amends for insults.[8]

These remedies are available not only to those directly injured by the crime, but even to those indirectly injured,[9] since canon 2211 specifies that redress is open to anyone—*quibuslibet personis*—who has suffered detriment from the crime. It is necessary only to establish that harm has arisen from the crime. Accordingly, reparation is available to all who have been injured, whether the harm was intentional or not on the part of the delinquents. Besides those directly injured, moreover, those who have suffered loss through the crime's effect upon another are also to be considered. Hence those to whom are transferred the rights of those directly injured, such as heirs and creditors, may also claim indemnity insofar as their rights have been affected. These indirect claims, however, are valid only when the secondary rights to indemnification have not been renounced by those who have been directly injured, or when these rights have not otherwise ceased.[10]

Article 2. Punishment

Canon 2231. **Si plures ad delictum perpetrandum concurrerint, licet unus tantum in lege nominetur, ii quoque de quibus in can. 2209, §§ 1-3, tenentur, nisi lex aliud expresse caverit, eadem poena; ceteri vero non item, sed alia iusta poena pro prudenti Superioris arbitrio puniendi sunt, nisi lex peculiarem poenam in ipsos constituat.**

A. *Legal Penalties*

According to canon 2231, co-agents, necessary cooperators, and effective cooperators all incur the penalty for the crime, as stated in the law. Since each is a true cause of the crime, and so, guilty of

[8] Roberti, p. 240; Michiels, *De delictis et poenis*, I, 347.

[9] Blat, *Commentarium*, V, 39.

[10] Roberti, pp. 240-241; Michiels, *De delictis et poenis*, I, 347.

the whole crime according to canon 2209, §§ 1-3, each is subject to the full legal penalty. It must be recalled here that the canonical legislation determining the basis of guilt and the causes which increase or diminish guilt has already been applied since it is postulated by canon 2231 that the cooperators are guilty according to canon 2209, §§ 1-3. But besides this, since there is now question of applying a penalty, the legislation governing the requisites for incurring penalties and the causes excusing from them must also be considered. Thus in a group of cooperators, who, as causes of the crime, are canonically responsible for it, not everyone will invariably incur the legal penalty. Differences in the apportionment of penalties among cooperators can occur from three sources: the nature of the penalty, the will of the superior, and the status of the subject.

1. *Differences consequent upon the nature of the penalty.* When the legal punishment is a vindictive penalty,[11] the distribution of this penalty among the guilty cooperators will usually be more uniform than in the case of censures.[12] In the former case only a morally imputable participation in the violation of the law is required; in the latter, contumacy[13] is also necessary. Should the contumacy cease before the penalty is incurred, the censure is not incurred according to the practical opinion, already explained, even though the act should thereafter be completed and help in effecting the crime. Moreover, a censure must be absolved when contumacy has ceased to exist;[14] the vindictive penalty, on the other hand, must run its course unless the superior should deign to grant a dispensation.[15]

[11] Canon 2286.

[12] Canon 2241, § 1.

[13] Canon 2242, § 2; Swoboda, *Ignorance in Relation to the Imputability of Delicts*, pp. 171-173; Noldin-Schoenegger, *De poenis ecclesiasticis*, p. 12; Crnica, *Modificationes in tractatu de censuris per codicem iuris canonici introductae*, p. 36; Chelodi, *Ius poenale*, p. 37. Raus expresses the opinion that those giving counsel incur censures only when mentioned in the law—*Institutiones canonicae* (2. ed., Lugduni-Parisiis: Emmanuelis Vitte, 1931), p. 692. This is contrary to canon 2231 and the common teaching of canonists.

[14] Canon 2248, § 2. "[absolutio] cum sit actus justitiae, concedi debet"—Bouuaert-Simenon, *Manuale juris canonici*, III, 344.

[15] Canon 2289.

Another reason for the unequal distribution of penalties among cooperators is the following consideration. *Latae sententiae* penalties are incurred automatically upon the commission of the crime, and so, in the absence of excusing causes, are meted out invariably to all the primary cooperators. But the *ferendae sententiae* penalties must be imposed in each case by the competent judge or superior. Accordingly, the guilt of the cooperator must be proved in court or be evident to the superior before the *ferendae sententiae* penalty can be inflicted. Thereupon, those cooperators whose guilt is not established escape the penalty. Moreover, with regard to *latae sententiae* penalties, which bind in both *fora,* the delinquent is excused from the observance of the penalty in the external forum when the penalty cannot be observed externally without infamy, until a declarative sentence is issued.[16] Here again individual cases may require some cooperators to observe the penalty externally while permitting others to ignore the external observance of the penalty, at least until the issuance of a declarative sentence.

Furthermore, there are penalties applicable only to certain persons; accordingly, when a crime is so punished, only the persons liable to the special penalty incur it, the other cooperators, of course, escaping the stated penalty. Thus suspension and the vindictive penalties peculiar to clerics[17] affect only clerics. There are, moreover, penalties which refer exclusively to the one directly contemplated by the law, e. g., the privation of both offices when a cleric presumes to accept a second office incompatible with the first;[18] suspension from the confering of orders;[19] privation of the fruits of a benefice, a dignity, or an office, or privation of the benefice, the office, or the dignity itself;[20] privation of the cardinalate;[21] and privation of the episcopacy.[22] Should there be cooperation in any of the crimes which are so penalized, the cooperators cannot be punished

[16] Canon 2232, § 1.
[17] Canon 2298.
[18] Canon 2396.
[19] Canon 2373.
[20] Canon 2381, n. 1, n. 2; 2384.
[21] Canon 2397.
[22] Canon 2398.

with penalties which are restricted to one person or one class of persons; so unless the canon in question contains other penalties applicable to them, these cooperators, not contemplated by the law, will escape all penalty.[23] Here, evidently, is a *lacuna legis,* since these cooperators are not within the meaning of the *ceteri vero non item* of canon 2231, who are subject to discretionary penalties. At present, only the cooperators detailed in canon 2209, §§ 1-3 are under consideration; later, the other cooperators will be discussed in connection with discretionary penalties. If, therefore, the cooperators according to canon 2209, §§ 1-3 are not capable of receiving the penalty stated in the law for the perpetrator of the crime, they escape all penalty, since the norm reserved by canon 2231 for the other cooperators is not to be applied to them.[24]

2. *Differences consequent upon the will of the superior.* The legislator in adding a penalty to a law can specify a penalty for certain classes of cooperators, while making no provision for other classes. This circumvents the usual norm of canon 2231 wherein it is stated that although only one be named in the law, nevertheless, all who have cooperated in the sense of canon 2209, §§ 1-3 are subject to the same penalty, unless the law expressly declares otherwise. The superior can, therefore, restrict the extension of the penalty by an express definition of its limitations. A similar effect may be attained, as has been seen, through the choice of penalties which are capable of application to only a particular class of cooperators.[25]

Under certain conditions, moreover, the judge has the power to apply the full penalty or to lessen it, to defer the penalty for a time, to refrain from inflicting the penalty, and finally, to commute the penalty to a penal remedy or penance.[26] This allows the judge scope in varying the penalty among cooperators, all of whom may

[23] Cf. Ciprotti, "De delicto retentionis officiorum incompatibilium"—*Apollinaris,* IX (1936), 54-55. Since only determinate penalties are discussed in this article, the possible use of canon 2222 is not adverted to; this will be considered in the following article of this chapter.

[24] Canon 2219, § 3.

[25] E. g., canons 2395; 2400.

[26] Canon 2223, §§ 1-3.

be equally guilty but differing in conditions of past offenses, repentance, and amendment. Sometimes, however, such modification of the penalty will depend upon the varying degrees of certitude regarding guilt reached by the judge in the case of the individual cooperators.[27]

3. *Differences consequent upon the status of the subject.* Unless they are expressly named, cardinals are not comprehended under the penal law, nor are bishops with reference to *latae sententiae* penalties of suspension and interdict.[28] Moreover, penalties can be inflicted and declared by judicial decree only by the Pope as binding the following:[29] the rulers of nations, their children and immediate successors, cardinals, legates of the Holy See, and all bishops, even titu-

[27] Cf. S.C.C. "Incriminationis", 31 iul., 1915—*AAS*, VIII (1916), 9-10; in this case, certain cooperators received a deferred sentence because the proof against them was less clear than the proof against their associates. With regard to the internal forum, these observations may be added. In case of doubt the confessor is, as was suggested before the Code, to decide if a censure has been incurred: "quare ad dignoscendum in foro conscientiae, utrum quis censuras incurrerit, discutienda est per confessarium uniuscujusque conscientia"—Joder, "Index casuum et censurarum in universa Ecclesia jure novissimo vigentium"—*Archiv fuer katholisches Kirchenrecht*, LXXIV (1895), 22. If the confessor absolves from censure while in error, the absolution is valid unless imparted under the condition *si preces veritate nitantur*: "Et si absolvens falso iudicet causes allatas esse veras, seu omnes conditiones necessarias adesse, cum de facto non adsint, et absolutionem impertiatur, non videtur quare ipsa dicenda non sit valida, nisi excipias casum, in quo ipse conditionem apponat: si preces veritate nitantur."—Crnica, *Modificationes in tractatu de censuris per codicem iuris canonici introductae*, p. 60; cf. canon 2242, § 3. Hence, even in cases where the cooperators are not held to the observance of the censure in the external forum, there can still be modifications of the penalty insofar as the confessor may decide that in certain cases the censure has been incurred, or may grant absolution to one cooperator sooner than to others even by error. It may be noted with regard to the first observation made that the only doubt to be settled by the confessor in relation to censures is subjective doubt on the part of the penitent; for if the doubt be objective, the censure cannot be incurred—cf. canons 2228, 2233; 2242, § 1.

[28] Canon 2227, § 3.

[29] Canons 2227, § 1; 1557, § 1.

lar. Boys under 14 years of age and girls under 12 [30] are excused from *latae sententiae* penalties, while those over this age-limit who have induced them to violate the law or who have cooperated with them in the sense of canon 2209, §§ 1-3, incur the legal penalty.[31]

[30] Canon 88; Dalpiaz, "De cadaverum crematione" — *Apollinaris,* VII (1934), 252-253; Berutti, "Utrum omnes minores a poenis latae sententiae eximantur usque ad expletum XIV aetatis annum"—*Jus Pontificium,* XVI (1936), 26-37; Blat, *Commentarium,* V, 74: Salucci, *Il Diritto Penale,* I, 147 note 1; Augustine, *Commentary,* VIII, 101; Ayrinhac-Lydon, *Penal Legislation,* p. 43; Cavigioli, *De censuris latae sententiae,* p. 21; Cerato, *Censurae vigentes,* p. 19; Chelodi, *Ius poenale,* p. 12 note 3; Ojetti, *Commentarium in codicem iuris canonici* (4 vols., Romae: Universitas Gregoriana, 1927-1931), II, 19-23; Maroto, *Institutiones iuris canonici* (2 vols., Romae: Apud Commentarium pro Religiosis, Vol. I, 3. ed., 1921; Vol. II, 1919), I, 493, 495; Schaefer, *De religiosis,* p. 986; Raus, *Institutiones canonicae,* p. 691. Some authors, invoking canon 6, state that in this matter the age of 14 applies to girls as well as to boys, since this opinion was held by some pre-Code canonists as Reiffenstuel (*Ius canonicum universum* [ed. novissima, 5 vols., Romae, 1831-1833], lib. 5, tit. 23, n. 5), Pichler (*Ius canonicum* [2 vols., Ravennae, 1741], lib 5, tit. 23, n. 1), and Sole (*De delictis et poenis,* p. 44). This position is held by Vermeersch-Creusen (*Epitome,* II, 210), Beste (*Introductio,* p. 895), Cappello (*De censuris,* p. 19), Roberti (p. 112), De Meester (*Juris canonici et juris canonico-civilis compendium* [nova ed., 3 vols. in 4, Brugis: Desclée, De Brouwer et Si, 1921-1928], IV, 155), Bouuaert-Simenon (*Manuale,* III, 333), Cocchi (*Commentarium in codicem iuris canonici* [5 vols. in 8, Taurinorum Augustae: Marietti, Vol. I, 5. ed., 1938; Vols. II-VIII, 4. ed., 1937], V. 74), Michiels (*Principia generalia de personis in ecclesia* [Lublin: Catholica Universitas, 1932], pp. 29-32), Sole (p. 24), and, somewhat doubtfully, also by Coronata (*Institutiones,* IV, 117 note 4). Ordinarily, it would be possible to follow the more benign opinion, but in this case there is no foundation for the application of canon 6, since, as Ojetti has demonstrated, there has never been a pre-Code *law* regarding the exemption of girls under the age of 14—*Commentarium,* II, 19-23. Accordingly, canon 6, which permits the pre-Code interpretation only in the case of the retention of the former law, is not pertinent, and the second opinion is without probability—Ojetti, *loc. cit.* Despite the psychological and jurisprudential arguments of Michiels, there is still no canonical reason to make an exception from canon 88, § 3, since as Chelodi in this regard says: "Legislator quod voluit expressit"—*Ius poenale,* p. 12 note 3.

[31] Canon 2230.

In practice, travelers (*peregrini*) are to be considered as free from the obligation to observe all particular laws, including particular penal laws, of the place in which they are staying, except those laws which provide for public order and legal solemnities.[32] The traveler is also bound to observe particular laws in the case where he is aware that scandal would result from his non-observance of the law.[33]

Regulars,[34] members of clerical institutes of simple vows who have received the privilege of exemption,[35] and nuns [36] who are not

[32] Canon 14, § 1 n. 2. Cocchi (*Commentarium*, I, 116), Maroto (*Institutiones*, I, 213), Roberti (p. 85), and Toso (*Ad codicem juris canonici commentaria minora* [5 vols., Romae: Marietti, Vol. I, 2. ed., 1921; Vols. II-V, 1927], I, 40-41) hold that *peregrini* are bound to the observance of particular penal laws, since, in their opinion, penal laws by their very nature provide for public order as required by canon 14. But Beste (*Introductio*, p. 72), Chelodi (*Ius poenale*, p. 30), Cappello (*De censuris*, p. 21), Vermeersch-Creusen (*Epitome*, III, 206-207) Crnica (*Modificationes in tractatu de censuris per codicem iuris canonici introductae*, p. 22), Ayrinhac-Lydon (*Penal Legislation*, p. 40), Sole (*De delictis et poenis*, p. 74), Cipollini (*De censuris latae sententiae*, pp. 16-17), Cavigioli (*De censuris latae sententiae*, p. 20), and, with regard to *censurae latae sententiae* but not *poenae ferendae sententiae*, Cerato (*Censurae vigentes*, pp. 19-20) exempt *peregrini* from the observance of particular penal laws except those which provide for public order or are concerned with the solemnities of acts according to canon 14, § 1 n. 2. Laws of public order are explained by Vermeersch-Creusen as laws guarding against harm to the community, rather than promoting the common good—*Epitome*, I, 63; cf. Van Hove, *De legibus*, p. 220; Cappello, *De censuris*, p. 21; Roelker, "The Traveler and the Local Statute"—*The Jurist*, II (1942), 106-116. Van Hove points out that the very basis of this controversy is itself unsettled—the end of penal laws; accordingly, while this is subject to discussion, *peregrini* cannot be held to the observance of particular penal laws except as regards public order and the solemnities of acts—*De legibus*, pp. 223-224; also, Roelker, *ibid.*, pp. 118-119. While the premise and conclusion of this matter are thus controverted, the favorable opinion may be followed in practice—canon 2219, § 1.

[33] Canon 2222; Roelker, "The Traveler and the Local Statute"—*The Jurist*, II (1942), 108-110.

[34] Canon 488, n. 7.

[35] Canon 618.

[36] Canon 488, n. 7. This case will be rare since nuns may be permitted to leave the monastery only in danger of death or of other grave harm—canon 601.

under the authority of the local ordinary,[37] are not bound to the observance of local laws and regulations except in cases specified by the common law.[38] When, however, they remain for some time [39] illegitimately outside their house, this privilege of exemption is lost and they become subject to local law.[40] But even when these religious remain outside their house legitimately they have the same obligation as the traveler to observe laws regarding public order.[41] Accordingly, exempt religious become subject to the regulations of the local ordinary in the following instances: 1) in cases specified

[37] Canon 500, § 2.

[38] Canon 615.

[39] "*Degere* supponit protractam quandam commorationem."—Vermeersch-Creusen, *Epitome*, I, 427. These authors require more than two days.—Vermeersch-Creusen, *loc. cit.*

[40] Canon 616, § 1.

[41] This obligation is not expressly adverted to by the authors who merely recite the cases of subjection to the local ordinary as related in the Code. However, it is clear that once outside the places enjoying exemption, religious cannot use their personal privilege to ignore particular laws of public order. The infraction of such laws would, according to their definition, mean the rendering of harm to the locality, not merely the failure to promote the common good. The natural law, therefore, would make exempt religious subject to local laws of public law, but this would not render them liable to penalties arising from positive law—Vermeersch-Creusen, *Epitome*, I, 63. Nevertheless, this subjection of the natural law should be indicative of the legislator's intention to include exempt religious under the rule of canon 14, § 1, n. 2. In view of canon 615, are exempt religious actually to be considered *peregrini?* The opinion offered here is in the affirmative since the conditions of canon 91 are fulfilled: 1) insofar as religious have a necessary domicile in the house in which they are stationed and a quasi-domicile in the place where they have actually resided for six months—Vermeersch-Creusen, *Epitome*, I, 120; 2) insofar as, for the purpose of subjection to particular law, exempt religious are outside their domicile when they go beyond their own house or territory; they, therefore, fulfill the definition of *peregrini*. Exempt religious are, therefore, by virtue of positive law, subject to local laws of public order and liable to punishments attached to these laws—canon 2226, § 1. Thus the condition of *peregrini* is to be considered as one of the cases expressed in the law, as related in canon 615, in which regulars are subject to the jurisdiction of the ordinary of the place. Otherwise, canon 615 would be interpreted as granting a privilege against the natural law.

by law;[42] 2) while remaining outside their house illegitimately for more than two days; 3) when outside their own house or territory if they are confronted with a local law of public order.

In view, therefore, of the rules just expressed regarding the exemption of certain persons from the penalty of the law and the reservation of judgment in certain cases to the Roman Pontiff, one can easily conceive of acts of natural cooperation among persons subject to the penalty of the law and other persons favored by some exemption. In these cases, there will be a difference in the distribution of penalties, even though all concerned are guilty to the same degree, morally.

This section, concerned with the legal penalties of cooperators, has shown that although the accomplices who are guilty according to canon 2209, §§ 1-3 incur the penalty as stated in the law for the perpetrator of the crime, nevertheless, there are, according to the law itself, many variations and exemptions of the stated penalty. These different modes of treating similar cooperators are due to three juridical considerations: the nature of the penalty, the will of the superior, and the status of the subject.

B. *Discretionary Penalties*

Canon 2231 applies a penalty determined in the law to those who cooperate in the sense of canon 2209, §§ 1-3; the other cooperators (*ceteri*) are rendered liable to indeterminate penalties at the discretion of the superior. In this latter group belong, as has been previously indicated, all cooperators referred to in canon 2209, § 4-7.[43] This would include facilitating cooperators, those who only partially had withdrawn their cooperation, negative cooperators, and subsequent cooperators. This list must, however, be revised insofar as subsequent cooperators, by express provision of canon 2209, § 7,

[42] Esswein gives a list of those matters in which by common law exempt religious are subject to the local ordinary—*The Extrajudicial Coercive Powers of Ecclesiastical Superiors*, pp. 89-91; also, but less completely, Chelodi, *Ius poenale*, p. 28 note 1, and Cappello, *De censuris*, p. 24.

[43] Cf. *supra* chapter 13, article 3; also Augustine, *Commentary*, VIII, 102; Blat, *Commentarium*, V, 76; De Meester, *Compendium*, IV, 155-156.

are to be punished only when the action performed by them, apart from any previous pact with the principal delinquent, is specifically punished in the law. This, in fact, agrees with the condition upon which the provision of canon 2231 is based—*Si plures ad delictum perpetrandum concurrerint.* In the case of subsequent cooperators there is no influence, even of a negative type, upon the crime, since the crime is complete in itself at the time when the subsequent cooperation is initiated. Hence only those are liable to the discretionary penalties of canon 2231 who are facilitating cooperators, cooperators who have made only partial withdrawal of cooperation, and negative cooperators.

Nevertheless, a question may be raised concerning negative cooperators. Are they also to be included under the term *ceteri* even though there is no formal cooperation attributed to them? It is to be noted that canon 2231 does not require positive acts of cooperation. The unqualified condition—*Si plures ad delictum perpetrandum concurrerint*—comprises negative cooperators, as may be seen from a comparison with canon 2209, § 6—*Qui in delictum concurrit suum dumtaxat officium negligendo.* Negative cooperators are, therefore, to be included in the list of the accomplices punishable with an indeterminate penalty at the discretion of the superior. Such punishment must, however, be done with due regard for canon 2209, § 6 which states that the guilt of these cooperators is proportionate to the obligation by which they are obliged by their office to impede the crime. By virtue of canon 2231, therefore, neglect of office as explained in canon 2209, § 6 becomes a canonical delict, with an indeterminate canonical sanction.

The punishment itself is left undefined. Nothing is determined in this regard other than liability to punishment according to the prudent judgment of the superior. There is no prescription demanding that any punishment be, in fact, applied. Penal capacity is described by the canon; the imposition of any actual punishment depends upon the superior.[44] This is true not only as to the application of penalties, but also as to the kind and the quantity of pun-

[44] Canon 2223, § 2.

ishment. The only requisite exacted by canon 2231 is that the punishment be other than the penalty determined in the law and that it be just—*alia iusta poena*. By this requirement it is evident that the penalties at the disposal of the superior in these cases must be at least less [45] in punitive value than the penalty of the law. This latter penalty is defined, by the proper canon, for the perpetrator of the crime, and is extended by canon 2231 to co-agents, necessary cooperators, and effective cooperators in the same crime, all of whom are juridically considered true causes of the crime. It would run counter to the mind of the legislator [46] to punish with greater penalties those who have had a minor part in the crime, as the facilitating cooperators, those who have, to some extent, withdrawn their cooperation, and the negative cooperators. Accordingly, these discretionary penalties must be less than the legal penalties. This is the maximum limit. The quality of justice, further stipulated, requires additionally that there be a proportion between the offense and the penalty.[47] This interpretation is confirmed by the words of canon 2231—*pro prudenti Superioris arbitrio*.

The situation sometimes arises in which the legal penalty cannot be applied to anyone, even a co-agent, other than the delinquent contemplated directly by the law. The solution to this problem has already been expounded in regard to the primary cooperators. But a new difficulty now arises. Since the penalty is incapable of application the cooperators according to canon 2209, §§ 1-3 escape all punishment due them according to the norm of canon 2231. But what about the remaining cooperators, who according to canon 2231 are to receive other just penalties at the discretion of the superior? Ciprotti [48] makes the point that the application of canon 2231 would be incongruous, since the condition of the secondary cooperators would be worse than that of the primary cooperators, insofar as the former could always be punished according to canon 2231 whereas

[45] Ciprotti, "De delicto retentionis officiorum incompatibilium"—*Apollinaris*, IX (1936), 54.

[46] Cf. canon 18.

[47] Wernz-Vidal, *Ius canonicum*, VII, 196, 211.

[48] "De delicto retentionis officiorum incompatibilium"—*Apollinaris*, IX (1936), 54-55.

the latter, the primary cooperators, could be punished only when scandal or the special gravity of the transgression so warrant.[49] The idea of other just penalties, therefore, demonstrates that canon 2231 seems to be unable to operate even in the case of secondary cooperators.

CONCLUSIONS

1. The canonical guilt due to cooperation in crime is essentially a moral imputation of the crime to the accomplice because of his cooperation.

2. Cooperation in crime by way of negligence, rather than by way of intent, is restricted to cases mentioned in canons 2316 (communication *in divinis* with heretics); 2324; 2348; 2370; 2373; 2381, n. 1; 2384; 2394, nn. 1, 3; 2398; 2404; 2408; 2411; 2412, n. 2; 2357 (sexual crimes committed with minors under sixteen years of age). Whether cooperation has actually occurred in any of these crimes must be determined from the facts of the case.

3. Since, co-agents, considered in canon 2209, § 1, must concur physically in the crime, and since they do this by performing executive or consummating physical acts, then the physical deficiency of the external act cannot be supplied by an executive moral act. Thus, the person who gave sufficient moral cooperation to be held by canon 2209, § 3 and, in addition, lent some slight physical aid would not be considered as physically concurring in the sense of canon 2209, § 1. Such a person would remain subject to canon 2209, § 3.

4. Only those who perform executive or consummating physical acts in concerted action are cooperators in the sense of canon 2209, § 1. By concerted action is meant either simultaneity of action or the explicit integration of successive cooperation so as to effect, of itself, the crime. This is the meaning of the words, *Qui communi delinquendi consilio simul physice concurrunt in delictum.*

5. Thus the complete cooperation of canon 2209, § 1 can be adequately distinguished from partial cooperation through physical

[49] Canon 2222.

aid, not by the intentions of the cooperators, but by the nature of their acts. Those who perform executive physical acts outside of concerted action or those who perform merely preparatory physical acts are subject to canon 2209, § 3 or § 4, whereas those who perform executive or consummating acts in concerted action are the co-agents of canon 2209, § 1. This positivist criterion is of great importance in the external forum since once the nature of the act and the presence or absence of concerted action is established the category of the cooperation is known without recourse to a subjective norm such as intent. The *dolus* may then be presumed with the performance of the external act in virtue of canon 2200, § 2.

6. There is no need of recourse to canon 2209, § 2 to establish the guilt of necessary cooperation when the law itself expressly names the cooperators, nor can the cited canon be invoked when the phraseology of the law restricts the delict to one member of what would ordinarily be necessary cooperation. There is, however, in this latter case a possible application of canon 2209, § 3 or § 4.

7. If the crime as mandated is not performed, but rather, if a lesser crime is substituted for it by the mandatary, this substituted crime is not to be ascribed to the one issuing the original mandate, except, possibly, by way of negligence, certainly, never by way of intent.

8. By interpreting, with regard to non-moral cooperation, the condition of canon 2209, § 3: *Si delictum sine eorum opera commissum non fuisset,* according to Heimberger and Michiels, as, *if without their work the crime could not have been committed,* one realizes more completely than by the usual factual interpretation the meanings of canon 2209, § 3 and § 4, and reduces to practicality the discrimination of effective physical cooperation and facilitating physical cooperation, besides following the canonical norm of restrictive interpretation in penal matters.

9. Incomplete withdrawal of cooperation is defined as any external effort, short of actual success, to render one's cooperation inefficacious, provided that this effort be made before the consummation of the crime. It is not necessary that the external effort actually

diminish the effect of the cooperation upon the commission of the crime but only that the effort be made earnestly, not fraudulently.

10. Accordingly, the concept of partial withdrawal of cooperation can be verified even in cases wherein it is intrinsically or extrinsically impossible to offset the cooperation already given.

11. Canonists have already decided that in cases of those committing the crime of abortion if repentance should remove contumacy before the consummation of the crime no censure is incurred. This doctrine is here applied to cooperation in any crime punished with *latae sententiae* censures. Thus, if the cooperator repents of his act so as to cease being contumacious before the consummation of the crime he will not incur the censure.

12. Ordinaries and religious superiors have the general duty of preventing all crimes so that if a crime be committed upon the occasion of their neglect and with some actual advantage from this neglect the ordinaries and the religious superiors are comprehended in the meaning of canon 2209, § 6.

13. Neglect of office in the sense of canon 2209, § 6 can arise in the case of ordinaries and religious superiors with regard to failure of vigilance, non-observance of the rules of residence and of visitation, failure to take due preventive measures.

14. Among the particular duties, the neglect of which can entail the guilt mentioned in canon 2209, § 6 are the care of the cloister and the exploration of the will in candidates to religious societies of women imposed upon local ordinaries and certain religious superiors; the duty of the metropolitan to report to the Holy See if a suffragan bishop should fall into excommunication, interdict, or suspension; the custody of the diocesan archives; vigilance as required of the vicar forane; the custody of the Blessed Sacrament, of the Holy Oils, and the care of the church; the pre-nuptial investigation; the obligation of the porter in refusing externs admittance to the cloister and in expelling those already admitted; the authentication of sacred relics.

15. Even when cooperators are morally guilty in the sense of canon 2209, §§ 1-3, they do not all necessarily receive the same

punishment as the perpetrator of the crime in accord with canon 2231 since the law itself has made several exceptions and variations of this penalty. These exceptions and variations are specifically described in chapter 16, article 2, section A. Those cooperators, however, who are not favored by these provisions, nonetheless receive the penalty as stated in the law.

16. Those cooperating in the sense of canon 2209, §§ 1-3 with regard to the crimes described in canons 2373; 2381, nn. 1-2; 2384; 2390; 2397; 2398 cannot be subjected to the same penalty as the perpetrator of the crime in accord with canon 2231 since these crimes are punished with penalties applicable only to the perpetrators. In these cases the cooperators escape all penalty, except as regards canon 2222. Similarly, only clerical cooperators in crimes punished by suspension and the vindictive penalties peculiar to clerics are subject to the penalty stated in the law.

17. When a traveler (*peregrinus*) cooperates in a crime against a local law, he is not to be punished unless the law is a matter of public order.

18. Exempt religious have the same obligation as travelers to observe particular laws of public order. Cooperating in crimes against such laws they immediately become subject to the stated penalty.

19. By virtue of the indeterminate canonical sanction of canon 2231 negative cooperation—or, the neglect of office upon the occasion of which and with the aid of which a crime has been committed, according to canon 2209, § 6—becomes a canonical delict. Canon 2209, § 6 merely states the degree of guilt; canon 2231 adds the indeterminate penalty required in canon 2195, § 1 to constitute a delict. A compilation of the possible forms of this new delict may be seen in conclusions 13 and 14.

BIBLIOGRAPHY

Sources

Acta Apostolicae Sedis, Commentarium Officiale, Romae, 1909-

Acta Sanctae Sedis, 41 vols., Romae, 1865-1908.

Bouscaren, T. Lincoln, *The Canon Law Digest*, 2 vols. and Supplement—1941, Milwaukee: Bruce, 1934-1941.

Bullarum Diplomatum et Privilegiorum Romanorum Pontificum Taurinensis Editio, 25 vols., Augustae Taurinorum, 1857-1872.

Canones et Decreta Sacrosancti Oecumenici Concilii Tridentini, Romae: ex typographia polyglotta S. C. de Propaganda Fide, 1882.

Codex Iuris Canonici Pii X Pontificis Maximi iussu digestus Benedicti Papae XV auctoritate promulgatus, Romae: Typis Polyglottis Vaticanis, 1917.

Codicis Dn. Ivstiniani Sacratissimi Principis ex Repetita Praelectione libri novem Priores, Lugduni, 1553.

Codicis Iuris Canonici Fontes cura Emi. Petri Card. Gasparri Editi, 9 vols., Romae (postea Civitate Vaticana): Typis Polyglottis Vaticanis, 1923-1939. (Vol. VII, VIII et IX ed. cura et studio Emi. Iustiniani Card. Serédi).

Corpus Iuris Canonici, ed. Lipsiensis 2., Aemilius Ludouicus Richter—Aemilius Friedberg, ed. anastatice repetita, 2 vols., Lipsiae: Tauchnitz, 1928.

Corpus Iuris Civilis, 3 vols., Berolini, 1928-1929.

Institutiones, quas recognovit Paulus Krueger;

Digesta, quae recognovit Theodorus Mommsen retractavit Paulus Krueger;

Codex Iustinianus, quem recognovit et retractavit Paulus Krueger;

Novellae, quas recognovit Rudolfus Schoell, et absolvit Guilelmus Kroll.

Decretales D. Gregorii Papae IX, una cum Glossis Restitutae, Romae, 1582.

Decretum Gratiani emendatum et notationibus Illustratum una cum Glossis, Gregorii XIII Pont. Max. iussu editum, 2 vols., Romae, 1582.

Digestum Vetus, Infortiatum, Digestum Novum, 3 vols., Lugduni, 1556-1557.

Fontes Iuris Romani Antejustiniani, Pars Prima, ed. Salvator Riccobono, Florentiae, 1909.

Friedberg, Aemilius, *Quinque Compilationes Antiquae*, Lipsiae, 1882.

Hinschius, Paulus, *Decretales pseudo-Isidorianae et capitula Angilrami*, Lipsiae, 1863.

Institutionum D. Iustiniani sacratissimi Imperatoris Libri Quatuor, Lugduni, 1553.

Jaffé, Philippus, *Regesta Pontificum Romanorum ab condita ecclesia ad annum post Christum natum MCXCVIII*, 2. ed. curaverunt S. Loewenfeld, F. Kaltenbrunner, P. Ewald, 2 vols. in 1, Lipsiae, 1885-1888.

Liber Sextus Decretalium, una cum Clementinis et Extravagantibus Earumque Glossis Restitutis, Romae, 1582.

Mansi, Ioannes, *Sacrorum Conciliorum Nova et Amplissima Collectio,* 53 vols. in 60, Paris, 1901-1927.

Migne, Jacques Paul, *Patrologiae Cursus Completus, Series Graeca,* 161 vols., Parisiis, 1856-1866.

——————, *Patrologiae Cursus Completus, Series Latina,* 221 vols., Parisiis, 1844-1864.

Monumenta Germaniae Historica,

Epistolae, II, pars II, *Gregorii I Papae Registrum Epistolarum,* ed L. M. Hartmann, Berolini, 1899.

Epistolae, III, tom. I, Epistolae Merowingici et Karolini Aevi (*S. Bonifatii et Lulli Epistolae,* ed. E. Dummler), Berolini, 1892.

Legum Sectio, I, tom. I, *Leges Visigothorum,* ed. K. Zeumer, Hannoverae et Lipsiae, 1902.

Legum Sectio, I, tom. II, pars I, *Leges Burgundionum,* ed. L. R. de Salis, Hannoverae, 1892.

Legum Sectio, I, tom. V, pars I, *Leges Alamannorum,* ed. K. Lehmann, Hannoverae, 1888.

Legum Sectio, II, tom. I, *Capitularia Regum Francorum,* ed. A. Boretino, Hannoverae, 1883.

Scriptores, VII, *Chronica Monasterii Casinensis,* ed. W. Wattenbach, Hannoverae, 1846.

Potthast, Augustus, *Regesta Pontificum Romanorum inde ab A. post Christum natum 1198 ad A. 1304,* 2 vols., Berolini, 1874-1875.

S. Romanae Rotae Decisiones seu Sententiae (ab anno 1909), Romae, 1912-

Thiel, Andreas, *Epistolae Romanae Pontificum Genuinae et quae ad eos scriptae sunt a S. Hilario usque ad Pelagium II,* Brunsbergae, 1868.

Reference Works

Aertnys, Josephus, *Theologia Moralis,* 7. ed., 2 vols., Paderbornae, 1906.

Alphonsus de Liguori, S., *Theologia moralis,* nova ed., 9 vols. in 4, Vensuntione, 1828.

Augustine [Bachofen], Charles, *A Commentary on Canon Law,* 8 vols., Vol. VIII, 3. ed., St. Louis: Herder, 1931.

Ayrinhac, H. A., and Lydon, P. J., *Penal Legislation in the New Code of Canon Law,* New York: Benziger Brothers, 1936.

Bartolus a Saxoferrato, *Omnia quae extant opera,* 10 vols., Venetiis, 1590.

Batiffol, Pierre, *Etudes d'Histoire et de Théologie Positive,* 1re serie, 4. ed., 2 vols., Paris, 1906; "Les Origines de la Pénitence," Vol. I, pp. 45-222.

Bernardus Guidonis, *Practica Inquisitionis Heretice Pravitatis,* ed. C. Douais, Paris, 1886.

Berutti, Christophorus, *Institutiones iuris canonici*, Vol. VI, *De delictis et poenis*, Taurini-Romae: Marietti, 1938.

Beste, Udalricus, *Introductio in codicem*, Collegeville, Minn.: St. John's Abbey Press, 1938.

Blat, Albertus, *Commentarium textus codicis iuris canonici*, *Liber V*, *De delictis et poenis*, Romae: Collegio Angelico, 1924.

Bonacina, Martinus, *Opera omnia*, Venetiis, 1687.

Bouuaert, F. Claeys, et Simenon, G., *Manuale juris canonici*, 3 vols., Gandae et Leodii: Prostat apud auctores in Seminariis Gandavensi et Leodiensi, Vols. I et III, 3. ed., 1930-1931; Vol. II, 1931.

Brunner, Heinrich, *Deutsche Rechtsgeschichte*, 2. ed., 2 vols., Leipzig und Muenchen: Verlag von Duncker & Humblot, 1906-1928.

Buckland, W. W., *A Text-book of Roman Law from Augustus to Justinian*, Cambridge: University Press, 1921.

Busenbaum, Hermanus, *Medulla theologiae moralis*, ed. novissima, Venetiis, 1688.

Cappello, Felix M., *Tractatus canonico-moralis de censuris*, 2. ed., Taurinorum Augustae: Marietti, 1925.

Cavigioli, Joannes, *De censuris latae sententia quae in Codice Iuris Canonici continentur commentarium*, Torino: Libreria Editrice Internazionale, 1918.

Cerato, Prosdocimus, *Censurae vigentes ipso facto a codice iuris canonici excerptae*, 2. ed., Patavii: Typis Seminarii, 1921.

Chelodi, Ioannis, *Ius de personis iuxta codicem iuris canonici*, 2. ed., Tridenti: Libr. Editr. Tridentum, 1927.

————, *Ius poenale et ordo procedendi in iudiciis criminalibus*, 4. ed., recognita et aucta a Vigilio Dalpiaz, Tridenti: Ardesi, 1935.

Chénon, Emile, *Histoire Generale du Droit Français Public et Privé des Origines à 1815*, 2 vols., Paris: Recueil Sirey, 1926-1929.

Cicognani, Amleto, *Canon Law*, authorized English version by J. O'Hara and F. Brennan, 2. ed., Philadelphia: The Dolphin Press, 1935.

Cipollini, Albertus, *De censuris latae sententiae iuxta codicem iuris canonici*, Taurini: Marietti, 1925.

Cocchi, Guidus, *Commentarium in codicem iuris canonici*, 5 vols. in 8, Taurinorum Augustae: Marietti, Vol. I, 5. ed., 1938; Vols. II-VIII, 4. ed., 1937-1938.

Coronata, Matthaeus Conte a, *Institutiones iuris canonici*, 5 vols., Taurini: Marietti, Vols. I-II, 2. ed., 1939; Vols. III-V, 1933-1936.

Crnica, Antonius, *Modificationes in tractatu de censuris per codicem iuris canonici introductae*, S. Mauritii Agaunensis: Typis Op. S. Augustini, 1919.

Dandinus, Anselmus, *De suspectis de haeresi*, Romae, 1703.

D'Annibale, Iosephus, *Summula theologiae moralis*, 3 vols., Reate, 1874.

——————, *In constitutionem apostolicae sedis commentarii*, 4. ed., Prati, 1894.

De Angelis, Franciscus, *Tractatus criminalis de delictis*, Neopoli, 1741.

De Meester, Alphonsus, *Juris canonici et juris canonico-civilis compendium*, nova ed., 3 vols. in 4, Brugis: Desclée, De Brouwer et Si, 1921-1928.

Dictionnaire Pratique des Connaissances Religieuses, Paris, Letouzey et Ané, 1925-1927.

Dreyer, W., *Die akzessorische Teilnahme*, Borna-Leipzig, 1911.

Du Cange, Charles, *Glossarium mediae et infimae latinitatis*, noveau tirage, 10 vols., Paris: Libraire des Sciences et des Artes, 1937-1938.

Eichmann, Eduard, *Das Strafrecht des Codex iuris canonici*, Paderborn, 1920.

Esswein, Anthony, *The Extrajudicial Coercive Powers of Ecclesiastical Superiors*, The Catholic University of America Canon Law Studies, n. 127, Washington, D. C.: The Catholic University of America Press, 1941.

Falchi, Giuseppino Ferrucio, *Diritto Penale Romano—Dottrine Generali*, Treviso: Vianello, 1930.

——————, *Diritto Penale Romano—I Singoli Reati*, Padova: R. Zannoni, 1932.

Ferreres, Ioannes, *Institutiones canonicae*, 2. ed., 2 vols., Barcinone, 1920.

Ferrini, Contardo, *Diritto Penale Romano*, Milano, 1899.

Funk, Francis X., *A Manual of Church History*, English translation by P. Perciballi, 2 vols., London: Burns, Oates, and Washbourne, 1931.

Genicot, Edwardus, et Salsmans, I., *Institutiones theologiae moralis*, 12. ed., 2 vols., Lovaniae: Museum Lessianum, 1931.

Gibalinus, Iosephus, *Disquisitiones canonicae de clausura regulari*, Lugduni, 1648.

Gonzalez-Tellez, Emmanuel, *Commentaria perpetua in singulos textus quinque librorum decretalium Gregorii IX*, 5 vols., Venetiis, 1699.

Gury, Jean Pierre, *Casus conscientiae*, 5. ed., 2 vols., Lugduni, 1874-1875.

Hefele, Carolus, et Leclercq, Henricus, *Histoire des Conciles*, 10 vols. in 19, Paris, 1907-1938.

Heimberger, J., *Aus dem Strafrecht des Codex Juris Canonici*, Sonderdruck aus der Bonner Festgabe fuer Ernst Zitelmann, Muenchen und Leipzig, 1923.

——————, *Die Schuld im Strafrecht des Codex Juris Canonici*, in Festgabe zum 60 Geburtstag von Gustav Aschaffenburg, Heidelberg, 1926.

Hinschius, Paul, *System des katholischen Kirchenrechts*, 6 vols., Berlin, 1869-1897.

Hollweck, Joseph, *Die kirchlichen Strafgesetze*, Mainz, 1899.

Kober, F., *Der Kirchenbann nach den Grundsaetzen des canonischen Rechts*, 2. ed., Tuebingen, 1863.

Kuttner, Stephan, *Kanonistische Schuldlehre von Gratian bis auf die Dekretalen Gregors IX*, Studi e Testi, n. 64, Città del Vaticano: Biblioteca Apostolica Vaticana, 1935.

Latini, Joseph, *Iuris criminalis philosophici summa lineamenta*, Taurini: Marietta, 1934.

Leage, R. W., and Ziegler, C. H., *Roman Private Law*, 2. ed., London: Macmillan, 1937.

Lee, Guy Carleton, *Historical Jurisprudence*, New York: Macmillan, 1900.

Lega, Michael, *De delictis et poenis*, 2. ed., Romae, 1910.

Lydon, P. J., *Ready Answers in Canon Law*, New York: Benziger Brothers, 1934.

Maroto, Philippus, *Institutiones iuris canonici*, 2 vols., Romae; Apud Commentarium pro Religiosis, Vol. I, 3. ed., 1921; Vol. II, 1919.

Majno, Luigi, *Commento al Codice penale*, 4. ristampa della terza edizione, Torino, 1924.

May's Law of Crimes, 4. ed. by Sears-Weihofen, Boston: Little, Brown, and Company, 1938.

Meier, Carl, *Penal Administrative Procedure against Negligent Pastors*, The Catholic University of America Canon Law Studies, n. 140, Washington, D. C.: The Catholic University of America Press, 1921.

Michiels, Gommarus, *Normae generales juris canonici*, Lublin: Universitas Catholica, 1929.

——————, *Principia generalia de personis in ecclesia*, Lublin, Universitas Catholica, 1932.

——————, *De delictis et poenis*, Vol. I, *De delictis*, Lublin: Universitas Catholica, 1934.

Moersdorf, Klaus, *Die Rechtssprache des Codex Juris Canonici*, Paderborn: Schoeningh, 1937.

Mommsen, Theodore, *Le Droit Penal Romain*, traduit par J. Duquesne, 3 vols., Paris, 1907.

Moriarty, Francis, *The Extraordinary Absolution from Censures*, The Catholic University of America Canon Law Studies, n. 113, Washington, D. C.: The Catholic University of America, 1938.

Morinus, Ioannes, *Commentarius historicus de disciplina in administratione sacramenti poenitentiae tredecim primis seculis in ecclesia occidentali et huc usque in oriental observata*, Parisiis, 1651.

Noldin, H., et Schoenegger, A., *De poenis ecclesiasticis*, 12. ed. (C.I.C. adaptata prima), Oeniponte, 1921.

Ojetti, B., *Commentarium in codicem iuris canonici*, 4 vols., Romae: Universitas Gregoriana, 1927-1931.

Ottaviani, Alaphridus, *Institutiones iuris publici ecclesiastici*, 2. ed., 2 vols., Romae: Typis Polyglottis Vaticanis, 1935-1936.

Panormitanus, Abbas (Nicolaus de Tudeschis), *Commentaria in quinque libros decretalium*, 5 vols. in 7, Venetiis, 1588.

Pennacchi, Ioseph, *Commentaria in constitutionem apostolicae sedis*, 2 vols., Romae, 1883.

Pichler, Vitus, *Ius canonicum*, 2 vols., Ravennae, 1741.

Raus, Joannes, *Institutiones canonicae juxta novem codicem iuris*, 2. ed., Lugduni-Parisiis: Emmanuelis Vitte, 1931.

Reiffenstuel, Anacletus, *Ius canonicum universum*, ed. novissima, 5 vols., Romae, 1831-1833.

Roberti, Franciscus, *De delictis et poenis*, 2. ed., Romae: Custodia Libraria Pontificii Utriusque Iuris, ...

Ryder, Raymond, *Simony*, The Catholic University of America Canon Law Studies, n. 65, Washington, D. C.: The Catholic University of America, 1931.

Salucci, Raffaele, *Il Diritto Penale secondo il Codice di Diritto Canonico*, 2 vols., Subiaco: Tipografia dei Monasteri, 1926-1930.

Schaefer, Timotheus, *De religiosis*, 3. ed., Romae: S.A.L.E.R., 1940.

Schmalzgrueber, Franciscus, *Jus ecclesiasticum*, 5 vols. in 12, Romae, 1843-1845.

Sherman, Charles, *Roman Law in the Modern World*, 2. ed., 3 vols., New York: Baker, Voorhis & Co., 1924.

Singer, Heinrich, *Die Summa des Magister Rufinus*, Paderborn, 1902.

Slafkosky, Andrew, *The Canonical Episcopal Visitation of the Diocese*, The Catholic University of America Canon Law Studies, n. 142, Washington, D. C.: The Catholic University of America Press, 1941.

Smith, S. B., *The New Procedure in Criminal and Disciplinary Causes of Ecclesiastics*, 2. ed., New York-Cincinnati, 1888.

Sole, Iacobus, *De delictis et poenis*, Romae: Pustet, 1920.

Stephenson, Carl, *Mediaeval History*, 2 vols., New York: Harper and Brothers, 1935.

Suarez, Franciscus, *Opera omnia*, ed. C. Berton, 26 vols., Parisiis, 1856-1866; Vol. XXIII, *De censuris in communi*.

Swoboda, Innocent, *Ignorance in Relation to the Imputability of Delicts*, The Catholic University of America Canon Law Studies, n. 143, Washington, D. C.: The Catholic University of America Press, 1941.

Thesaurus, Carolus, *De poenis ecclesiasticis praxis absoluta et universalis, cum notis et accessionibus earundem poenarum ab anno MDCLIII ad currentem usque MDCCLX inflictarum locupletata ab Ubaldo Giraldi a S. Cajetano*, Romae, 1760.

Thomas Aquinas, S., *Summa theologica*, ed. altera Romana, 6 vols., Romae, 1894.

Toso, Albertus, *Ad codicem juris canonici commentaria minora*, 5 vols., Romae: Marietti, Vol. I, 2. ed., 1921; Vols. II-V, 1927.

Vacandard, E., *L'Inquisition*, Paris, 1907.

Van Hove, A., *Commentarium Lovaniense in codicem iuris canonici*, Vol. I, Tom. I, *Prolegomena*, Mechliniae-Romae: H. Dessain, 1928; Vol. I, Tom. II, *De legibus ecclesiasticis*, Mechliniae-Romae: H. Dessain, 1930.

Vermeersch, Arthurus, *Theologiae moralis principia, responsa, consilia*, 4 vols., Romae: Universita Gregoriana, Vols. I, III, IV, 2. ed., 1926-1927; Vol. II, 1928.

Vermeersch, A., et Creusen, J., *Epitome iuris canonici*, 2. ed., 3 vols., Mechliniae: Dessain, 1924.

Wernz, Franciscus X., *Ius decretalium*, Tom. VI, *Ius poenale Ecclesiae catholicae*, Prati, 1913.

Wernz, F., et Vidal, P., *Ius canonicum*, 7 vols. in 8, Romae: Apud Aedes Universitatis Gregorianae, 1923-1938.

Articles

Baumer, A., "De iure poenali pro delinquentibus minoris aetatis in codice iuris canonici et novissimo schemate codicis poenalis helvetici"—*Apollinaris*, VI (1933), 453-495.

Berutti, Christophorus, "Utrum omnes minores a poenis latae sententiae eximantur usque ad expletum XIV aetatis annum"—*Jus Pontificium*, XVI (1936), 26-37.

Brys, J., "De poena in procurantes abortum"—*Collationes Brugenses*, XXXIV (1934), 42-46.

Ciprotti, Pius, "De delicto retentionis officiorum incompatibilium"—*Apollinaris*, IX (1936), 44-57.

Dalpiaz, V., "De cadaverum crematione"—*Apollinaris*, VII (1934), 252-253.

Goyeneche, S., "Consultationes"—*Commentarium pro Religiosis et Missionariis*, XVII (1936), 343-345.

Joder, J. Chr., "Index casuum et censurarum in universa ecclesia jure novissimo vigentium"—*Archiv fuer katholisches Kirchenrecht*, LXXIV (1895), 18-25.

Kinane, J., "Cooperators and the *ipso facto* Punishments Decreed against Crime"—*The Irish Ecclesiastical Record*, 5. Series, XXXIII (1929), 68-70.

Kuttner, Stephan, "Damasus als Glossator"—ZSS, kan. Abt., XXIII (1934), 380-390.

——————, "Eine Dekretsumme des Johannes Teutonicus" — ZSS, kan. Abt., XXI (1932), 141-189.

——————, "The Father of the Science of Canon Law"—*The Jurist*, I (1941), 141-189.

Luenenborg, "Der Versuch im Strafrecht des Codex Juris Canonici"—AKKR, CXI (1931), 369-399.

Pistocchi, Mario, "Concorso di più persone in uno stesso delitto"—*Mon. Eccl.* XLVII (1935), 226-239.

————, "L'obligazione emergente dal delitto"—*Mon. Eccl.*, XLVIII (1936), 52-54.

Roelker, Edward, "The Traveler and the Local Statute"—*The Jurist*, II (1942), 105-119.

Teodori, I., "Lectio librorum prohibitorum"—*Apollinaris*, IV (1931), 435-437.

Periodicals

Apollinaris, Romae, 1928-

Archiv fuer katholisches Kirchenrecht, Innsbruck, 1857-1861; Mainz, 1862-

Collationes Brugenses, Brugis Flandrorum, 1896-

Commentarium pro Religiosis (later, *Commentarium pro Religiosis et Missionariis*), Romae, 1920-

Irish Ecclesiastical Record, The, Dublin, 1864-

Jurist, The, Washington, D. C., 1941-

Jus Pontificium, Romae, 1921-

Monitore Ecclesiastico, Il, Romae, 1876-

Zeitschrift der Savigny-Stiftung fuer Rechtsgeschichte, kanonistische Abteilung, Weimar, 1911-

Abbreviations

AAS—*Acta Apostolicae Sedis*.

AKKR—*Archiv fuer katholisches Kirchenrecht*.

ASS—*Acta Sanctae Sedis*.

Bullarium Romanum—*Bullarum Diplomatum et Privilegiorum Sanctorum Romanorum Pontificum Taurinensis Editio*.

C.—Codex (Iustinianus).

CpRM—*Commentarium pro Religiosis et Missionariis*.

Comp.—Compilatio.

D.—Digestum (Iustinianum).

Ep.—Epistola.

Fontes—*Codicis Iuris Canonici Fontes cura . . . Gasparri editi*.

h. t.—hoc titulo, i. e., the same title as in the previous citation.

JE—Jaffé, *Regesta Pontificum Romanorum*, 2. ed., y. 590-881, revised by P. Ewald.

JK—*ibid.*, up to y. 589, revised by F. Kaltenbrunner.

JL—*ibid.*, y. 882-1198, revised by S. Loewenfeld.

Mansi—*Sacrorum Conciliorum Nova et Amplissima Collectio*.

MPG—Migne, *Patrologia Graeca*.

MPL—Migne, *Patrologia Latina*.

N.—Novellae (Iustinianae).
Mon. Eccl.—*Il Monitore Ecclesiastico.*
P. Sent.—*Iulii Pauli Libri Quinque Sententiarum ad Filium.*
S.C.C.—Sacra Congregatio Concilii.
S.C.de Rel.—Sacra Congregatio de Religiosis.
S.C. de Sacr.—Sacra Congregatio de disciplina Sacramentorum.
S.C.P.F.—Sacra Congregatio de Propaganda Fide.
S.R.R.—Sacra Romana Rota.
y.—year.
ZSS—Zeitschrift der Savigny-Stiftung.

ALPHABETICAL INDEX

Accessoriness, 69, 70, 71
Accompany, 50
Accomplices, Cf. Persons
Action,
  concerted, 91
  positive and external, 3, 67
Acts,
  executive, 75, 85, 91
  preparatory, 75, 85
Aid, 24, 52, 59, 60, 121, 163
Aid, intellectual, 110
Alanus, 56
Approbation, 54
Association, 25, 26, 27
Authority, lent to crime, 33, 54, 58, 106

Bartholomaeus Brixiensis, 56
Bartolus a Saxoferrato, 105
Believers in heresy, 50
Bernardus Parmensis de Botone, 33, 54, 55, 56, 57
Bishop, duties of, 151

Capitularia Regum Francorum, 21
Censure, 64, 80, 142
Circumstances,
  personal, 95, 96
  real, 95
Co-agents, 84, 134
Command, 18, 45, 53, 59
Common agreement, lack of, 4
Common end or purpose, 2
Common intention, lack of, 4
Common knowledge of end, or agreement, 2, 4
Common purpose, 3
Communicatio in crimine criminoso, 29, 30, 51
Communication
  with excommunicate, 28, 46, 50
  with criminal, 28

Complicity,
  Cf. Cooperation;
    defined, 1
    in strict sense, 48
    kinds of, 6
    presumed, 12, 44
    specified, 121
Contumacious, 26
Contumacy, 80, 143, 144, 171
Cooperation,
  Cf. Complicity;
    attempted, 73, 107
    effective, 63, 104, 120
    efficacious, 73
    facilitating, 123, 126
    formal, 1, 2, 3, 61, 62
    intellectual, 110, 120, 124, 126, 133
    material, 1, 4, 5, 61, 62, 100, 101
    moral, 84, 116, 118, 124, 133
    necessary, 6, 23, 34, 98
    negative, 5, 12, 40, 110, 124, 126, 133, 146, 179
    partial, 104, cf. Participation, partial
    physical, 84, 85, 92, 110, 111, 120, 124, 132
    subsequent, 5, 24, 110, 113, 124, 126, 133, 161
Cooperation in ecclesiastical law,
  abortion, 40, 59, 61, 80, 88, 93, 137, 138
  adultery, 35, 40
  alienation of church property, 37, 49
  conspiracy, 42, 44, 46, 47, 76
  disobedience, 76
  dueling, 37, 58, 59, 61, 76, 79
  forcing woman into religious life, 58

fornication, 36, 46
fraud, 58
homicide, 45
idolatry, 42
incendiarism, 45, 47
incest, 46
lay investiture, 37, 46
marriage, illicit, 46
marriage with religious, 36, 76, 99
marriage with clerics in major orders, 36, 76, 99
mutilation, 45
murder, 42, 43
pillaging, 45
plundering bishop's house, 46
perjury, 43
rape, 31, 42, 43, 45, 76, 102, 163
rebaptism, 39
remarriage after divorce, 35
removal of Sacred Species, 76
schism, 46
simony, 36, 41, 163
subordination, 76
superstition, 40
theft of ecclesiastical goods, 42

Cooperation in Roman law,
explained, 8
in crimes against life, 10
in crimes against the state, 9
in crime of price manipulation, 16
in crimes of superstition, 13
in crimes of violence, 13
in sexual crimes, 15
in damage, 18
in *iniuria*, 18
in theft, 16

Cooperative unity, 2, 3

Crime,
attempted, 67, 73, 125, 133
elements of, 2

Crimes,
accessorial, 62, 71, 121
of omission, 149
of subsequent cooperation, 166
list of, 99, 100, 101, 102, 156
requiring necessary cooperation, 101
permanent, 162
special, 121, 166

Consent, 43, 45, 48, 49, 50, 54, 121

Counsel, 24, 31, 47, 48, 53, 54, 56, 59, 62, 64, 108, 109, 125, 133, 137, 138

Counsel, non-effective, 53, 60, 125

Culpa, 11, 76, 147

Damages, 168
Damasus, 57
Defend, 49, 50, 53
Defenders, 31, 51
Defense, 54
Deliberate will, 3
Delictum, 115
Dispositions, subjective, 50, 72
Dolus, 11, 24, 77, 79, 80, 129, 147, cf. Intent, criminal

Exceptions, legal, 5, 174

Favor, 30, 31, 48, 53, 59, 60, 121, 163
Favor, non-effective, 53
Fear, 55
Friendship, 27

Germanic law,
faida, 21
fredus, 21, 26
penal system, 21

Guido de Baysio, 54
Guilt, 66, 67, 68, 69, 72, 114, 123, 127, 128, 131, 136, 138
Guilt, canonical concept of, as applied to cooperators, 66
Guilt, multiple, 166

Help, 47
Hostiensis, 56

Ignorance, 46, 55
Inciting, 50

Ioannes Andreae, 56, 57
Ioannes Galensis, 57
Ioannes Teutonicus, 54
Imputability, 66, 67, 68, 71
Intent, criminal, 4, 24, 80
Intent, criminal, in Germanic law, 24

Jurisprudence of this study, 2

Law, penal, required in formal co-operation, 3
Leges Barbarorum, 21
Lex Aquilia, 11, 18, 51
Lex Cornelia de sicariis et veneficis, 11
Lex Julia de adulteriis coercendis, 15
Lex Julia de vi privata, 13
Lex Julia de vi publica, 13

Mandate, 32, 56, 62, 64, 105, 121, 124, 133
Metropolitan, duties of, 156

Necessity, 46
Negligence, 3, 49, 67, 76

Obligation of preventing crime, 149
Office,
  explained, 146
  neglect of, 149
Omission, 55, 125
Ope consilio, 16
Ordinaries, duties of, 151

Panormitanus, 50, 51, 54
Participation,
  complete, 70, 84
  partial, 70, 84
Pastor, duties of, 158
Penalties *ab homine*, 30
Penalty, 62, 63, 64, 131, 140, 142
Penalty, discretionary, 62, 141, 173, 178
Penalty, legal, 170
Peregrini, 176
Persons considered accomplices
  advocates, 31, 76
  associates, 25, 39, 42
  authors of crime, 40, 41, 42, 58
  brother, 53
  children, 43
  cleric, 32, 40, 41, 43, 50
  cleric in major orders, 35, 36
  companions, 26, 50, 53
  consecrator, 36, 41
  consort, illicit, of nun, 23
  Christian, 15
  decurio, 15
  descendents, 53
  druggist, 119
  father, 41
  followers, 26, 39, 59
  governors, 13
  grand-nephews, 53
  guardians, 14, 24
  householders, 19
  inhabitants, 14
  intermediary, 41, 58
  Jew, 12, 15, 43
  joint agents, 39
  judges, 14, 17, 31, 51, 58, 76
  keepers of inns and stables, 19
  layman, 40, 41
  lawyers, 51
  magistrate, 13
  master, 18, 19, 22
  masters of ships, 19
  monks, 41, 45
  nephews, 53
  notaries, 31, 51, 58
  nun, 23, 35, 36, 45
  nurses, 88
  officials, 76
  owner, 13, 14, 15
  physician, 12, 88
  pimps, 40
  pirates, 44
  prelate, 36
  priest, 43
  procurators, 14, 15, 76
  publishers, 18
  relatives, 15, 43, 44

religious, 36
seconds, 58
servants, 10, 43
slaves, 12, 14, 15, 17, 18, 19, 22
soldier, 12, 14
sons, 10, 17
spectators, 33, 59, 61
supporters, 30, 31, 59
tenants, 14
wards, 14
widows, 14
wife, 17, 43
writers, 18
youth, 32
Permission, 121
Perpetrators, single, 96
Popes,
Alexander III, 32, 49
Anacletus II (antipope), 47
Benedict V (antipope), 31
Boniface VIII, 52, 53, 57
Celestine I, 26
Clement III (antipope), 46
Clement V, 53
Clement VIII, 59
Clement XIV, 59
Cornelius I, 30
Damasus I, 26, 40
Felix III, 28
Gelasius I, 27, 28, 36, 42
Gelasius II, 47
Gregory I, 30, 43
Gregory II, 31, 43
Gregory III, 44
Gregory V, 46
Gregory VII, 37, 46
Gregory IX, 52, 53
Gregory XIII, 59
Hadrian II, 37
Honorius I, 30, 43
Honorius III, 52
Hormisdas, 27, 42
Innocent II, 47
Innocent III, 28, 29, 31, 32
Innocent IV, 32
Iulius II, 33
John VIII, 44
John IX, 45
John XXII, 53
Leo I, 27, 28, 30, 41
Leo IV, 44
Lucius I, 37
Lucius III, 31, 51
Martin I, 31
Nicholas I, 29, 31, 44
Nicholas II, 32
Paschal II, 37, 46
Paul IV, 58
Paul V, 60
Pelagius I, 42
Pius IX, 60
Sixtus V, 59
Stephan I, 39
Urban VIII, 60
Victor I, 39
Virgilius, 42
Precept, 48, 154
Presence, 24, 32, 33, 58, 68, 93, 112
Principle of objectivity, 72, 94, 96, 98
Principle of subjectivity, 72, 96, 99
Procedure on suspicion, 27
Pseudo-Isidore, 37

Ratification, 53, 56, 164
Ratify, 53, 60
Receiving, 50
Religious, exempt, 176
Religious superior, duties of, 154
Remedies, penal, 155
Repentance, 56, 131, 135, 144

Shelter, 53
Simon de Bisiniano, 54
Simul, 89
Subjective dispositions, 50
Support, 30
Supporters, 51

Tancredus, 56
Thomas Aquinas, 61
Travelers, 176

Vicar general, duty of, 153
Violence, 55

Will to commit a crime, 55, 67
Withdrawal of cooperation, 131
Withdrawal of cooperation, complete. 131
Withdrawal of cooperation, incomplete, 137

BIOGRAPHICAL NOTE

The writer of this dissertation was born in Philadelphia, April 24, 1914. After his completion of the elementary course in St. Ignatius's Parochial School, he attended St. Joseph's Preparatory School. In 1930 he entered St. Charles' Seminary, Overbrook, and in 1936 received the degree of Bachelor of Arts. He was ordained to the priesthood June 3, 1939. After enrolling in the School of Canon Law at the Catholic University of America in September 1939, he received the degree of Bachelor of Canon Law in 1940, and the degree of Licentiate in Canon Law in 1941.

CANON LAW STUDIES

1. Freriks, Rev. Celestine A., C.PP.S., J.C.D., Religious Congregations in Their External Relations, 121 pp., 1916.
2. Galliher, Rev. Daniel M., O.P., J.C.D., Canonical Elections, 117 pp., 1917.
3. Borkowski, Rev. Aurelius L., O.F.M., J.C.D., De Confraternitatibus Ecclesiasticis, 136 pp., 1918.
4. Castillo, Rev. Cayo, J.C.D., Disertacion Historico-Canonica sobre la Potestad del Cabildo en Sede Vacante o Impedida del Vicario Capitular, 99 pp., 1919 (1918).
5. Kubelbeck, Rev. William J., S.T.B., J.C.D., The Sacred Pentitentiaria and Its Relations to Faculties of Ordinaries and Priests, 129 pp., 1918.
6. Petrovits, Rev. Joseph J.C., S.T.D., J.C.D., The New Church Law On Matrimony, X-461 pp., 1919.
7. Hickey, Rev. John J., S.T.B., J.C.D., Irregularities and Simple Impediments in the New Code of Canon Law, 100 pp., 1920.
8. Klekotka, Rev. Peter J., S.T.B., J.C.D., Diocesan Consultors, 179 pp., 1920.
9. Wanenmacher, Rev. Francis, J.C.D., The Evidence in Ecclesiastical Procedure Affecting the Marriage Bond, 1920 (Printed 1935).
10. Golden, Rev. Henry Francis, J.C.D., Parochial Benefices in the New Code, IV-119 pp., 1921 (Printed 1925).
11. Koudelka, Rev. Charles J., J.C.D., Pastors, Their Rights and Duties According to the New Code of Canon Law, 211 pp., 1921.
12. Melo, Rev. Antonius, O.F.M., J.C.D., De Exemptione Regularium, X-188 pp., 1921.
13. Schaaf, Rev. Valentine Theodore, O.F.M., S.T.B., J.C.D., The Cloister, X-180 pp., 1921.
14. Burke, Rev. Thomas Joseph, S.T.D., J.C.D., Competence in Ecclesiastical Tribunals, IV-117 pp., 1922.
15. Leech, Rev. George Leo, J.C.D., A Comparative Study of the Constitution, "Apostolicae Sedis" and the "Codex Juris Canonici," 179 pp., 1922.
16. Motry, Rev. Hubert Louis, S.T.D., J.C.D., Diocesan Faculties According to the Code of Canon Law, II-167 pp., 1922.
17. Murphy, Rev. George Lawrence, J.C.D., Delinquencies and Penalties in the Administration and Reception of the Sacraments, IV-121 pp., 1923.
18. O'Reilly, Rev. John Anthony, S.T.B., J.C.D., Ecclesiastical Sepulture in the New Code of Canon Law, II-129 pp., 1923.

19. Michalicka, Rev. Wenceslas Cyrill, O.S.B., J.C.D., Judicial Procedure in Dismissal of Clerical Exempt Religious, 107 pp., 1923.
20. Dargin, Rev. Edward Vincent, S.T.B., J.C.D., Reserved Cases According to the Code of Canon Law, IV-103, pp., 1924.
21. Godfrey, Rev. John A., S.T.B., J.C.D., The Right of Patronage According to the Code of Canon Law, 153 pp., 1924.
22. Hagedorn, Rev. Francis Edward, J.C.D., General Legislation on Indulgences, II-154 pp., 1924.
23. King, Rev. James Ignatius, J.C.D., The Administration of the Sacraments to Dying Non-Catholics, V-141 pp., 1924.
24. Winslow, Rev. Francis Joseph, A.F.M., J.C.D., Vicars and Prefects Apostolic, IV-149 pp., 1924.
25. Correa, Rev. Jose Servelion, S.T.L., J.C.D., La Potestad Legislativa de la Iglesia Catolica, IV-127 pp., 1925.
26. Dugan, Rev. Henry Francis, A.M., J.C.D., The Judiciary Department of the Diocesan Curia, 87 pp., 1925.
27. Keller, Rev. Charles Frederick, S.T.B., J.C.D., Mass Stipends, 167 pp., 1925.
28. Paschang, Rev. John Linus, J.C.D., The Sacramentals According to the Code of Canon Law, 129 pp., 1925.
29. Pointek, Rev. Cyrillus, O.F.M., S.T.B., J.C.D., De Indulto Exclaustrationis necnon Saecularizationis, XIII-289 pp., 1925.
30. Kearney, Rev. Richard Joseph, S.T.B., J.C.D., Sponsors at Baptism According to the Code of Canon Law, IV-127 pp., 1925.
31. Bartlett, Rev. Chester Joseph, A.M., LL.B., J.C.D., The Tenure of Parochial Property in the United States of America, V-108 pp., 1926.
32. Kilker, Rev. Adrian Jerome, J.C.D., Extreme Unction, V-425 pp., 1926.
33. McCormick, Rev. Robert Emmett, J.C.D., Confessors of Religious, VIII-266 pp., 1926.
34. Miller, Rev. Newton Thomas, J.C.D., Founded Masses According to the Code of Canon Law, VII-93 pp., 1926.
35. Roelker, Rev. Edward G., S.T.D., J.C.D., Principles of Privilege According to the Code of Canon Law, XI-166 pp., 1926.
36. Bakalarczyk, Rev. Richardus, M.I.C., J.U.D., De Novitiatu, VIII-208 pp., 1927.
37. Pizzuti, Rev. Lawrence, O.F.M., J.U.L., De Parochis Religiosis, 1927. (Not printed).
38. Bliley, Rev. Nicholas Martin, O.S.B., J.C.D., Altars According to the Code of Canon Law, XIX-132 pp., 1927.
39. Brown, Mr. Brendan Francis, A.B. LL.M., J.U.D., The Canonical Juristic Personality with Special Reference to Its Status in the United States of America, V-212 pp., 1927.

40. Cavanaugh, Rev. William Thomas, C.P., J.U.D., The Reservation of the Blessed Sacrament, VIII-101 pp., 1927.
41. Doheny, Rev. William J., C.S.C., A.B., J.U.D., Church Property: Modes of Acquisition, X-118 pp., 1927.
42. Feldhaus, Rev. Aloysius H., C.PP.S., J.C.D., Oratories, IX-141 pp., 1927.
43. Kelly, Rev. James Patrick, A.B., J.C.D., The Jurisdiction of the Simple Confessor, X-208 pp., 1927.
44. Neuberger, Rev. Nicholas J., J.C.D., Canon 6 or the Relation of the Codex Juris Canonici to the Preceding Legislation, V-95 pp., 1927.
45. O'Keefe, Rev. Gerald Michael, J.C.D., Matrimonial Dispensations, Powers of Bishops, Priests and Confessors, VIII-232 pp., 1927.
46. Quigley, Rev. Joseph A.M., A.B., J.C.B., Condemned Societies, 139 pp., 1927.
47. Zaplotnik, Rev. Johannes Leo, J.C.D., De Vicariis Foraneis, X-142 pp., 1927.
48. Duskie, Rev. John Aloysius, A.B., J.C.D., The Canonical Status of the Orientals in the United States, VIII-196 pp., 1928.
49. Hyland, Rev. Francis Edward, J.C.D., Excommunication, Its Nature, Historical Development and Effects, VIII-181 pp., 1928.
50. Reinmann, Rev. Gerald Joseph, O.M.C., J.C.D., The Third Order Secular of Saint Francis, 201 pp., 1928.
51. Schenk, Rev. Francis J., J.C.D., The Matrimonial Impediments of Mixed Religion and Disparity of Cult, XVI-318 pp., 1929.
52. Coady, Rev. John Joseph, S.T.D., J.U.D., A.M., The Appointment of Pastors, VIII-150 pp., 1929.
53. Kay, Rev. Thomas Henry, J.C.D., Competence in Matrimonial Procedure, VIII-164 pp., 1929.
54. Turner, Rev. Sidney Joseph, C.P., J.U.D., The Vow of Poverty, XLIX-217 pp., 1929.
55. Kearney, Rev. Raymond, A., A.B., S.T.D., J.C.D., The Principles, of Delegation, VII-149 pp., 1929.
56. Conran, Rev. Edward James, A.B., J.C.D., The Interdict, V-163 pp., 1930.
57. O'Neil, Rev. William H., J.C.D., Papal Rescripts of Favor, VII-218 pp., 1930.
58. Bastnagel, Rev. Clement Vincent, J.U.D., The Appointment of Parochial Adjutants and Assistants, XV-257 pp., 1930.
59. Ferry, Rev. William A., A.B., J.C.D., Stole Fees. V-135 pp., 1930.
60. Costello, Rev. John Michael, A.B., J.C.D., Domicile and Quasi-domicile, VII-201 pp., 1930.
61. Kremer, Rev. Michael Nicholas, A.B., S.T.B., J.C.D., Church Support in the United States, VI-1930.

62. Angulo, Rev. Luis, C.M., J.C.D., Legislation de la Iglesia sobre la intencion en la application de la Santa Misa, VII-104 pp., 1931.
63. Frey, Rev. Wolfgang Norbert, O.S.B., A.B., J.C.D., The Act of Religious Profession, VIII-174 pp., 1931.
64. Roberts, Rev. James Brendan, A.B., J.C.D., The Banns of Marriage, XIV-140 pp., 1931.
65. Ryder, Rev. Raymond Aloysius, A.B., J.C.D., Simony, IX-151 pp., 1931.
66. Campagna, Rev. Angelo, Ph.D., J.U.D., Il Vicario Generale del Vescovo, VII-205 pp., 1931.
67. Cox, Rev. Joseph Godfrey, A.B., J.C.D., The Administration ot Seminaries, VI-124 pp., 1931.
68. Gregory, Rev. Donald J., J.U.D., The Pauline Privilege, XV-165 pp., 1931.
69. Donohue, Rev. John F., J.C.D., The Impediment of Crime, VII-110 pp., 1931.
70. Dooley, Rev. Eugene A., O.M.I., J.C.D., Church Law On Sacred Relics, IX-143 pp., 1931.
71. Orth, Rev. Raymond Clement, O.M.C., J.C.D., The Approbation of Religious Institutes, 171 pp., 1931.
72. Pernicone, Rev. Joseph M., A.B., J.C.D., The Ecclesiastical Prohibition of Books, XII-267 pp., 1932.
73. Clinton, Rev. Connell, A.B., J.C.D., The Paschal Precept, IX-108 pp., 1932.
74. Donnelly, Rev. Francis B., A.M., S.T.L., J.C.D., The Diocesan Synod, VIII-125 pp., 1932.
75. Torrente, Rev. Camilo, C.M.F., J.C.D., Las Processiones Sagradas, V-145 pp., 1932.
76. Murphy, Rev. Edwin J., C.PP.S., J.C.D., Suspension Ex Informata Conscientia, XI-122, pp., 1932.
77. Mackenzie, Rev. Eric F., A.M., S.T.L., J.C.D., The Delict of Heresy in its Commission Penalization, Absolution, VII-124 pp., 1932.
78. Lyons Rev. Avitus E., S.T.B., J.C.D., The Collegiate Tribunal of First Instance, XI-147 pp., 1932.
79. Connolly, Rev. Thomas A., J.C.D., Appeals, XI-195 pp., 1932.
80. Sangmeister, Rev. Joseph V., A.B., J.C.D., Force and Fear as Precluding Matrimonial Consent, V-211 pp., 1932.
81. Jaeger, Rev. Leo A., A.B., J.C.D., The Administration of Vacant and Quasi-vacant Episcopal Sees in the United States, IX-229 pp., 1932.
82. Rimlinger, Rev. Herbert T., J.C.D., Error Invalidating Matrimonial Consent, VII-79 pp., 1932.
83. Barrett, Rev. John D.M., S.S., J.C.D., A Comparative Study of the Third Plenary Council of Baltimore and the Code, IX-221 pp., 1932.

84. Carberry, Rev. John J., Ph.D., S.T.D., J.C.D., The Juridical Form of Marriage, X-177 pp., 1934.
85. Dolan, Rev. John L., A.B., J.C.D., The Defensor Vinculi, XII-157 pp., 1934.
86. Hannan, Rev. Jerome D., A.M., S.T.D., LL.B., J.C.D., The Canon Law of Wills, IX-517 pp., 1934.
87. Lemieux, Rev. Delisle A., A.M., J.C.D., The Sentence in Ecclesiastical Procedure, IX-131 pp., 1934.
88. O'Rourke, Rev. James J., A.B., J.C.D., Parish Registers, VII-109 pp., 1934.
89. Timlin, Rev. Bartholomew, O.F.M., A.M., J.C.D., Conditional Matrimonial Consent, X-381 pp., 1934.
90. Wahl, Rev. Francis X., A.B., J.C.D., The Matrimonial Impediments of Consanguinity and Affinity, VI-125 pp., 1934.
91. White, Rev. Robert J., A.B., LL.B., S.T.B., J.C.D., Canonical Ante-Nuptial Promises and the Civil Law, VI-152 pp., 1934.
92. Herrera, Rev. Antonio Parra, O.C.D., J.C.D., Legislation Ecclesiastica sobra el Ayuno y la Abstinencia, XI-191 pp., 1935.
93. Kennedy, Rev. Edwin J., J.C.D., The Special Matrimonial Process in Cases of Evident Nullity, X-165 pp., 1935.
94. Manning, Rev. John J., A.B., J.C.D., Presumption of Law in Matrimonial Procedure, XI-111 pp., 1935.
95. Moeder, Rev. John M., J.C.D., The Proper Bishop for Ordination and Dismissorial Letters, VII-135 pp., 1935.
96. O'Mara, Rev. William A., A.B., J.C.D., Canonical Causes For Matrimonial Dispensations, IX-155 pp., 1935.
97. Reilly, Rev. Peter, J.C.D., Residence of Pastors, IX-81 pp., 1935.
98. Smith, Rev. Mariner T., O.P., S.T.L., J.C.D., The Penal Law For Religious, VII-169 pp., 1935.
99. Whalen, Rev. Donald W., A.M., J.C.D., The Value of Testimonial Evidence in Matrimonial Procedure, XIII-297 pp., 1935.
100. Cleary, Rev. Joseph F., J.C.D., Canonical Limitations on the Alienation of Church Property, VIII-141 pp., 1936.
101. Glynn, Rev. John C., J.C.D., The Promoter of Justice, XX-337 pp., 1936.
102. Brennan, Rev. James H., S.S., A.M., S.T.B., J.C.D., The Simple Convalidation of Marriage, VI-135 pp, 1937.
103. Brunini, Rev. Joseph Bernard, J.C.D., The Clerical Obligations of Canons, 139 and 142, X-121 pp., 1937.
104. Connor, Rev. Maurice, A.B., J.C.D., The Administrative Removal of Pastors, VIII-159 pp., 1937.
105. Guilfoyle, Rev. Merlin Joseph, J.C.D., Custom, XI-144 pp., 1937.
106. Hughes, Rev. James Austin, A.B., A.M., J.C.D., Witnesses in Criminal Trials of Clerics, IX-140 pp., 1937.

107. Jansen, Rev. Raymond J., A.B., S.T.L., J.C.D., Canonical Provisions for Catechetical Instruction, VII-153 pp., 1937.

108. Kealy, Rev. John James, A.B., J.C.D,, The Introductory Libellus in Church Court Procedure, XI-121 pp., 1937.

109. McManus, Rev. James Edward, C.SS.R., J.C.D., The Administration of Temporal Goods in Religious Institutes, XVI-196 pp., 1937.

110. Moriarity, Rev. Eugene James, J.C.D., Oaths in Ecclesiastical Courts X-115 pp., 1937.

111. Rainer, Rev. Eligius George, C.SS.R., J.C.D., Suspension of Clerics, XVII-249 pp., 1937.

112. Reilly, Rev. Thomas F., C.SS.R., J.C.D., Visitation of Religious, VI-195 pp., 1938.

113. Moriarty, Rev. Francis E., C.SS.R., J.C.D., The Extraordinary Absolution from Censures, XV-334 pp., 1938.

114. Connolly, Rev. Nicholas P., J.C.D., The Canonical Erection of Parishes, X-132 pp., 1938.

115. Donovan, Rev. James Joseph, J.C.D., The Pastor's Obligation in Prenuptial Investigation, VII-322 pp., 1938.

116. Harrigan, Rev. Robert J., M.A., S.T.B., J.C.D., The Radical Sanation of Invalid Marriages, VIII-208 pp., 1938.

117. Boffa, Rev. Conrad Humbert, J.C.D., Canonical Provisions for Catholic Schools, VII-211 pp., 1939.

118. Parsons, Rev. Anscar John, O.M. Cap., J.C.D., Canonical Elections, XII-236 pp., 1939.

119. Reilly, Rev. Edward Michael, A.B., J.C.D., The General Norms of Dispensation, X-156 pp., 1939.

120. Ryan, Rev. Gerald Aloysius, A.B., J.C.D., Principles of Episcopal Jurisdiction, XII-172 pp., 1939.

121. Burton, Rev. Francis James, C.S.C., A.B., J.C.D., A Commentary on Canon 1125, X-222 pp., 1940.

122. Miaskiewicz, Rev. Francis Sigismund, J.C.D., Supplied Jurisdiction according to Canon 209, XII-340 pp., 1940.

123. Rice, Rev. Patrick William, A.B., J.C.D., Proof of Death in Prenuptial Investigation, VIII-156 pp., 1940.

124. Anglin, Rev. Thomas Francis, M.S., J.C.D., The Eucharistic Fast, VIII-183 pp., 1941.

125. Coleman, Rev. John Jerome, J.C.D., The Minister of Confirmation, VI-153 pp., 1941.

126. Downs, Rev. John Emmanuel, A.B., J.C.D., The Concept of Clerical Immunity, XI-163 pp., 1941.

127. Esswein, Rev. Anthony Albert, J.C.D., Extrajudicial Penal Powers of Ecclesiastical Superiors, X-144 pp., 1941.

128. Farrell, Rev. Benjamin Francis, M.A., S.T.L., J.C.D., The Rights and Duties of the Local Ordinary Regarding Congregations of Women Religious of Pontifical Approval, V-195 pp., 1941.
129. Feeney, Rev. Thomas John, A.B., S.T.L., J.C.D., Restitution in Integrum, VI-169 pp., 1941.
130. Findlay, Rev. Stephen William, O.S.B., A.B., J.C.D., Canonical Norms Governing the Deposition and Degradation of Clerics, XVII-279 pp., 1941.
131. Goodwine, Rev. John, A.B., S.T.L., J.C.D., The Right of the Church to Acquire Property, VIII-119 pp., 1941.
132. Heston, Rev. Edward Louis, C.S.C., PhD., S.T.D., J.C.D., The Alienation of Church Property in the United States, XII-222 pp., 1941.
133. Hogan, Rev. James John, S.T.L., J.C.D., Judicial Advocates and Procurators, VIII-200 pp., 1941.
134. Kealy, Rev. Thomas M. A.B., Litt.B., J.C.D., Dowry of Women Religious, IX-152 pp., 1941.
135. Keene, Rev. Michael James, O.S.B., J.C.D., Religious Ordinaries and Canon 198.
136. Kerin, Rev. Charles A., S.S., M.A., S.T.B., J.C.D., The Privation of Christian Burial, XVI-279 pp., 1941.
137. Louis, Rev. William Francis, M.A., J.C.D., Diocesan Archives, X-101 pp., 1941.
138. McDevitt, Rev. Gilbert Joseph, A.B., J.C.D., Legitimacy and Legitimation, X-247 pp., 1941.
139. McDonough, Rev. Thomas Joseph, A.B., J.C.D., Apostolic Administrators, X-217 pp., 1941.
140. Meier, Rev. Carl Anthony, A.B., J.C.D., Penal Administrative Procedure Against Negligent Pastors, XI-240 pp., 1941.
141. Schmidt, Rev. John Rogg, A.B., J.C.D., The Principles of Authentic Interpretation in Canon 17 of the Code of Canon Law, XII-331 pp., 1941.
142. Slafkosky, Rev. Andrew Leonard, A.B., J.C.D., The Canonical Episcopal Visitation of the Diocese, X-197 pp., 1941.
143. Swoboda, Rev. Innocent Robert, O.F.M., J.C.D., Ignorance in Relation to the Imputability of Delicts, IX-271 pp., 1941.
144. Dubé, Rev. Arthur Joseph, A.B., J.C.D., The General Principles for the Reckoning of Time in Canon Law. VIII-299 pp., 1941.
145. McBride, Rev. James T., A.B., J.C.D., Incardination and Excardination of Seculars., XX-585 pp., 1941.
146. Król, Rev. John J., J.C.L., The Defendant in Contentious Trials, IX-207 pp., 1942.
147. Comyns, Rev. Joseph J., C.SS.R., J.C.L., The Papal and Episcopal Administration of Church Property.

148. Barry, Rev. Garrett Francis, O.M.I., J.C.L., Violation of the Cloister.
149. Bolduc, Rev. Gatien, C.S.V., A.B., S.T.L., J.C.L., Les études dans les religions cléricales.
150. Boyle, Rev. David John, M.A., J.C.L., The Juridic Effects of Moral Certitude on Pre-Nuptial Guarantees.
151. Canavan. Rev. Walter Joseph, M.A., Litt.D., J.C.L., Profession of Faith.
152. Desrochers, Rev. Bruno, A.B., Ph.D., S.T.B., J.C.L. The Premier Concile Plénier de Québec et le Code de Droit Canonique.
153. Dillon, Rev. Robert Edward, A.B., J.C.L., Common Law Marriage.
154. Dodwell, Rev. Edward John, Ph.D., S.T.B., J.C.L., The Time and Place for the Celebration of Marriage.
155. Donnellan, Rev. Thomas Andrew, A.B., J.C.L., The Obligation of the Missa pro Populo.
156. Eltz, Rev. Louis Anthony, A.B., JC.L., Cooperation in Crime.
157. Gass, Rev. Sylvester Francis, M.A., J.C.L., Ecclestiastical Pensions.
158. Guiniven, Rev. John Joseph, C.SS.R., J.C.L., The Precept of Hearing Mass on Sundays and Holy Days of Obligation.
159. Gulczynski, Rev. John Theophilus, J.C.L., The Desecration and Violation of Churches.
160. Hammill, Rev. John Leo, M.A., J.C.L., The Obligations of the Traveler according to Canon 14.
161. Haydt, Rev. John Joseph, A.B., J.C.L., Reserved Benefices.
162. Huser, Rev. Roger John, O.F.M., A.B., J.C.L., The Crime of Abortion in Canon Law.
163. Kearney, Rev. Francis Patrick, A.B., S.T.L., J.C.L., The Principles of Canon 1127.
164. Linahen, Rev. Leo James, S.T.L., J.C.L., De Absolutione Complicis in Peccato Turpi.
165. McCloskey, Rev. Joseph Aloysius, A.B., J.C.L., The Subject of Ecclesiastical Law according to Canon 12.
166. O'Neill, Rev. Francis Joseph, C.SS.R., J.C.L., The Dismissal of Religious in Temporary Vows.
167. Prince, Rev. John Edward, A.B., S.T.B., J.C.L., The Diocesan Chancellor.
168. Riesner, Rev. Albert Joseph, C.SS.R., J.C.L., Apostates and Fugitives from Religious Institutes.
169. Stenger, Rev. Joseph Bernard, J.C.L., The Mortgaging of Church Property.
170. Waldron, Rev. Joseph Francis, A.B., J.C.L., The Minister of Baptism.
171. Willett, Rev. Robert Albert, J.C.L., The Probative Value of Documents in Ecclesiastical Trials.
172. Woeber, Rev. Edward Martin, M.A., J.C.L., The Interpellations.

www.ingramcontent.com/pod-product-compliance
Lightning Source LLC
LaVergne TN
LVHW050242080826
844660LV00012B/585

9780813223452